Northwestern University

STUDIES IN *Phenomenology &*

Existential Philosophy

Husserl
An Analysis of His Phenomenology

Paul Ricoeur

Translated by Edward G. Ballard

and Lester E. Embree

Husserl

AN ANALYSIS

OF HIS PHENOMENOLOGY

NORTHWESTERN UNIVERSITY PRESS

1 9 6 7   EVANSTON

Northwestern University Press
Evanston, Illinois 60208-4210

Sixth paperback printing 1999

Printed in the United States of America

ISBN 0-8101-0530-6

The paper used in this publication meets the minimum require-
ments of the American National Standard for Information
Sciences—Permanence of Paper for Printed Library Materials,
ANSI Z.39.48-1984

Contents

[ix]

Foreword

To BE FORCED to spend years in the concentration camp of a highly civilized yet warlike and confused enemy is to feel oneself invited to make a new examination of what is termed civilization and its basis in experience and thought. Professor Paul Ricoeur accepted the challenge of this invitation by setting for himself the task of mastering and expounding just that German philosophy which seeks a new and unprejudiced view of life at its foundations. Upon achieving possession of this phenomenological philosophy, Ricoeur undertook to develop it further and, appropriately enough, in just the direction designed to throw light upon that strange division or fault in human nature which from time to time is manifested in such phenomena as Nazi concentration camps.

As part of the discipline which led to his mastery of phenomenological philosophy, Ricoeur made a number of translations and studies of Husserl's writings. Happily he was led to publish many of these, thus contributing materially toward bringing French philosophy to its present leading position in the development of phenomenology. Professor Herbert Spiegelberg has pointed out that Ricoeur is "the best informed French historian of phenomenology" [1] and has added that his translations and analyses of Husserl's work have created a unique instrument for entering into the thought of the Founder of Phenomenology. The first seven phenomenological studies and analyses collected and translated in the present volume form an important part of this instrument and provide, moreover, the appropriate link to Ricoeur's own original

1. *The Phenomenological Movement*, II (The Hague, 1960), 563. A selected bibliography of Husserl's writings is included on pp. 163–67 of Vol. I, together with references to complete bibliographies. A complete list of Ricoeur's writings up to June 30, 1962, will be found in Dirk Vansina, "Bibliographie de Paul Ricoeur," *Revue philosophique de Louvain*, LX (August, 1962), 394–413.

philosophy, a transition clarified in the last two articles of this collection.

The following translations are offered both as a perceptive and critical view of Husserl's phenomenology and as a presentation of the preparatory phase of Ricoeur's own work. Originally they were published at various times and under differing circumstances. Yet in spite of not being composed as a single book, they express a consistent and unified interpretation of the most influential part of Husserl's phenomenology. A brief account of some of the recurrent themes and main views will be helpful both in pointing up this unity and in introducing the essays. The themes selected for brief notice in this preface are the body, the self, intersubjectivity, objectivity, and the tension in Husserl's philosophy between idealism and realism. These themes will be developed just sufficiently to indicate the manner in which Husserl's philosophy is analyzed in these essays and related to the tradition (e.g., to Kantianism) and to later philosophy (e.g., to existentialism).

Although a few philosophers have endeavored to study objects as if they were obviously given just as they really are, it is no new thing to observe, as Husserl observed, that inquirers do not unambiguously confront an unquestionably external world. The novelty of Husserl's philosophy lies first in offering techniques (*epoché* and the reductions) for removing the prejudices which ordinarily are interposed between ourselves and phenomena as they are presented, and secondly in developing interpretations of the self and its phenomenal world. The beliefs basic to this descriptive method and to the idealistic interpretation of its results have a rich and complex history. The first essay in this collection seeks specifically to place Husserlian phenomenology within its historical setting and then briefly to set forth its internal development. It functions in this collection as an anticipation of the general drift of the essays to follow.

The article on *Ideas I* (cf. n. 1, p. 13 below) is introductory and general. The details and defense of the interpretation which it sketches are set forth in the summaries and detailed notes which Ricoeur appended to his translation of this work. Unfortunately, the plan of the present volume renders it impossible to include this valuable commentary.

In the same article Ricoeur outlines his opposition to the Neo-Kantian interpretation which tends to make of Husserl a sort of Platonic realist inconsistently combined with a subjective idealist. This Neo-Kantian view is said to represent the Husserlian transcendental reduction as a slip into psychologism and the eidectic reduction as an effort to regain balance by clutching at Platonism in the form of a doctrine of the eidos ego. Then this criticism attempts to catch Husserl in a dilemma: either the originary ego to which the reductions lead as the constituting source of its experience is not cognized, although it may be conscious, or else it is cognized but only as a natural and non-transcendental thing. Ricoeur shows both in the essay on *Ideas* and especially in "Kant and Husserl" that in fact Husserl's philosophy falls into neither of these traps.

Another point in this interpretation of *Ideas* enables us to contrast Ricoeur's view, at least with respect to emphasis, with that of Eugen Fink. Fink has held that the primary theme of *Ideas* is the "origin of the world" in transcendental subjectivity (cf. n. 2, p. 15 below). Ricoeur does not flatly disagree with this view. He holds only that it is not primary; rather, the theme of "the origin of the world" is a guide to Husserl's inclusive philosophical purpose, which is the phenomenological interpretation of the ego and its constitutive function. The world, originating in transcendental subjectivity, is to be viewed as a limitation placed upon this ego. It is the index of the ego's possibilities. In other words, the management of the problem of the origin of the world is seen as tributary to the more basic question concerning the nature and function of the transcendental ego. Thus, Ricoeur's interpretation of *Ideas* situates it within the perspective defined by the *Cartesian Meditations*.

Ricoeur is constantly concerned with analyzing and evaluating this idealistic and egological interpretation of phenomenology, which reaches its high point in *Cartesian Meditations*. An important reason for this concern lies in the confused state of many of the current opinions about the relation between the egological doctrine and existential philosophy. One of these opinions finds Husserl to be the immediate parent of existentialism, indeed all but an existentialist himself; another presents him as only incidentally and accidentally related to existentialism. Ricoeur's reflections on the question of this relationship are especially interesting, since his own philosophy was elaborated at a point where these trends join.[2]

For instance, in the essay on *Ideas II* (cf. n. 1, p. 36), Ricoeur takes pains to show that the doctrine of the psycho-physical body, which is developed there, is in no way the incarnate body investigated by some of the existentialists. Husserl is not concerned with formulating an irreducible experience of "my body," as Marcel is, but only wishes to determine the sense in which sensation belongs to the body. Nor is sensation understood as an existentialist phenomenon depend-

2. Husserl's influence upon Ricoeur's philosophy is perhaps only slightly greater than Marcel's; cf. *Gabriel Marcel et Karl Jaspers, philosophie du mystère et philosophie du paradoxe* (Paris, 1947).

ent upon the owned body. The body, too, is developed as a thing, an object, though an incomplete object, and man himself is objectified and regarded as the possible object of a science (e.g., of psychology or sociology). These doctrines are contributions to Husserl's lifelong effort to formulate a foundation for the science of psychology, and in no way do they compromise his quest for a beginning in philosophy. Thus, Husserl never dreams of objectifying the transcendental ego. Rather, he develops this ego in contrast to the objects of science and as their ground.

In the essay entitled "Existential Phenomenology," number eight in this collection, Ricoeur goes so far as to recognize in the theme of the owned and lived body one of the three most characteristic themes of existentialism. In addition, he points out that this is just the theme which places a limit upon the Husserlian technique of reduction. Neither the body, through which I am inserted in the world, nor its involuntary behavior will allow of our suspension of their existence.[3] Such limits to the *epoché* (bracketing) point both toward possible difficulties within Husserl's philosophy and toward directions in which phenomenology might be developed (some of which Ricoeur will explore).

However, in his later writings Husserl draws far closer to the notion of the owned and incarnate body. In the fifth of the *Cartesian Meditations* (cf. n. 1, p. 82 below), as Ricoeur notes, the ego is reduced to its own unique, concrete experience, and at this point it coincides with its body and its world. However, in this movement of his thought, Husserl's purpose is still to understand the nature of objectivity as related to its origin in the ego. Far from sharing in the preoccupations of existentialists, Husserl remains faithful to his ideal of philosophy as the complete science, certain of its own foundations because they are grounded in absolute self-evidence.

The contributions to existentialist philosophy which develop out of *Ideas II* are to be found in the elaboration of the notion of spirit (*Geist*) and in the personal and intersubjective lived world—although even here Husserl's interests lay more in the direction of a phenomenology of culture and in particular in analyzing the intentive processes by which spirit, the object of the human sciences, is constituted. Still, Husserl does elaborate the notion of a personal self, bearer of spirit, who with other personal selves is the creator of culture and its world; this personal self is viewed by Ricoeur as something between the pure transcendental ego and the empirical ego or psyche. In it, perhaps, one

3. *La Philosophie de la volonté;* Vol. I: *Le Volontaire et l'involontaire* (Paris, 1950), p. 76. English translation by Erazim V. Kohák, *Freedom and Nature: The Voluntary and the Involuntary* (Evanston, Ill., 1966).

may see the traits of the concrete subject of some existential philosophies beginning to take form. However, this notion of the personal "I" must undergo many changes before emerging as the individualized self, or even as *das Man,* of a Heidegger. In general, existentialism is obligated to Husserl rather for its phenomenological method and for particular analyses than for its interests and specific themes.

Although the Husserlian ego is not an existentialist self, it is an even further cry from the formal subject of Kantian philosophy; its self-knowledge is not theoretical. Much less is it identical with a Platonic form. As Ricoeur points out in the articles on *Cartesian Meditations,* the eidos ego is a personal self which can speak of each of its experiences as "mine." Its eidetic status is derived by imaginative variations upon one's own self and is not induced from a generalizing observation of many selves, nor is it the object of a Platonic intellectual intuition. In this doctrine of the self, one may say that Husserl put the eidos ego, an essence in the sense of being a unity of sense, back into existence and thus took an important step toward rendering possible a more immediate grasp of the existent self; that is, he took a step toward grasping the *sum* of the *cogito.* However, Husserl is not interested in working out a view of the self's freedom, or of its creativity, or of its destructive power. Although his rejection of a merely formal self and his approach to the concrete self may seem to have opened up this line of thought, he is concerned, rather, with the constitution of objectivity in the subject. Even though he describes consciousness as transcendence, he limits the use of this notion to an epistemological function which manifests a kinship to rationalism quite as much as to existentialism. In fact, Husserl is concerned with transcendence primarily as directed by one type of transcendental guide: the object, or the world of objects. His ideal from first to last envisaged the sciences, those "highest achievements of the human spirit," and sought to secure an appropriate foundation for them and to distinguish between their own content and their phenomenological basis. Ricoeur adds, however, that the scientific ideal of rationality displays a new function in *The Crisis of European Sciences* (cf. n. 1, p. 44 below). There it becomes the distinctive Idea or task of Western history, so that when the vision of this Idea became obscured—as happened during the Renaissance—man's existence itself became narrowed and proportionately impoverished in meaning. In this respect, the Idea of rationality seems at least remotely to approach the status of an existential project. It suggests, as Ricoeur notes, the possibility of connecting a critical philosophy with an existential project by way of a reflection upon history.

However, the question may well be asked—and Ricoeur is quick to ask it—how Western man, whose sense and existence is a dependency upon and a function of history, can at the same time be a transcendental ego, the source of all sense. The idealistic and monadic doctrine of the ego, worked out in the *Cartesian Meditations*, seemed to require Husserl to discover the source and foundation of all objective sense within the self. To this end, therefore, he reduced the reality of the object to the "seen." Then that which is present with evidence is reduced to noematic unities of sense (the cogitata); the cogitata are integrated into the cogitationes or noeses, and the latter in turn are integrated into the monadic ego. Thus, though the world remains important as the transcendental guide in phenomenology, phenomenology as a whole becomes in the *Cartesian Meditations* an egology, the explication of the self and of its self-constitution, of the Other, of the objective world, and of communities of persons. Thus, the idealism is completed by this reduction or leading back of all reality to its origin in performances of the ego. The weight of objectivity now comes to be shifted from the individual's full perception of an intended object to an intersubjectively constituted sense which can give general validity to the presumption of objectivity. Clearly, this doctrine is as different from the abstract self of Kantianism as it is from the dramatic preoccupations of existentialism.

Ricoeur is no less concerned in pointing to the uniqueness of Husserl's philosophy than in relating it to tradition. This complex objective requires him to expound this philosophy and its development. His intention, however, does not prevent him from ferreting out the difficulties internal and native to Husserl's philosophy. A number of such difficulties are indicated, the chief of which is the problem of relating Husserl's phenomenological method and its immediate outcome in the description of phenomena to his metaphysical decision to make an idealistic interpretation of these phenomena. Ricoeur locates the decisive moment of this shift in the second of the *Cartesian Meditations* where the act of abstention, initiating the transcendental reduction, explicitly becomes an act negating all reality-claims except those derivable from the ego's cogitationes. Thus, the presence of a thing is reduced to my present, and the notion of an in-itself of realism or naturalism is completely expelled, and its being is reduced to a sedimented moment of egological constituting. Ricoeur makes it quite clear that he himself cannot follow this use of the phenomenological method through to the extreme of "dogmatic idealism."

Husserl's metaphysical decision in favor of this idealism led directly to the problem of transcendental solipsism. Husserl heroically faced up to this test of egology without ontology. He viewed his task not as eliminating a doubt concerning the natural existence of others but rather as determining the source of the sense of the Other. Can this sense be seen to be constituted in transcendental subjectivity? Ricoeur throws some doubt upon the success of Husserl's effort to constitute in me (in my subjectivity) the sense of the Other as an other self; once he even suggests that a sounder recognition of the realities involved is offered in the descriptions of empathy in *Ideas II* or, by way of contrast, in Kant's practical philosophy. However, Ricoeur's primary aim, aside from getting at the sense and organization of Husserl's complex analyses, is often directed toward a grasp of the delicate balance which Husserl sought to maintain between the demands of idealism, which required purity and radicalness in the vision of origins, and the demands of realism, which required faithfulness to the concrete and concentration upon the objective in experience. For just this reason he found it necessary to follow the treatment of the problem of intersubjectivity through to the end.

Thus, Ricoeur finally broaches the task of adjusting the egological doctrine of *Cartesian Meditations* to the views on Western man's involvement in the historical task as expressed in the *Crisis*. In "Husserl and The Sense of History," [4] the sixth essay of this collection, he points up the strange paradox of all-including history which must be included within the all-including transcendental ego. But he sees at least a verbal exit from this impasse in that the first inclusion is real whereas the latter is intentional. Nevertheless, the problem of solipsism remains a serious one for the Husserlian philosophy of the ego, and its ghost refuses to be laid in the *Crisis*. After all, one of its tasks was to formulate the foundation of objectivity within transcendental subjectivity, and its later doctrine of objectivity is expressed chiefly in terms of intersubjective community. Thus, a flawless solution to the problem of intersubjectivity would seem to be quite necessary. Ricoeur makes every effort to do full justice to Husserl's insights and subtleties, without, however, hesitating in the end to point to their persistent difficulty: the incompletely resolved tension between their idealistic and realistic tendencies.

The achievements and advantages of a phenomenological philosophy offer a promise, and its difficulties extend a warning. Together its achievements and problems indicate the way to its appropriate development. The manner in which Ricoeur has utilized this opening is outlined in the last article, "Methods and Tasks of a Phenomenology of the Will." This essay summarizes many of the developments in the author's *La Philosophie de la volonté* and opens the way to the mature

4. This essay may be regarded as leading up to Ricoeur's *Histoire et vérité* (Paris, 1955), as the author himself points out. Cf. p. 7 and pp. 42 ff. English translation by Charles A. Kelbley, *History and Truth* (Evanston, Ill., 1965).

elaboration of his philosophy in the two volumes of *Finitude et culpabilité*.[5] In this essay the author describes the elements and modalities of willing—motive, consent, decision, action—while seeking to preserve their continuity. Being unhampered by Husserl's rationalist preoccupation with objectivity, he is led to conclude that willing is no less meaning-giving than perception. Then, warned by Husserl's commitment to transcendental idealism, he moves on, by way of a second and ontological reflection upon the division or "fault" within human will, to approach a hermeneutic of the myth of evil and an ontology of the fault which characterizes the human person and is perceptible even prior to the elaboration of an ethic. Thus, he pursues a clearer vision and understanding of that disproportionality which tradition has assigned to human nature itself and which has eventuated not only in the acts of destruction and revenge which punctuate history, but also in the confusions and blindness which have attended the philosophic effort to comprehend history.

May we also suppose that this ontological "fault" is exhibited in Husserl's philosophy in its realistic-idealistic tension? The movement from Husserl to Ricoeur is a movement toward a more critical awareness of the presupposition of the finality of the scientific ideal of rigor and objectivity along with an accompanying suspicion that radicalness in philosophy is not to be attained by way of an egology without ontology. The self and the world stand in delicate balance. How is this balance to be understood? The nature and degree of the interpenetration of man and the world is surely one of the most obscure problems in philosophy. Husserl's contribution to its understanding is notable but scarcely final. What at least is evident is that confusion and excess in the existential interpretation of this balance become manifest in history as mass illusion or as inhumanity. Happily European philosophers generally, Edmund Husserl and Paul Ricoeur in particular, have not been content idly to ignore this problem.

Edward G. Ballard

5. The first volume of this work, *L'Homme faillible* (Paris, 1960) has been translated by Charles Kelbley under the title *Fallible Man* (Chicago, 1965). An account of Ricoeur's philosophy will be found in Dirk Vansina, "Esquisse, orientation et signification de l'entreprise philosophique de Paul Ricoeur," *Revue de métaphysique et de morale*, LXIX (March–July, 1964), 179–208; (July–October, 1964), 305–32.

TRANSLATORS'

Preface

OCCASIONALLY in our translations of technical words we have added notes in order to specify the sense as we have understood it and the rationale for our choice of terms. All translators' remarks are clearly indicated except for some additions to or changes in the bibliographical notes. With the author's permission we have adapted paragraphing and italicizing to English usage. For convenience we have supplied the English for all German titles and ordinarily have translated the German terms and sentences which Ricoeur left untranslated.

We decided to translate the author's French citations of Husserl rather than to quote the standard English translations. We were led to this decision owing to the fact that Ricoeur himself is a recognized authority in translating Husserl's German and, furthermore, he often worked from manuscripts in the Husserl Archives which differ in some particulars from the later published texts. Page references to the standard German or English editions, however, are provided.

Each of the editors or publishers mentioned in the following list, numbered to correspond with our Table of Contents, has granted permission to use the articles by Paul Ricoeur as indicated; we wish to express our appreciation to them for their cooperation and generosity:

1. "Husserl (1859–1938)," from the appendix contributed to the third edition of E. Bréhier, *Historie de la philosophie Allemande*, Bibliothèque d'histoire de la philosophie (Paris, Vrin, 1954), pp. 166–69, 183–85, 186–96.
2. "Introduction à 'Ideen I' de Edmund Husserl," in *Idées directrices pour une phénoménologie pure*, trans. Paul Ricoeur (Paris, Gallimard, 1950), pp. xix–xxxix.
3. "Analyses et problèmes dans 'Ideen II' de Husserl," *Revue de métu-*

physique et de morale, LVI (October–December, 1951), 357–94; and LVII (January–March, 1952), 1–16.

4. "Etudes sur les 'Méditationes Cartésiennes' de Husserl," *Revue philosophique de Louvain,* LII (1954), 75–109.

5. The essay on the Fifth Cartesian Meditation, included on pp. 115–42 below, was contributed by the author specifically for this collection and has not been published previously.

6. "Husserl et le sens de l'histoire," *Revue de métaphysique et de morale,* LIV (July–October, 1949), 280–316.

7. "Kant et Husserl," *Kantstudien,* XLVI (September, 1954), 44–67.

8. "Phénoménologie existentielle," *Encyclopédie Française,* XIX (Paris, Larousse, 1957), 10.8–10.12.

9. "Méthodes et tâches d'une philosophie de la volonté," in *Problèmes actuels de la phénoménologie,* ed. H. L. Van Breda (Paris, Desclée de Brouwer, 1952), pp. 113–40.

Our work in translating the last essay, *"Méthodes et tâches d'une philosophie de la volonté,"* was made easier by Professor Erazim V. Kohàk of Boston University who kindly made a draft of his translation available to us.

To Professor Dorian Cairns we are grateful for generous advice on many problems. We have profited greatly from consulting his unpublished *Guide for Translating Husserl* and his translation of *Cartesian Meditations* (The Hague, 1960)

To the author himself, Professor Paul Ricoeur, we are obligated not only for his good will and patient cooperation but also for explicit and expert assistance with many difficult points in the translation.

We hasten to add that any mistakes in translation are our own.

EDWARD G. BALLARD
LESTER E. EMBREE

Husserl
An Analysis of His Phenomenology

1 / Introduction: Husserl (1859–1938)

[I] HUSSERL AND THE PHENOMENOLOGICAL MOVEMENT

ALL OF PHENOMENOLOGY is not Husserl, even though he is more or less its center.

Phenomenology has a past which situates it within the history of occidental philosophy and connects it with the Leibnizian and Kantian sense of "phenomenon" (*Erscheinung*, not *Schein*). Hegel, of course, understood phenomenology to be a thorough inspection of all the varieties of human experience, not only epistemological experience, but also ethical, political, religious, aesthetic, and everyday experience. But phenomenology in Husserl's sense does not tie in with Hegel's philosophy. There are two themes in the *Phenomenology of the Spirit* which do not arise in Husserl: tragedy, which refers to the fertility of the "negative," and logic, which expresses the necessary connection of all forms of spirit into a unitary development. Thus, Husserl never produced a phenomenology of the spirit. According to Husserl, the phenomenon is not the appearing of a being which can be reached in an absolute knowing.

Husserl is connected to Kant not only through the idealistic interpretation of his method but likewise in descriptions which continue the Kantian analysis of mind (*Gemüt*); although, in the *Critique* this analysis tends to remain in the shadow of epistemological preoccupations. Likewise, phenomenology matches the spirit of Hume in depth. By reason of its taste for what is "originary," "full," "present," and beyond the abbreviations and symbols of discourse, it continues the great English tradition of criticizing language and extends its discipline of thought into all sectors of experience, experience of significations, of things, of values, and of persons. Finally, phenomenology is still more radically related to Descartes, to the Cartesian doubt and

[3]

cogito. The reduction which it effects from false evidences, from what is "self-understood" or a "matter of course" (*Verständlichkeit*), to the true phenomenon, to the genuine appearing, is quite in line with the Cartesian doubt. But in Husserl the cogito becomes something other than a first truth upon which other truths should follow in a chain of reasons. The cogito is the only field of phenomenological truth, and within it all claims to sense are brought before the presences which make up the phenomenon of the world. Thus, phenomenology continues the transcendental of Kant, the originary of Hume, and the doubt and cogito of Descartes. In no way does it represent a sharp mutation in philosophy.

Beyond this, phenomenology is a vast project whose expression is not restricted to one work or to any specific group of works. It is less a doctrine than a method capable of many exemplifications of which Husserl exploited only a few. Thus, it is necessary to look for phenomenology in the work of the psychologists of the Munich school— Pfänder, Geiger—as well as in Max Scheler, in Heidegger, in Hartmann, and also in Jaspers, even if none of these thinkers ever believed that phenomenology was the *philosophia prima*, the science of sciences. In Husserl himself the method was mixed with an idealistic interpretation which takes up a major portion of the published work and tends to place phenomenology on a plane with turn-of-the-century Neo-Kantianism. As for the parts of his work where the method is applied effectively, principally in the manuscripts, they do not constitute one homogeneous body of work with a single direction of orientation. Husserl abandoned along the way as many routes as he took. This is the case to such a degree that in a broad sense phenomenology is both the sum of Husserl's work and the heresies issuing from it. It is the sum of Husserl's own variations and in particular the sum of the genuinely phenomenological descriptions and the philosophical interpretations by which he reflects upon and systematizes his method.

[II] THE PHENOMENOLOGY OF SIGNIFICATION

LET US first consider the critique of psychologism and the conception of logic expressed in the first volume of the *Logical Investigations*.[1] The question is whether the facts of the understanding, concepts, and judgments should be studied as psychological facts,

---

1. *Logische Untersuchungen*, 1st ed., 2 vols. (Halle, 1900–1901); 2d ed., 3 vols. (Halle, 1913–21). Hereafter, this book will be referred to as *Logical Investigations*. The second edition brings the Fifth and Sixth Investigations to the level reached by *Ideas I* [cf. n. 1, p. 13 below].

consequently with all the subjective conditions which accompany them in their formation, or whether they should be considered as general elements of representation, elements independent of the consciousness we can have of them. The historical study of Kant near the turn of the century led to the complete destruction of the psychological interpretation sometimes given to Criticism. The categories designate not the products of an individual conscious activity, or even a social one, but rather the first elements of knowable reality. They are not subjective processes but rather objective data upon which the theoretician of knowledge works, just as the arithmetician works on the properties of numbers.

Husserl's anti-psychologism, however, presents itself under a perspective foreign to Kantianism. His logicism is linked to a dual movement of ideas: in the first place, it is related to the studies of pure logic towards which Trendelenburg (from 1840) and Erdman (1892) had been led after the collapse of the Hegelian dialectic; and in the second place, mainly, it is linked to a movement issuing from the mathematical sciences. This movement sought to re-establish in opposition to Kant the Leibnizian thesis according to which mathematics is an "extension of general logic." Mathematical judgments are not synthetic, as Kant believed, but rather analytic. Thereafter a rigor in demonstration was sought which had not been attained by the great mathematicians of the Eighteenth Century. All of the indemonstrable postulates introducing immediate intuitions without logical value were hunted down. Mathematical notions were analyzed to their simplest elements, and the general goal was to introduce nothing into deduction other than these elements and the relations by which they are combined. This same movement concluded in Germany with the works of Hilbert and Cantor, in England with those of Russell, and in Italy and France with logistics.

Logic, then, in Husserl had no goal other than that of separating out the general conditions of deduction. For him the primary question was one of distinguishing and isolating the elementary concepts entering into classical logical thought (concepts much more numerous than classical theory had made them out to be) and showing which of them are absolutely irreducible. In a general manner, classical logic, the logic of the syllogism, would then appear as no more than a particular case of the general theory of reasoning.

The second volume of the *Logical Investigations* opens with an analysis of signification; it already makes use of principles of phenomenological method not clarified until the Fifth and Sixth Investigations, investigations devoted to intentionality and categorial intuition. It is important to notice that the first question of phenomenology is:

What does signifying signify? Whatever the importance subsequently taken on by the description of perception, phenomenology begins not from what is most silent in the operation of consciousness but from its relationship to things mediated by signs as these are elaborated in a spoken culture. The first act of consciousness is designating or meaning (*Meinen*). To distinguish signification from signs, to separate it from the word, from the image, and to elucidate the diverse ways in which an empty signification comes to be fulfilled by an intuitive presence, whatever it may be, is to describe signification phenomenologically.

The empty act of signifying is nothing other than intentionality. If intentionality is that remarkable property of consciousness to be a consciousness of . . . , of moving out from itself toward something else, then the act of signifying contains the essence of intentionality. And it even reveals the two intentive processes (*visées*). When I mean or intend something, there is a first intending which goes to the sense,[2] which is like a stable object (*Gegenstand*) to all the acts of signifying which intend the *same thing*. Here we have the phenomenological root of logic, for there is something determinate in the sense which is intended. But this analysis which renders logic possible also goes beyond it, since there can be absurd significations, that is to say significations where the sense is actually intended but where there is no possibility of an intuitive fulfillment. Then, there is a second intending which goes to presence and which resolves itself finally into intuition. Perception is its fundamental form. There is also an intuiting of the articulations of judgment and discourse, or categorial intuition, and there are other modes of intuition—Husserl never terminated the list.

By turning his back on a phenomenology of signification in his last philosophy, Husserl abandons a way seen at the beginning of his work, one which could be called the original dialectic of sense and presence and which is best illustrated by the empty-full relationship described in the *Logical Investigations*. It is true, however, that he does not abandon it insofar as he discerns an anticipating of the unity of sense within the perceiving which permits the determination of the flux of appearances of the thing. This phenomenology of "sense," rather than the clumsy hypostatizing of "significations in themselves" to which the anti-psychologistic polemic occasionally led, constitutes the essential Platonism of the early period.

2. [We translate the French *sens* as "sense." This term usually refers to the object or objectivity intended, i.e., the noematic or object-side of consciousness. The term "meaning" is reserved for the (noetic) process or act of intending such a sense; thus, sometimes it renders *visée* (cf. p. 36 below).—Trans.]

Moreover, phenomenology itself is possible because intentionality goes to the sense. This is the sense which determines presence, just as much as presence fulfills the sense. Thanks to an intuition bearing on the essence of "acts" and their "contents," we are able to distinguish expression, sign, signification—empty signification and fulfilled signification—sensuous intuition, and categorial intuition. All phenomenology takes place on the level of an intuition of an eidos. It does not stop with the individual and incommunicable subjective process [3] but rather reaches for the intelligible internal articulation and universal signification in the subjective process. In short, it is a signification which more or less comes to fulfill either immanent perceiving or the imagining of this perceiving, which by means of variations precipitates out the "sense" within the crucible of phenomenological analysis.

After the *Logical Investigations* Husserl's works follow two paths: [4] On the one hand, descriptive themes never cease to be enriched and to overflow the initial logical framework; [5] on the other hand, Husserl continues to refine the philosophy of his method and thus to mix a phenomenological philosophy [6] with a phenomenology actually practiced. This mixture is evidenced in the title: *Ideas Pertaining to a Pure Phenomenology and Phenomenological Philosophy*. Neither of these ways has priority over the other. The reduction was used before being reflected upon,[7] and long afterwards Husserl was still using descriptive themes to elicit the reduction. The fact is that the idealistic interpretation of the method does not necessarily coincide with its actual practice, as many of his disciples have pointed out. Beginning in 1929,

3. [We translate the French *vécu* as "subjective process" or "subjective life" depending on the context. Here we follow Professor Cairns, who in translating *Cartesianische Meditationen* (cf. n. 1, p. 82) usually renders the German equivalent, *Erlebnis*, in this manner. Other translators have used "lived experience."—Trans.]

4. Husserl's actual phenomenology is contained in the very considerable number of manuscripts placed in order by the Husserl Archives at Louvain, many of which are published in the series *Husserliana*, (The Hague, 1950–   ).

5. *Formale und Transcendentale Logik, Jahrbuch für Philosophie und Phänomenologische Forschung* (1929). French translation by Susanne Bachelard, *Logique Formale et Logique Transcendentale* (Paris, 1957). This book—hereafter referred to as *Formal and Transcendental Logic*—represents the final state of Husserl's logical work, as viewed within the perspective of transcendental idealism.

6. This phenomenological philosophy finds its extreme expression in *Cartesian Meditations* [cf. n. 1, p. 82 below]. Also see *Nachwort zu meinen Ideen*, published with *Ideen III, Husserliana IV*, ed. Marly Biemel (The Hague, 1952), 138–62. [English translation by W. R. Boyce-Gibson, published as preface to *Ideas* (cf. n. 1, p. 13 below).]

7. Cf. the lecture course of 1907 entitled *Die Idee der Phänomenologie*, published in *Husserliana II*, ed. W. Biemel (The Hague, 1950). [English translation by William P. Alston and George Nakhnikian, *The Idea of Phenomenology* (The Hague, 1964).]

phenomenology experienced a resurgence both descriptively and systematically.

[III] THE DESCRIPTIVE THEMES

FROM THE START Husserl confers on the notion of intentionality its full breadth: every consciousness is a consciousness of . . . (Here "consciousness" signifies not the individual unity of a "flux of subjective processes" but rather each distinct cogitatio turned toward a distinct cogitatum.) Hence, there will be as many species of intentionality, as many "consciousnesses," as there are ways in which a cogito may be turned toward something, for example, toward the actual, the inactual, the past, the willed, the loved, the desired, the judged, and so on. From a strictly descriptive point of view, intentionality avoids the alternatives of realism and idealism. Insofar as it appears to a consciousness, one can say that the object *transcends* that consciousness and likewise that the object is *in* that consciousness; but it is there specifically by virtue of being intentional and not by virtue of being a really inherent part of consciousness. Intentionality only signifies that consciousness is, in the first place, outside of itself and that it is so in manifold ways among which logical objectivity is only a modality of the second degree and perception is the most fundamental modality.

Husserl evades his own logicism and moves away from critical philosophies of judgment by asserting the primacy of perception among intentional acts. In this primacy we have the standard for all presence "in flesh and blood." Likewise perceiving uncovers the horizonal structure of consciousness; every present consciousness is discovered to be exceeded by a horizon of perceivability which confers on the world its strangeness and abundance. In turn this horizon gives rise to a reflection on the temporality encountered in the perceiving of even the most stable of objects. In short, perception never ceases to reveal how living goes beyond judging. At the end of this road is the theme of "being-in-the-world" explicated by the phenomenology of the later Husserl, by Heidegger, and by the French existentialists.

At the same time this description develops a critique;[8] in effect,

8. Initially Husserl conceived this criticism as a strict science, the foundation of the exact sciences, excluding all pathos and concrete ethics; cf. "Philosophie als strenge Wissenschaft" ("Philosophy as Strict Science"), *Logos*, I (1911), 289–341. [Q. Lauer has translated this essay into English, and it appears in two places: *Cross Currents*, VI (1956), 227–46 and 325–44, and *Edmund Husserl: Phenomenology and the Crisis of Philosophy* (New York and Evanston, Ill., 1965), pp. 71–148.—Trans.]

phenomenology carries out a frontal attack on a conviction belonging to all Galileans. The first truth of the world is not the truth of mathematical physics but the truth of perception; or rather the truth of science is erected as a superstructure upon a first foundation of presence and existence, that of the world lived through perceptually.

Husserl can thus maintain the transcendence of the perceived with respect to consciousness by a criticism of the critique of "secondary qualities," all the while denying the existence in-themselves of the things perceived. This difficult and original setting up of the problem of reality is phenomenology's essential philosophical contribution. The distinction between the noema and the noesis in every consciousness permits the analysis of consciousness to be conducted so that alternatively there are noematic analyses, that is to say analyses dealing with the objective face of the subjective process (the perceived as such, the imagined as such, etc.), and noetic analyses, dealing with attentional modalities, with the power of the "ego" of the cogito, and with the temporality of the subjective flux of adumbrations [9] of things. There is no way to convey even an approximate notion of the patience and rigor of these analyses. *Ideas II*, devoted to the constitution of the thing, of the psyche, and of cultural and personal realities, is a good example of this work. There it appears clearly that "constituting" is not constructing, even less creating, but rather the unfolding of the intendings of consciousness which are merged together in the natural, unreflective, naïve grasp of a thing.

[IV] FROM DESCRIPTIVE TO TRANSCENDENTAL PHENOMENOLOGY

THE PHENOMENOLOGICAL "reduction" is presented as the explication of the method practiced in the description of phenomena and simultaneously as the elaboration of a transcendental philosophy implying a genuine metaphysical decision concerning the ontological status of these phenomena.

The reduction was born from a skeptical crisis posterior to the discovery of intentionality yet concerning the very possibility of intentionality, that is to say, ultimately concerning the reference of a consciousness to a transcendence. The essence of consciousness is also

---

9. [The French here is *sillouettes*, a translation of Husserl's *Abschattungen*. Professor Ricoeur also uses *profil* and *esquisse* for this term. We shall translate it as "adumbration"; other translators have used "perspectival variation" (cf. p. 102 below)—Trans.]

its enigma. The crisis was resolved, not by the distinction between reflective consciousness and the spatial thing, as in Descartes, but by the separation between the supposed in-itself status and the pure appearing of the object itself. In *Ideas I* this separation is prepared by an investigation into the precariousness and temporality of this appearing, for, placed in flux, the object is ready for the reduction to its successive appearances. The hypothesis that the world could be nothing, that is to say that adumbrations could cease to come together into a thing of some sort, completes the resolution of being into appearing. Thus presented, the reduction seems to be a removal of being. In *Ideas I* consciousness is called a "remainder," a phenomenological "residue." In the purely methodological sense of the operation this means that one abstains from pronouncing (*epoché*) on the ultimate ontological status of the appearing and that one occupies oneself only with the pure appearing. But more and more Husserl interprets this conquest of appearing in defiance of unmotivated believing in the in-itself as a decision about the very sense of being.

The *Cartesian Meditations* are the most radical expression of this new idealism for which the world is not only "for me" but draws all of its being-status "from me." The world becomes the "world-perceived-in-the-reflective life." Constitution becomes a gigantic project of progressively composing the signification "world" without an ontological remainder.

In addition, the Fourth Meditation contains Husserl's outline of the passage from a phenomenology "turned toward the object" to a phenomenology "turned toward the ego," where "the ego continuously constitutes itself as being." The cogitatum is grasped in the cogito and this in the ego which lives "through" its thinkings. Phenomenology is the unfolding of the ego, thereafter termed "monad" in the Leibnizian manner. It is the "explication of self" (*Selbstauslegung*).

Phenomenology is obliged to at least two things for this radicalism. In the first place it advances the theme of temporality; this theme was perceived very early. The present, we are told in the *Lectures on Inner-Time Consciousness*,[10] "retains" the immediate past, which is not a represented memory but a "just now" implied in the consciousness of the "now." This analysis, originally destined to resolve a psychological enigma, that of the persistence of an identical object in consciousness, becomes one of the main keys to the constitution of the ego by the ego;

---

10. *Vorlsungen zur Phänomenologie des inneren Zeitbewusstseins*, ed. M. Heidegger, *Jahrbuch*, IX (1928), 367–496. These lectures date from 1905–10. [English translation by James S. Churchill, *The Phenomenology of Internal Time Consciousness* (Bloomington, Ind., 1964).]

in the large number of manuscripts devoted to time (Group C),[11] the "living present" appears as the origin of temporalization by reason of its dialectical structure of "flowing persistence." In turn this primordial temporalization serves to elucidate the consolidation of acquired evidences whose origin has vanished. A non-positional transversal intentionality inherent in the succession which consciousness makes with itself is thus placed at the origin of the "thetic" consciousness which posits things or significations as in-themselves. We cannot overestimate the importance of this theme, which in fact was elicited by Husserlian idealism, even if that idealism could not survive this radical motivation. Just here we have one of the crossroads where the Kierkegaardian meditation on the instant meets with the Husserlian reflection on the living present; Heidegger will not forget it.

In addition, the identification of phenomenology with egology leads to the promotion of a second great problem, that of the existence of the Other. Phenomenology very clearly comes to bay with the paradox of solipsism, for only the ego is constituted primordially. The importance of the Fifth Meditation (on the constitution of the Other) stems from this paradox; Husserl labored over this Meditation for many years. The constitution of the Other plays the same role in Husserl that the existence of God does in Descartes in preserving the objectivity of my thoughts. But if the ego appears able to be transcended only by another ego, this other ego must itself be constituted precisely as *outsider* but still *in* the sphere of experience belonging to the ego. This problem is one of the great difficulties of Husserlian phenomenology. Respect for the naïve experience of intersubjectivity and the philosophical radicalism inherited from the older Meditations are so closely mixed together that it is difficult to separate the descriptions from the idealistic content.

[V] From Transcendental Idealism to Genetic Phenomenology

Husserl's works had a strange destiny: their author reworked them over and over again, and sometimes when they were judged ready for publication their problems had already been left behind. Transcendental idealism underwent a profound revision after

---

11. The system of classifying Husserl's manuscripts is explained by H. L. Van Breda, "The Husserl Archives in Louvain," *Journal of Philosophy and Phenomenological Research,* VII (March, 1947), 487–91.

1929.[12] At first glance this revision is a true revolution which leads phenomenology into the neighborhood of French existential phenomenology. In reality, however, the descriptions of the last period continue those of the preceding period; only the idealistic interpretation of the method is overturned.

Husserl searches further and further below the judgment for the order of experience and the origin of the predicative order. At the same time he accentuates the notion of passive genesis as prior to the active operations of positing, juxtaposing, supposing, etc. Finally the world appears as a totality inaccessible to doubt, not acquired through the addition of objects, and inherent in "living." This life-world (*Lebenswelt*) is the "pre-given passive universal in all judgmental activity." Thus, Husserl pushes the tendencies of descriptive phenomenology to the limit, abandoning the dialectic of empty signification and full presence elaborated earlier in the *Logical Investigations*. He engages in a "genealogical" investigation which definitely appears to move from below to above without the return of a contrary movement from the signified to the lived.

But the decisive fact is the progressive abandonment, upon contact with the new analyses, of the idealism of the *Cartesian Meditations*. The reduction less and less signifies a "return to the ego" and more and more a "return from logic to the antepredicative," to the primordial evidence of the world. The accent is placed no longer on the monadic ego; instead the accent is placed on the totality formed by the ego and the surrounding world in which it is vitally engaged. Thus, phenomenology tends toward the recognition of what is prior to all reduction and what cannot be reduced. In sum, only the Galilean universe is reduced. The irreducibility of the life-world signifies that the Platonic-mathematical conversion cannot be carried out all the way. The being of the world is manifest in such a manner that all truth refers back to it.

Owing to this impressive mutation beginning from primarily logical preoccupations, phenomenology was prepared for the astonishing encounter with existential meditation coming from horizons quite foreign to Husserl—the tireless worker so temperate and so honest.

12. *Die Krisis der Europäischen Wissenschaften und die transcendentale Philosophie* (*The Crisis of European Sciences and Transcendental Philosophy*), hereafter referred to as *Crisis* [cf. n. 1, p. 144 below]. Also see *Erfahrung und Urteil, Untersuchungen zur Genealogie der Logik*, hereafter referred to as *Experience and Judgment*; Husserlian texts completed and connected by L. Landgrebe, following Husserl's indications, 1st ed. (Prague, 1939); 2d ed. (Hamburg, 1954).

2 / An Introduction to Husserl's *Ideas I*

To Mikel Dufrenne

THERE CAN BE NO QUESTION of viewing the whole of Husserlian phenomenology within this limited space. Furthermore, we are prevented at the present time from attempting a comprehensive and definitive interpretation of Husserl's work by the enormous mass of unpublished material deposited at the Husserl Archives at Louvain. There are 30,000 handwritten pages there, almost all in shorthand, which represent a considerably larger volume of work than that published during the philosopher's lifetime. The transcription and the partial or total publication of these manuscripts is projected by the Archives under the direction of Dr. H. L. Van Breda. Only the completion of this undertaking will allow Husserl's thought to be fully tested. The presentation offered here is based almost entirely on the texts published during Husserl's life.

The goal of this introduction is, therefore, quite modest. There is first the question of drawing together several themes issuing from the internal examination of *Ideas I* developed in our commentary; [1] then

1. [Ricoeur is referring to his running commentary, which appears in the footnotes to his French translation of *Ideas I* but is not included in the present collection. *Ideas I* is the short title for *Ideen zu einer reinen Phänomenologie und phänomenologischen Philosophie, erstes Buch, Allgemeine Einfuhrung in die reine Phänomenologie*, published in *Jahrbuch für Philosophie und Phänomenologische Forschung* (1913), ed. E. Husserl, and also published in *Husserliana III*, ed. Walter Biemel (The Hague, 1950). English translation by W. R. Boyce-Gibson, *Ideas, General Introduction to Pure Phenomenology* (New York, 1931). French translation by Paul Ricoeur, *Idées directrices pour une phénoménologie;* Vol. I: *Introduction générale à la phénoménologie pure* (Paris, 1950). Our page references will be to the pagination of the *Jahrbuch* edition and the first three unchanged German editions; we have used the letter *I* preceding the page numbers to refer to *Ideas I* in those editions. This pagination also appears on the margins of the French and *Husserliana III* editions.—Trans.]

there is the matter of outlining the history of Husserl's thought from the *Logical Investigations* to the *Ideas* with the aid of the most important manuscripts of the period 1901–11.

[I] THE DEVELOPMENT OF REFLECTION WITHIN *Ideas I*

IT IS PARTICULARLY difficult to treat *Ideas I* as a book to be understood in itself. What makes things difficult, in the first place, is the fact that while meant as the first book of a work in three books, it is the only one which Husserl allowed to be published. We have been able to consult *Ideas II* at the Husserl Archives. This volume is a very precise study of problems concerning the constitution of the physical thing, the psycho-physical ego, and the person seen from the viewpoint of the human sciences. Thus, it is the application of a method which was presented in *Ideas I* only in principle and through a few highly abbreviated examples. According to the Introduction to *Ideas I*, *Ideas III* was to found first philosophy upon phenomenology; unfortunately, the definitive transcription of *Ideas III* was not finished when we ended our work of translating *Ideas I*.

In addition, *Ideas I* presupposes precise logical cognitions to be found in the *Logical Investigations*. These cognitions are usually treated by allusion in the present work and cannot be understood technically without recourse to the *Logical Investigations*. Furthermore, to grasp the exact connection between the *Logical Investigations* and the central notion of transcendental phenomenology, recourse must be had to *Formal and Transcendental Logic*, which shows the passage from formal logic to its transcendental foundation in phenomenology.

Finally, it must be added that *Ideas I* is a book whose sense lies hidden; one is inevitably inclined to search for this sense elsewhere. At every turn one gets the impression that the essential is not being said, that the effort is to impart a new vision of the world and of consciousness, rather than to say something definitive about the world and about consciousness, something which perhaps could not be understood at all without the acquisition of this new vision.

The key to the philosopher's work escapes us even in a reading of the *Cartesian Meditations*, a work appearing twenty years after *Ideas I*. The most explicit text that we have raises the most embarrassing questions. This text is not even by Husserl himself but by Eugen Fink, who was Husserl's assistant for several years and who knew from within not only the published work but also a good part of the manuscript material and, above all, the living thought of the master. We are speaking of the famous article entitled "Die phänomenologische Philosophie Edmund Husserls in der gegenwärtigen Kritik." [2] One might suspect that this article represents merely Fink's interpretation, or a self-interpretation by Husserl at some point while under the influence of Fink. In any event, Husserl has accredited this article in the clearest manner: "I rejoice in being able to say that it contains not one phrase with which I do not perfectly agree and recognize explicitly as the expression of my own convictions" (*Preface*). Therefore, we have no right to neglect this text. We shall return to it in attempting to elucidate questions which the direct reading of *Ideas I* leaves hanging.

1. "Essences and Eidetic Cognition"

Ideas I opens with a very difficult chapter on logic that the reader can temporarily omit in order to understand the spiritual (*spirituel*) movement of the whole book. But it will be essential to reintegrate this chapter along the way in order finally to grasp the status of phenomenology as a science. Even if we ignore for the moment the swarm of technical difficulties of a somewhat local character, an uncertainty weighs on the over-all interpretation of this chapter. If phenomenology is to be "presuppositionless," in what sense does it presuppose a logical framework? Initially it is impossible to answer this question, for the response would be just the law of the spiritual movement of *Ideas I* which we are going to attempt to grasp. This law is at first supported by a logic and a psychology, then through a spiral motion it changes level, is freed from these initial supports, and finally emerges as primary and without presuppositions. Only at the end of this deepening movement is phenomenology in a position to found the science which at first elicited it.

The goal of this chapter on logic is to show first that it is possible to erect a non-empirical, eidetic science of consciousness, and second, to understand the essences of consciousness as the supreme genera which will be found again throughout the whole "region" consciousness (as contrasted to the "region" nature). Thus, phenomenology might appear to be dependent upon this twofold logical analysis of essences and regions. But in fact, this analysis will be raised to the level of the subject which is constituting with respect to those sciences which gave it its initial status. In particular one sees that the "region" consciousness is not coordinated with the "region" nature, but that the latter is referred to the former and even in a very special sense of the word is included in it. Thus, one can suspect that the phenomenology

2. Eugen Fink, "Die phänemenologische Philosophie Edmund Husserls in der gegenwärtigen Kritik," *Kantstudien*, XXXVIII (1933), pp. 319–83.

which earlier appeared to isolate its object within a total reality (nature and consciousness) might be able to found the other sciences and even its own methodology by founding logic itself universally; so it appears in *Formal and Transcendental Logic.*

Let us set this complex relationship of logic and phenomenology aside for the moment, since the third part of this Introduction will be devoted to the historical problem of the passage from the *Logical Investigations* to the *Ideas.*

2. "Fundamental Phenomenological Considerations"

Ideas I describes an ascending path which leads to what Husserl calls the reduction or, perhaps better, the "suspension" of the natural thesis of the world (thesis = positing). This movement is as yet only the inverse, the negative, of a formative, or perhaps even creative, operation of consciousness called "transcendental constitution." What is this thesis of the world? What is reduction? What is constitution? What is constituted? What is this transcendental subject which disengages itself from natural reality and engages in the work of constitution? These things cannot be directly told but must be achieved by the spiritual discipline (*ascèse*) of the phenomenological method. Also it is difficult to say at what point within *Ideas I* one is actually using the famous phenomenological reduction, a fact which is quite disconcerting to the reader. In Part Two the reduction is spoken of from without and in very enigmatic and even confusing terms (I, §§ 27–32, 33, 56–62). The most important analyses of Part Two are below the level of the reduction and, according to Fink, it is not certain that the analyses of the third and fourth parts go beyond the uncertain level between the preparatory psychology and the truly transcendental philosophy.

Leaving the enigmatic Chapter One, which gets ahead of the spiritual discipline to come, let us consider the analyses of Part Two, which prepare for the phenomenological reduction by setting out from the level of psychological reflection. They are still within the "natural attitude," which is just what is to be reduced. They include two movements:

(1) Chapter Two contains the study of the intentionality of consciousness, that remarkable property of consciousness to be a consciousness of . . . , an intending of transcendence, a bursting out towards the world.[3] This chapter points up the study by the discovery

---

3. *"Eclatement vers le monde . . ."* Cf. J.-P. Sartre, "Une idée fondamentale de la phénoménologie de Husserl," *N.R.F.* (1939), pp. 129–32; reprinted in Sartre's *Situations I,* 1947. [Ricoeur by no means restricts himself to the term

of a reflection which is the revelation of consciousness to itself as a bursting out beyond itself. What is this analysis aiming at? It can be called phenomenological in the broad sense of a description of phenomena such as they offer themselves to intuition but not in the strict sense of the transcendental phenomenology introduced by reduction and constitution. The goal is modest. It is a matter of preparing to free oneself from the natural attitude by shattering the naturalism which is only one of its least subtle manifestations. In Husserlian language, the "region" consciousness is other than the "region" nature. It is perceived differently, it exists differently, it is certain differently. An entirely Cartesian method of beginning is evident at this point. This is one path, but not the only one, since the *Formal and Transcendental Logic* proceeds along an altogether logical route (and an important manuscript of the *Crisis* discerns five different routes). This path is not without dangers. It immediately leads one to think that the reduction consists in subtracting something (dubitable nature) and retaining a residue from the subtraction (indubitable consciousness). Such a mutilation, leaving only a psychological consciousness and not the transcendental subject, is a counterfeit of the true reduction. But the pedagogical procedure of *Ideas I*, which is more Cartesian than Kantian, will risk this confusion.

(2) Chapter Three straightens out the analysis. Consciousness is not only different from reality, but reality is relative to consciousness in the sense that it announces itself as a unity of sense in a diversity of convergent "adumbrations." The mind (*esprit*) is thus oriented towards the notions of reduction and constitution. That the appearances harmonize differently, even that they do not harmonize at all, is shown not to be contrary to the essence of an object and of the world. In this limiting hypothesis, made up by the imagination but opposed by no essence, the world would be annihilated (I, § 49). From this point on nature is no longer just dubitable, it is also contingent and relative; consciousness is no longer merely indubitable but also necessary and absolute (I, §§ 54–55).

A mind thus prepared perceives that it is brought little by little into

---

"transcendence" in discussing the problem of the intentionality of consciousness (cf. pp. 8 of this text), partly because he does not wish to risk confusion with the existentialist sense of this term (cf. p. 99 below), partly also because the complex and somewhat enigmatic character of this characteristic of consciousness is best expressed with the help of a variety of metaphors. Later he will make use of such terms as *"se dépasser"* (which will usually be translated as "to go beyond," e.g., pp. 93 f.), or *"les opérations de transfert"* (e.g., p. 141), or *"transgresser"* (cf. n. 6, p. 119 below), and other phrases, as in the present textual passage, to refer to this property of consciousness or to some one of its facets.—Trans.]

harmony with the reduction, and the reduction leads on to an analysis which never stops moving beyond itself.

(3) If now one is inclined to approach the famous phenomenological reduction, then one must attempt to grasp the "natural thesis," "reduction of the thesis," and "transcendental constitution" en bloc. To think it possible to define the natural attitude while maintaining this same attitude is illusory. The reduction itself reveals the natural attitude as the "thesis of the world," and at the same time constitution gives a positive sense to the reduction. For this reason all that is said about the natural thesis is initially obscure and inclined to confusion. In particular, one is tempted to try a Cartesian or Kantian schema, the first in line with Chapter Two and the second in line with Chapter Three. Thus, it might be said that the thesis of the world is the illusion that perception is more certain than reflection, or else that this thesis is the naïve believing in the existence in-itself of the world. The reduction would then be something like methodological doubting or else recourse to consciousness as the a priori condition for the possibility of objectivity. These are only some among the several possible routes of approach. In particular, the reduction is not doubting, since it leaves believing intact without participating in it. Hence, properly speaking, the thesis is not believing but rather something which contaminates belief. Nor is the reduction the discovery of a regulative action of the mind, since consciousness continues to be a subject of intuition and not of construction.[4] The intuitionism at the base of the Husserlian epistemology is not destroyed by transcendental phenomenology. On the contrary, Husserl never ceases to deepen his philosophy of perception in the broad sense of a philosophy of seeing. Therefore, the natural thesis is something mixed with an undoubted belief and, what is more, one which is intuitive at its root. Hence, Husserl has a principle in view which is involved in believing without being believing and which contaminates the seeing without being this seeing itself, since the seeing will emerge in its authentic form from the phenomenological reduction.

We move on toward the essential point by noting that the thesis of the world is not a positive element that could go on to cancel the reduction understood as a negative moment. On the contrary, the reduction removes a limitation and thus frees the whole sweep of consciousness. What allows us to affirm this liberation is precisely the link between theses, reduction, and constitution. If constitution is to be the essential positive moment of consciousness, the reduction must be the lifting of a prohibition that weighs upon it.

4. Husserl, "Postscript to my 'Ideas . . .'" [cf. above p. 7, n. 6].

What prohibition can limit the consciousness that believes in the world and sees the world in which it believes? Pursuing our metaphors, we may say that the thesis of the world is consciousness caught up in its believing; it is captive of seeing, woven into the world into which it transcends itself. But this is still misleading, for it remains to be understood what subject is captive in this way, since this captivity in no way inhibits the psychological freedom of attention which is turned here and there and considers this and that. This freedom remains a freedom within a matrix which is precisely the natural attitude. But to understand the thesis of the world is already to realize oneself not merely as the psychological but as the transcendental subject. In other words, it is already to have reached the summit of phenomenology (a summit that as yet is only a provisional one).

Consequent upon our inability to reach the radical understanding of the transcendental subject in a single step, by relation to which the thesis of the world derives its sense, the analysis in *Ideas I* leaves the reduction dangerously associated with the notion of the destruction of the world and the notion of the relativity of the world to the absolute of consciousness. Moreover, the Kantian (and even Cartesian) atmosphere of this pedagogical hyperbole is no longer useful in Part Four for enabling us to understand how intuition marks the ultimate "legitimation" of all believings, be they mathematical, logical, perceptual, etc. In fact, the reduction, far from destroying intuition, emphasizes its primitive or originary character. If intuition is to be the ultimate for all constitution, then the "thesis of the world" should be some sort of modification of intuition.

Husserl uses a surprising expression to start us off in the right direction. He calls the intuition that can "legitimize" all signification envisaged by consciousness the "originary giving intuition" (*originär gebende Anschauung*). That intuition can be *giving* (*donatrice*) is at first glance an expression more enigmatic than clarifying. Nevertheless, I believe Husserl would be understood if one could understand that the constitution of the world is not a formal legislation but the very giving of seeing by the transcendental subject. Then it could be said that in the thesis of the world I see without knowing that I give. But the "ego" of the "I see" in the natural attitude is not on the same level as the "ego" of the "I give" in the transcendental attitude. The first "ego" is mundane; and the world toward which it transcends itself is mundane. The spiritual discipline of phenomenology brings about a differentiation between the "ego" and the world because it elicits the transcendental "ego" out of the mundane "ego." Hence, since the transcendental "ego" is the key to constitution, and constitution the key to the reduction, and the reduction the key to the thesis of the world, then it is quite understandable that Husserl can speak only very enigmatically when beginning, as he does in *Ideas I*, with the thesis of the world.

I think that each of us is invited to rediscover in himself this act of transcendence. Thus, I will risk an outline of the "existential" sense of the thesis of the world. Initially I am lost and forgotten in the world, lost in the things, lost in the ideas, lost in the plants and animals, lost in others, lost in mathematics. Presence (which can never be disavowed) is the occasion of temptation; in seeing there is a trap, the trap of my alienation; there I am external, diverted. Now it is evident how naturalism is the lowest stage of the natural attitude, the level that leads to its re-engagement. For if I lose myself in the world, I am then ready to treat myself as a thing of the world. The thesis of the world is a sort of blindness in the very heart of seeing. What I call living is hiding myself as naïve consciousness within the existence of all things: "In natural living I live the fundamental form of all 'actual' life." [5] Thus, the spiritual discipline of phenomenology is a true conversion of the sense of intentionality, which is first the forgetting of consciousness, and then its discovery of itself as given.

This is why intentionality can be described both before and after the phenomenological reduction; before, it is an encounter; after, it is a constitution. And it continues to be the common theme of pre-phenomenological psychology and of transcendental phenomenology. Reduction is the first free act because it is the one that liberates from mundane illusion. Through it I apparently lose the world that I truly gain.

3. "Methods and Problems of Pure Phenomenology"

In *Ideas I* not only are the problems of constitution situated in a certain indeterminate zone between intentional psychology and a phenomenology which is frankly transcendental,[6] but they are deliberately kept within narrow limits. Only the constitution of "transcendences" is considered, and then principally the transcendence of nature, which is considered as the touchstone of the phenomenological attitude (I, §§ 47 and 56). This is quite reasonable if one begins by passing over the more subtle transcendences, such as the psychological ego, which are "founded" in nature by the intermediacy

5. "Im naturlichen Dahinleben lebe ich immerfort in dieser Grundform alles aktuellen Lebens" (I, pp. 50–51).

6. This is why Husserl insists on the distinction between "phenomenological psychology" and "transcendental phenomenology" at such length in his "Postscript to my 'Ideas . . .'"

of the body (I, § 53). A very minor place is made for the transcendence of logical essences, which nevertheless provided the principal analyses of the *Logical Investigations* (I, §§ 59–60). There is no doubt that the natural attitude also includes logic, that the reduction concerns it, and that there is a problem of constituting the logico-mathematical disciplines, as outlined in the third chapter of Part Four. This outline is important because it shows very well that logic itself has a transcendental root in a primordial subjectivity. The *Logical Investigations* are integrated, not repudiated. This is shown most abundantly in *Formal and Transcendental Logic*. But in *Ideas I* the psychological method of initiating phenomenology does not open up a clear view of this grafting of logic onto the new phenomenological tree. Generally speaking, the *Ideas* have their center of gravity in a phenomenology of sensuous perception. From this fact a number of residual problems develop, to which allusion is made at the close.

In the third part the problems of constitution are very carefully presented with reference to the notion of noema. This notion is developed slowly and through long methodological preparations (Chapter One), and not without a return to the themes of the first phenomenological analysis (reflection, intentionality, etc.), but this time reaching up to another level in the spiral movement of the analysis (Chapter Two). Chapter Three is a study of the noema (from the Greek *nous*, mind). The noema is the correlate of consciousness, but it is considered as constituted in consciousness. But (a) this constitution is still described as the parallelism of certain characters of the noema (object-side of consciousness) and certain characters of the noesis (subject-side of consciousness) (I, § 98); (b) this constitution provisionally leaves out of consideration the material of the act (or hyle) which is animated by the constituting form (I, §§ 85, 86, 97). Owing to this twofold limitation, constitution does not appear as creative here. But from time to time courageous breakthroughs in the direction of the radical problems of phenomenological philosophy indicate that consciousness is what "prescribes" the mode of givenness and the structure of all correlates of consciousness by its "configuration," and by its "interconnection." Inversely, every unity of sense announced in consciousness is the *index* of these interconnections of consciousness (I, §§ 90, 96).

But the phenomenological exercises of this Third Part—entitled noetico-noematic analyses—do not carry out this promise. These exercises consist in a separation and a study of correlation between the traits of the object intended (noema) and the traits of the conscious intending (noesis). The most remarkable analyses are devoted to the "characters of belief" (certitude, doubting, questioning, etc., on the

noetic side; actual, doubtful, problematic, etc., on the noematic side).
One by one all of the characters of the "intended" as such are constituted—all except the one reserved for the fourth part. These characters are constituted in the sense that the doubtful, for example, or the
actual, are included in the very "sense" of the "intended as such" and
appear as correlative to a character which belongs to the conscious
intending. Bit by bit, the "intended as such" becomes filled out with all
of the characters which ultimately amount to reality itself.

Perhaps the residual problems of Part Three are more important
than the explicit analyses. Everything points to the supposition that if
the problems of constitution treated in *Ideas I* concern the transcendences announced in the lived subjective process (*vécu*)—that is, the
object-side of the subjective life—then the more radical problem of
the constitution of the ego, of the subject-side of the ego, remains. The
sense of the ego, whose free gaze "traverses" all of its acts, remains
indefinite. The *Logical Investigations* asserted that the ego is outside
among the things and that subjective life is only an interconnected
bundle of acts which does not require the referential center of an ego.
In *Ideas I* Husserl retracts this pronouncement; there is an un-reduced
pure ego. But is this pure ego the most radical transcendental subject?
Nothing indicates this to be the case. On the contrary, it is clearly
affirmed that it is itself constituted in a specific sense (I, p. 163). And
in fact, a breach in Husserl's silence on these difficult problems is
opened by the problem of time. Moreover, the date of the writing of
such a work as *Lectures on Inner-Time Consciousness* (1904–10)
provides evidence that the most radical problems of egology are contemporaneous with the birth of transcendental phenomenology itself.

A group of important manuscripts is devoted to this question.[7] In
Ideas I even the interconnection of time implies that reflection is
possible only in consequence of the "retention" of the immediate past
in the present. But still more radically, it is seen that the enigma of the
sensuous matter, whose diversity ultimately harbors the basic configurations where transcendences appear, resides in the immanent connection of flux lived through. Now the constitution of transcendences
leaves as residue just this hyle (matter), this manifold of adumbrations. Thus, by this means, constitution is glimpsed at another degree
of depth. Even though this be so, ego, temporality, and hyle form a
trilogy that calls for a proto-constitution only remotely envisaged in
Ideas I.

---

7. In the classification of manuscripts set up by E. Fink and L. Landgrebe in
1935, this is Group D: *Primordiale Konstitution* (*Urkonstitution*).

4. "Reason and Actuality"

IF ONE ABSTRACTS from the deliberate omissions in the analysis on the side of the subject and the correlative difficulties on the side of the object, then one last gap still remains to be filled in between what we shall henceforth call the "sense" of the noema and actuality. An attempt has been made to constitute the sense of the noema, for example, the sense of the tree that I perceive over there determined as green, gnarled, and further characterized as perceived with certainty, doubt, conjecture, etc. To constitute this sense of the tree, according to Part Three, is to show that it is correlative to certain structures of consciousness. The very term "noema" signifies that there is more in the subject than the subject itself and that a specific reflection uncovers for every moment of consciousness its implied correlate. Thus, phenomenology appears as a reflection not only on the subject but also on the object *in* the subject.

Something essential is still missing from this constitution, namely the "fullness" of perceived presence, the "quasi-fullness" of the imaginary, or the "simply intended" of determinations merely signified. Transcendental phenomenology aspires to integrate into the noema its own relation to the object, i.e., its "fullness," which completes the constitution of the whole noema. This final change of course in *Ideas I* is of the highest importance. In effect, the whole theory of evidence set forth in the *Logical Investigations* is based upon the fulfilling of empty significations by the "originary" presences (presence in the original, in person) of the thing itself, of the idea itself, etc. (Sixth Investigation, Part Two). The universal function of intuition—be it intuition of the empirical individual, of the essences of things, of essence-limits in mathematics, or of regulative Ideas in the Kantian sense—is to fulfill the "emptiness" of signs by the "fullness" of presences. To constitute actuality is to refuse to leave its "presence" outside the "sense" of the world.

Thus in Part Four, *Ideas I* leads us to the initial difficulty that brought forth the interpretation of the thesis of the world. Transcendental phenomenology would be established if we could show effectively that intuition is "prescribed" by an "interconnection of consciousness." But *Ideas I* promises more than it produces. The "relation to the object," it is affirmed, "is the most intimate moment of the noema . . . the point most central to the core." The actual object represents "an index that refers back each time to perfectly determined systems of consciousness which present a teleological unity" (I, pp. 268–69, 303).

All of transcendental phenomenology hangs upon this twofold possibility: on the one hand, of affirming the primacy of intuition over all construction; on the other hand, of making the point of view of transcendental constitution triumph over the naïveté of natural man. In his "Postscript" (p. 4) Husserl emphasizes the unity of these two requirements: transcendental subjectivity issuing from the reduction is itself a "field of experience," "described" and not "constructed."

[II] DIFFICULTIES IN AN OVER-ALL INTERPRETATION OF *Ideas I*

THE PHENOMENOLOGY elaborated in *Ideas I* is incontestably an idealism, even a transcendental idealism. This term itself is not in the *Ideas* though it is encountered in later unpublished manuscripts, in *Formal and Transcendental Logic*,[8] and in the *Cartesian Meditations*.[9] Furthermore, Landgrebe unhesitatingly groups the most important analyses of constitution around this term in his Analytical Index to *Ideas I,* and Husserl employs it to characterize the *Ideas* in "Postscript to my 'Ideas . . . ,'" when he contrasts "transcendental-phenomenological idealism" to "psychological idealism." Finally, though, it is impossible to characterize this idealism definitively on the basis of *Ideas I* alone; it remains in the state of a project, promise, or claim. The most carefully worked out parts of *Ideas I* are either fragments of an intentional psychology (Part Two) or exercises in the direction of a radical constitution of reality, but still below the level of the idealism envisaged (Parts Three and Four). Finally, "pure consciousness," "transcendental consciousness," "the absolute being of consciousness," and "originary giving consciousness" are names for a consciousness that fluctuates among several levels or, as it might be said, is described at different phases of the spiritual discipline. Hence issue the errors of interpretation of which Husserl complained so constantly and bitterly. If subsequent phases be interpreted while remaining at the level of departure, the level of intentional psychology, then transcendental idealism would appear to be only a subjective idealism. The "being" (*étant*) of the world is reduced in a destructive sense to the "being" of consciousness just as this being is revealed in the most ordinary internal perception. But then it becomes impossible to reconcile this crude idealism with the persistent philosophy which is

8. See § 66, "Psychological and Phenomenological Idealism."
9. See § 40, "Transition to the Question of Transcendental Idealism" and § 41, "Genuine Phenomenological Explication of the 'ego cogito' as Transcendental Idealism."

not contradicted once from the *Logical Investigations* (1900–1) to *Experience and Judgment* (1939).[10] It is intuition, be it under its sensuous form or under its categorial or eidetic form, that "legitimates" the sense of the world and that of logic in the widest use of this word (pure grammar, formal logic, *mathesis universalis,* etc.). Transcendental idealism is of such a nature that intuition is not repudiated but founded.

Neo-Kantian critics believed they could discern an inconsistent mixture of Platonic realism and subjective idealism in *Ideas I,* these disparate elements being united through the artifice of language in the Kantian style. As Fink has shown thoroughly,[11] there never was any Platonic realism in Husserl, not even in the *Logical Investigations,* as we shall soon be reminded. Nor is there a subjective idealism masked by Kantian language. But now these points must be shown.

Nothing is more difficult than fixing the final sense of the Husserlian idealism as reached by the progress of reflection. In *Ideas I* we have only one path among others directed towards a center which cannot be seen from outside. Hence, we must take a chance on an interpretation and then see if the signposts scattered throughout *Ideas I* agree with it. Here Fink's interpretation presents itself and should be accepted at least tentatively, since Husserl at one time recognized it as his own.[12]

Husserl's "question," writes Fink [13] is not Kant's. Kant poses the question of validity for a possible objective consciousness. This is why he remains within a certain matrix which is still in the natural attitude. The transcendental subject of Kant is an a priori form of the world (*apriorische Weltform*), a mundane, though formal, subject immanent in the world (*weltimmanent*). The true differentiation of the level of the absolute subject is not effected. Husserl's question, according to Fink, is the question of the origin of the world.[14] It is, no doubt, the question involved in myths, religions, theologies, and ontologies, where it is not yet scientifically elaborated. Only phenomenol-

10. E. Levinas, *La Théorie de l'intuition dans la phénoménologie de Husserl* (Paris, 1930), pp. 101–74; reprinted (Paris, 1963). J. Héring, in his discussion with L. Chestov, has shown convincingly that there is no autocracy of reason and logic in Husserl but rather a reign of intuition in all of its forms. Cf. Héring, "Sub specie aeterni," *Revue d'histoire et de philosophie religieuses* (1927) in response to "Momento mori," *Revue Phil.* (January, 1926).

11. Fink, *op. cit.,* pp. 321–26, 334–36.

12. In another article Fink speaks of the "risk" of his interpretation: "Das Problem des Phänomenologie E. Husserls," *Revue Inter. de Phil.* (January, 1939), p. 227.

13. Fink, *Kantstudien,* pp. 336 ff.

14. *Ibid.,* p. 338. On Husserl and Kant, cf. G. Berger, *Le Cogito dans la philosophie de Husserl* (Paris, 1941), pp. 121, 133.

ogy places the unity of the "being" (*étant*) and "form" of the world in question and does not naïvely have recourse to another "being" or to a world behind the world. It is precisely the enterprise of overcoming all worldly (*welthaft*) forms of explanation, of founding, and of producing a new concept of science which is transcendent to the world (*welttranzendent*) rather than immanent in the world (*weltimmanent*). Phenomenological philosophy claims to found even the sphere of the problem to which Criticism is related in its own way. It is a philosophy that shows the inclusion of the world—of its "being," of its sense, of essences, logic, mathematics, etc.,—in the absolute nature of the subject.

(1) This is why the principal operation—reduction—is a conversion of the subject itself which frees it from the limitation of the natural attitude. The subject which is hidden from itself as part of the world discovers itself as the foundation of the world.[15]

If this interpretation is correct, it might be wondered why Husserl did not say so at the beginning of *Ideas I*. But to be precise, the question itself cannot be understood before the methodological movement which elaborates it. There is no intramundane motive prior to phenomenology. The project of the transcendental problem of the world arises through the phenomenological reduction. For this reason all description of the natural attitude in its own terms is a mistake. To be even more radical, phenomenology is not a natural possibility of man. It is in conquering oneself as man that the pure subject inaugurates phenomenology. Thereafter, phenomenology, unmotivated in the natural attitude, can give only poor or equivocal reasons—Cartesian or Kantian—for its own emergence. Only the reduction reveals what mundane believing is and sets this believing up as "transcendental theme." As far as it is enunciated in the letter and spirit of the natural attitude, the reduction appears to be only the mundane inhibition of intramundane believing in the being (*être*) of the world.[16]

(2) These misapprehensions of the reduction are misapprehensions of constitution, for the transcendental subject is not at all external to the world; on the contrary, it is the foundation of the world. Husserl's constant affirmation signifies this: that the world is the correlate of absolute consciousnesses; that actuality is the index of the radical configurations of consciousness. To discover the transcendental subject is precisely to found believing in the world.

Every new dimension of the ego is a new dimension of the world.

15. Fink, *Kantstudien*, pp. 341–43.
16. *Ibid.*, p. 359; in favor of this interpretation, see *Cartesian Meditations*, § 41 [cf. n. 1, p. 82 below]. G. Berger, *op. cit.*, pp. 43–61, gives a noteworthy exposition of the phenomenological reduction with all of its difficulties.

In this sense intentionality remains the theme common to intentional psychology and to phenomenological philosophy.[17] But whenever the phenomenological reduction is cut down to psychological consciousness, the sense of the ego is brought down to that of a simple for-itself (*pour soi*) of a mental nature or to a powerless thinking that leaves the in-itself outside. Insofar as the reduction is a "limitation" within the world and not a "non-limitation" (*Einschränkung, Entschränkung*),[18] beyond the world, the world is outside consciousness as another region. In transcending the world, "a-regional" consciousness includes it and all other regions as well.

On the other hand, the phenomenological method consists in performing an explication of the ego with the phenomenon of the world as a guiding thread. Thus, there are several levels of truth concerning constitution, just as there is a progressive deepening of the reduction. At the most superficial level, that of intentional psychology, constitution retains a moment of receptivity evidenced by the doctrine of the hyle. In anticipation of the highest level, *Ideas I* already calls constitution the simple correlation between noema and noesis. But, Fink assures us, on the highest level, transcendental intentionality is "productive," "creative." [19] These two momentous words are countersigned by Husserl.

There are, therefore, three concepts of intentionality: that of psychology, which is synonymous with receptivity; that of *Ideas I,* which is dominated by the noema-noesis correlation and of which it is difficult to say whether it is receptive or creative; and that of true constitution, which is productive and creative.

Eugen Fink indicates that reflection on the transcendental ego itself implies a third ego. "The reflecting spectator that looks upon (*zuschaut*) the believing in the world, in the actuality of its living operation, without cooperating with it . . ." [20] It is basically for this ego that the transcendental ego in its stream of life is a believing in the world. It effects the reduction. It is the "theoretical transcendental spectator" which uncovers believing in the world as foundational of the world.

17. The *Cartesian Meditations* proposes this developed formula of the cogito: "ego-cogito-cogitatum," p. 87.

18. Fink, *Kantstudien*, p. 359.

19. *Ibid.,* p. 373. But, as we have said above, this "creating" is so little a "making" in the mundane sense that it is a "seeing." Here I agree with G. Berger, *op. cit.,* pp. 97–100: "One must learn to unite two concepts that we are in the habit of contrasting: Phenomenology is a philosophy of *creative intuition.* . . . Evidence, the completed form of intentionality, is constituting" (p. 100). This creating "beyond action and passion" (p. 103) is a "creation by intuition" (p. 107).

20. Fink, *Kantstudien*, pp. 356 f.

That the most extreme difficulties are elicited by this interpretation is hardly necessary to observe. In what sense and at what level of the spiritual discipline of phenomenology is subjectivity still a plurality of consciousnesses, an intersubjectivity? Is the most radical subject God? Or does the question of "the origin," scientifically elaborated by transcendental phenomenology, dissipate the natural man and problems of religion as if they were myths? Only study of the manuscripts on *Urkonstitution* would permit the proper expression of these questions.[21]

[III]   THE BIRTH OF *Ideas I*

ONLY WHEN ONE CLARIFIES *Ideas I* from the vantage point of later development does it acquire a sense and, conversely, clarify the rough sketches from which it comes.

Often it is said that Husserl was a realist in 1901 and an idealist in 1911. What has just been said about the hierarchical character of phenomenological reflection puts us on our guard against such comparisons; they err in being superficial and in interpreting the development of Husserl's thought horizontally. The *Ideas* are not at all in opposition to the *Logical Investigations,* because phenomenology in the meantime elicited a new dimension of consciousness, another level of reflection and analysis.

It is said that the *Logical Investigations* take the truths of logic out of subjectivity which *Ideas I* reinclude in subjectivity. But the subjectivity that Husserl struggled against in 1901 is not that which he upheld in 1911. If the idealism of the *Ideas* were subjective, then the *Ideas* would contradict the *Logical Investigations.* Husserl was so little aware of such a contradiction that he never ceased to alter the *Logical Investigations* so that they would agree with *Ideas I;* thus the Fifth and Sixth Investigations were reworked in the second and third editions of 1913 and 1922. The material of the first four investigations was reworked within the framework of the first part of *Formal and Transcendental Logic.*

It is true that in *Ideas I* it is hard to see how logic fits in with phenomenology (I, cf. §§ 146–49). This is because the method of introduction in *Ideas I* is more psychological than logical. But on the other hand, the most superficial reading of *Formal and Transcenden-*

21. Marvin Farber, who has so carefully and faithfully studied the *Logische Untersuchungen* in *The Foundations of Phenomenology,* 1st ed. (Cambridge, Mass., 1943); 2d ed. (New York, 1962) criticized the Husserlian idealism too curtly (cf. pp. 543–49).

tal Logic leaves no doubt: logic can continue to be perfected on the level of the apriorism of formal essences (Part One), then carried en bloc to the level of transcendental philosophy (Part Two). *Experience and Judgment* confirms this interpretation.

One can say generally that the *Prolegomena to Pure Logic* (which forms the first part of the *Logical Investigations*) and the first four Investigations of Volume Two are on a line that moves from formal logic to transcendental logic and passes through *Formal and Transcendental Logic* to *Experience and Judgment,* while the Fifth and Sixth Investigations, the *Ideas,* and the *Cartesian Meditations* are on another line that goes from the psychological cogito to the transcendental cogito. One needs to orient oneself within Husserl's work, just as in that of Leibniz. Each is a labyrinth with several entries and perhaps several centers, each relative to different perspectives on the total work. Comparison between the *Logical Investigations* and *Ideas I* is, therefore, not simple, because the two works are neither on the same plane of reflection nor on the same line of entry to the heart of phenomenology.

In order, therefore, to discover a contradiction between the great work on logic and *Ideas I,* it would be necessary to attribute a Platonism to the former which is not there and a subjective idealism to the latter which is its counterfeit. In fact, such a supposed Platonism would already be on the level of the problem-set (*problématique*) of the *Ideas,* though opposed to it in advance. Conversely, subjective idealism would return us to the previously combatted psychologism. We have already sufficiently emphasized the unique nature of the idealism of *Ideas I.* On the other hand, the "neutrality" of the *Logical Investigations* in relation to the problem-set of *Ideas I* cannot be too strongly emphasized. The task of the *Prolegomena* and the first four Investigations is the elucidation of the objective structures of propositions and of formal objectivities (whole and part, dependent and independent parts, abstract and concrete parts, etc.). The objectivity of these structures in no way implies the existence of essences in a Cosmos of Ideas. The notion of essence implies only an intelligible invariant that resists empirical and imaginative variations. The notion of the intuition of essences implies only the possibility of "fulfilling" logical significations in a manner analogous to the way in which perception ordinarily "fulfills" the empty significations which refer to things.[22]

The objectivity of these structures must constantly be recaptured from the subjective illusion that mixes up concepts, numbers, es-

22. E. Levinas, *op. cit.,* pp. 143–74.

sences, logical structures, etc., with the individual psychological operations which intend them. Objectivity must be continuously reconquered. Transcendental idealism always assumes this first victory over psychologism. One can even say that the logicism of the *Prolegomena* is a permanent protective parapet around transcendental idealism.

This is why *Formal and Transcendental Logic* begins by giving complete scope to objective formal logic [23] before taking it to another level where objectivity is related to a more radical subjectivity.[24] Only a flat, horizontal, view of Husserl's thought would prevent understanding that the passage from "logicism" to transcendental subjectivity is made without repudiating anything. But the passage is not indicated at the period of the first edition of the *Logical Investigations*. The Fifth and Sixth Investigations in their original form provide nothing more than a descriptive psychology of intentionality and the "fulfilling" of empty significations by the fullness of intuition or evidence.

Beginning in 1907 Husserl was fully conscious of the limited bearing of the last two Investigations. He saw in them only a sample of "descriptive psychology" or "empirical phenomenology," which he already distinguished from the future "transcendental phenomenology." [25]

What happened between 1901 and 1907? Six years after the appearance of the *Logical Investigations* Husserl went through a period of discouragement. The University of Göttingen set aside the minister's plan to name him professor "ordinarius" of philosophy. He came to have doubts about himself and his existence as a philosopher. In his *Notizbuch* of September 25, 1906, he passionately proposes to himself the realization of a critique of reason. In consequence of failing to reach clarity on the most radical problems, he writes: "I am unable to live in truth and veracity. I have tasted sufficiently of the torments of obscurity and doubt where I am tossed about in every direction. I must achieve internal coherence." [26]

The notion of a transcendental phenomenology, of a transcendental idealism reached by means of the phenomenological reduction,[27] finds its first public expression in the five lectures that bear the title of *The Idea of Phenomenology*.[28]

23. "The Full Idea of Formal Logic," pp. 42 ff.
24. "Psychologism and the Laying of a Transcendental Foundation for Logic," pp. 135–56.
25. Unpublished text of September, 1907, listed under B II 1 in the Husserl Archives at Louvain.
26. Text and information extracted from Dr. Biemel's Introduction to *Die Idee der Phänomenologie*.
27. The first allusion to the reduction dates from Autumn, 1905: *Seefelder Blattern*, A VII 5.
28. Summer Semester, 1907, F I 43.

As numerous short manuscripts of the period 1907–11 show, a true skeptical crisis is at the origin of the phenomenological question. A gap seems to run between "the subjective process of consciousness" and the object: "How can it move beyond itself and encounter its object with certainty?" [29] This question returns in a thousand forms in the manuscripts of this period. Phenomenology was born under the menace of a true solipsism, a true subjectivism, although no trace of this perilous situation is found in *Ideas I.* At the outset the most urgent task is "to elucidate the essence of cognition and the objectivity of cognition" (First Lecture). The question remains like a sting: "How can the subjective process move, so to speak, beyond itself?" [30] (Second Lecture). This is why the *erkenntnis-theoretische* reduction appears as an exclusion of transcendence and a withdrawal into immanence. At that period the restrictive character of the reduction is incontestable. The image of a switching off (*Ausschaltung*) is found in this Third Lecture. And at the same time a clear vision of the goal is affirmed: this goal is to recognize the relation to transcendence as a "character internal to the phenomenon" grasped in its immanence. And then the Fourth Lecture introduces intentionality as a new dimension of immanence. There are two immanences, "immanent in the sense of something really inherent" and "immanent in the sense of intentionality." [31] This latter is what the *Ideas* call the noema. Thus, the philosopher appears to have closed himself up in himself only in order the better to understand intentionality as a structure of consciousness rather than as an intra-objective relation. The Fifth Lecture can then go on to the theme of constitution, which is likewise distinguished by a victory over skepticism. The immanent data that once appeared as simply contained in consciousness, "as if in a box," "play the role of appearance." These appearances themselves are not the objects and do not contain the objects, but "somehow create the objects for the ego." Confronted by this first sketch of phenomenology, the reader has difficulty suppressing the feeling that absolute existence is lost and that the matrix of consciousness has only been enlarged to introduce the *phenomenon* of the world into it. Some later manuscripts fail to come up even to this initial achievement and echo the internal battle which left the philosopher prey to the shadow of the in-itself, never reached but ever lost.[32] It seems that the first attempt at

29. "Wie kann sie über sie hinaus und ihre Objekt zuverlässig treffen?"
30. "Wie kann das Erlebnis sozusagen über sie hinaus?"
31. ". . . *das reel Immanent and das im intentionalem Sinn Immanent.*"
32. Manuscript III 9 II: *Das Problem der Erkenntnistheorie, die Auflösung des Empirischen "Seins" in Zusammenhänge des absoluten Bewusstseins* (The Epistemological Problem, the Dissolution of Empirical "Being" [*être*] in the Context of Absolute Consciousness). "All objectivities are 'appearances' in a

transcendental idealism continued to be branded by the very subjectivism that it attempted to defeat.

The transition to the *Ideas* is reached in the October-November Course of 1910 entitled "Foundation Problem of Phenomenology." [33] It contains the germs of most of the themes of *Ideas I*, even of *Ideas II*, in particular of empathy (*Einfühlung*). This course opens with a remarkable description of the natural attitude and its prediscovered world (*vorgefundene*). In the Second Chapter the reduction is presented again, more exactly than in *Ideas I*, as an elimination of nature and the owned body (*corps propre*). Thus, the natural attitude seems to be intelligible by itself within the framework of reflection of natural man. From his point of view the reduction appears as a "self-limitation" of the sphere of immanence, the sphere of immanence being what "remains" when the positing of empirical existence is removed. Everything which Fink regretted in *Ideas I* is displayed here. But on the other hand, the skeptical undertones and evident philosophical anxiety seem to have disappeared; at the same time the future direction of thinking is clearly revealed. It is strongly affirmed that the believing in physical nature remains intact but merely is not used, and that solipsism is avoided by the very fact that the *solus ipse* of psychological consciousness is also put out of play. In the Third and Fourth Chapters the phenomenological experience, separated out in this manner by the reduction, is enlarged from the intuition of the present to the temporal horizons of expectation and reminiscence. Thus, subjectivity has its temporal breadth restored to it. This movement is remarkable because it is oriented towards the auto-constitution of immanent time, even before the problem of the constitution of nature is formulated. The problem of the unity of the flux of subjective life (Chapter Four) even takes precedence over considerations concerning intentionality. Only in Chapter Five is "what belongs to the cogitatio by virtue of being intentional" called up and examined. The reduction of nature to the "perceived" and to the "remembered" leads directly to the radical affirmation that in phenomenology nature is no more than "the index of a certain regulation of consciousness as pure consciousness." Even

specific sense, that is, they are unities of thought, unities in diversities, which on their side (as consciousness) form the absolute in which all objectivities are constituted." Manuscript III 9 III speaks of the "enigma" (*Rätsel*) of consciousness: "In thought itself everything must be 'legitimized' (as Lotze already perceived but without proper application). Do I not see then that I cannot first posit a being before thought but rather can only found it in thought and on the basis of the motives of thought?" Similarly, Manuscript III 9 IV, *Transzendenzprobleme*, Summer Semester, 1909.

33. Text prepared by L. Landgrebe. Some pages are from the beginning of October, 1910; the main part comes from the first part of the Winter Semester, 1910–11. Manuscripts III 9 IVa and F I.

more strongly put, "The true existence of the thing is the index of certain determined interconnections of appearances that call for a determinate description." Here some of the most radical affirmations of *Ideas I* and the *Cartesian Meditations* can be recognized. The experience of nature is thus integrated with the temporal flux of subjective processes. Finally (Chapter Six), the last extension of the phenomenological field, empathy, permits considering a plurality and a community of subjects within the framework of the reduction of nature; here each subject is "presented" to itself, and to each all others are "presentiated" (*Vergegenwärtigung*), not as parts of nature but as pure consciousnesses.

The stage of *Ideas I* is thus reached.

In summary: First, from the methodological point of view, there is no difficulty in the transition from "logicism" to transcendental phenomenology if the latter be taken at a level sufficiently elevated and removed from all intentional psychology and all subjective idealism. In 1929 Husserl was able to write *Formal and Transcendental Logic,* wherein he enlarged and reinforced the "logicism" before radically integrating it into transcendental phenomenology.

Second, from the point of view of the history of Husserl's thought, transcendental phenomenology had a difficult birth before developing to the point of correctly presenting the problem of the integration of objective logic and, generally speaking, of the several forms of intuition into phenomenology. The development of Husserl's thought from 1905 to 1911 appears to us to consist in an effort to subordinate the understanding of the natural attitude more and more to the phenomenological reduction and to clarify the reduction by the transcendental constitution of the world. At the beginning the natural attitude is understood as "experience of the physical" itself, and the reduction is elicited by a skeptical crisis. It is presented as a limitation of the ego by way of expelling nature.[34]

34. Merleau-Ponty places himself at the other limit toward which phenomenology tends in its last phase: here phenomenology "reflects" only to elicit from every sort of naïveté the assurance that the world is always "already there." It "reduces" our participation in the presence of the world only in order to break off our familiarity with the world momentarily and to restore "astonishment" to us before the strangeness and the paradox of a world which situates us. It turns to essences only in order to gain distance and reconquer the "facticity" of our being-in-the-world. (*Avant-Propos* to *La Phénoménologie de la perception* [Paris, 1945].) One may also consult A. de Waelhen's lecture given at the Collège Philosophique, "*De la phénoménologie à l'èxistentialisme*." This last turn in the Heideggerian direction cannot yet be seen in *Ideas I,* where the negative moment of the reduction is not yet absorbed into the positive moment of constitution. But the clear indication that this is the direction which will be taken is given by the identification of constituting and seeing in the theme of originary giving consciousness.

Since *Ideas I* is clarified on the one hand by taking a stand more advanced in phenomenological philosophy and on the other hand by comparing it to the first outlines of the transcendental idealism, the work appears as witness to an intermediary period where the first psychological and even subjective motives for the reduction are not yet integrated into the final project of phenomenology.[35] Perhaps these motives could not be integrated, if it is true that the ultimate sense of phenomenology can only be approached by definitely equivocal steps. No doubt this is the reason why Husserl saw fit in 1928 to republish *Ideas I* a third time without modification, even though thousands of other pages, completed and following upon *Ideas I*, continued to be denied to the public in the name of the intellectual rigor and the scrupulous taste for perfection that were the rare virtues of the master of Göttingen and Freiburg.

35. No one more than Husserl had the sense of being on the way and even of being at the beginning. He claimed for himself "the seriousness of the beginning." He aspired to merit the title of a "genuine beginner," on the path of that phenomenology which is itself at the "beginning of the beginning" ("Postscript to my '*Ideas* . . . ,'" p. 21).

3 / Husserl's *Ideas II:* Analyses and Problems

In his introduction to the handsome German edition of Husserl's *Cartesian Meditations,* Professor S. Strasser has recently recounted the curious fate of the principal works of the founder of phenomenology. Three times—in the periods of the *Ideas* (1911–ca. 1925), of the *Cartesian Meditations* (1928–31), and of the *Crisis* (1931–36)—Husserl attempted to combine into one comprehensive work the philosophical interpretation of his method and phenomenological exercises that would be at once the application and justification of phenomenology. Each time endless reworkings and scruples over wording frustrated the original undertaking. Thus it was that the public came to know only the systematic exposition that should have served as an introduction to the whole of the *Ideas: Ideas I, Introduction to Pure Phenomenology and Phenomenological Philosophy.* Even though complete, *Ideas II* and *Ideas III* remained unpublished. Similarly, the French edition of the *Cartesian Meditations* was not followed by the publication of the original German text. This latter work underwent a total recasting which was never completed. Beginning at the end of 1930 Husserl was engrossed with the great work of which only a fragment was to be published in 1935 in a Belgrade journal under the title "The Crisis of the European Sciences and Transcendental Phenomenology." The philosopher's labor and integrity seem continually to have provoked a movement beyond any given achievement; thus, the opposing need for a definitive, perhaps pre-emptory, formulation of the systematic unity of his work was thwarted. As this need was best met by extensive expositions of doctrine, it is understandable that the expositions of his research should have been constantly sacrificed. For those of us who now have access to the unpublished manuscripts, thanks to the admirable work of the Husserl Archives at Louvain, it is important that we can check the systematic and programmatic character of the theses of *Ideas I* by the analyses of *Ideas II*, which is entitled *Phenomenological Investigations into the Constitution of Reality in its Totality.*[1]

We are doubly interested here. On the one hand *Ideas II* tests the method of "intentional analysis" advanced in *Ideas I;* and on the other hand the analyses of *Ideas II* retrospectively clarify the idealistic doctrine, which after 1905 was the interpretation of the phenomenological method. Upon this doctrine the systematic expression in *Ideas I,* and especially in *Cartesian Meditations,* is founded. It is important clearly to distinguish these two aspects of Husserl's work that were so often confused by their author himself under the ambiguous term "constitution."

In an important sense, exercises in "constitution" are exercises in intentional analysis. They consist in beginning with a "sense" already elaborated in an object that has a unity and a permanence before the mind and then separating out the multiple intendings that intersect in this "sense." This is where the name "intentional analysis" comes from. In *Ideas I* this method is practiced on the privileged example of the perceived object. Thus, one ascends from the indivisible stability of the thing, such as it "appears" visually in the flux of profiles, aspects, outlines, or adumbrations through which consciousness anticipates and claims the unity of the thing. Intentional analysis always takes for its "transcendental guide" an object—a sense—in which the intentive processes (*visées*) of consciousness are united. It never begins directly with the untamed generative power of consciousness. Its implicit rationalism carries it toward the one, the order, the system into which it goes beyond itself as toward a pole. Some unity is always the Ariadne's thread in the manifold of consciousness. Such a method in no way prejudges the ultimate sense of consciousness, for it entails a methodological rather than a doctrinal idealism and resolves to hold reality only as a sense for consciousness and to spell out the diverse syllables of sense in temporal "moments" and functional "strata."

Husserl interprets this sense "for" consciousness as a sense "in" consciousness. At the same time he makes a metaphysical decision about the ultimate sense of reality and exceeds the methodological prudence by which consciousness is only interrogated. The *Cartesian Meditations* draw all the consequences of such a decision with an exemplary philosophic courage. The return to the ego leads to a mon-

1. [*Phänomenologische Untersuchungen zur Konstitution,* in *Husserliana IV,* ed. W. Biemel (The Hague, 1952). Our short title will be *Ideas II.* Professor Ricoeur worked from a manuscript, but he has provided pagination adjusted to *Husserliana IV.* Textual references to this work are designated by the letters *II.*—Trans.]

adism according to which the world is primordially thc sense that my ego lays out. Husserl, lucidly assuming the responsibility of "transcendental solipsism," tries to find something in the understanding of the Other that would resolve the extraordinary paradox of constituting "in" me the primary "outsider," the primordial "Other," which, pulling me out of the domination of subjectivity, reorganizes the sense of the world around it and inaugurates the intersubjective adventure of objectivity.

Ideas II remains on the near side of the properly philosophical set of problems and unfolds its analyses within the limits of the methodological idealism which we have just characterized. The "transcendental guide" of the intentional analysis is the notion of "reality in its totality" (*die gesamte Realität*). This theme is articulated in two stages: reality as nature and reality as "the human-spiritual world" (*geistige Welt*). Nature itself is analyzed into "material nature" and "animal or psychic nature." The "thing," "the soul," and "the spirit" (*esprit*) [2] are thus the three directive themes, the three regulative objects of the investigation.

At first glance, this passage from below to above reproduces an entirely traditional schema for reality and the interrelationship of the sciences. But we must not lose sight of the fact that it is always a question of constituting these directive objects in consciousness. In other words, we seek to discover these objects at the terminus of the conscious intending in which they are evidenced and, therefore, to speak about nature in an attitude other than the natural one; that is, to speak about nature and reality transcendentally. Moreover, it is equally a question of constituting the points of contact among these objects, of "founding" "strata" one in another. Between the two levels of nature, just as between nature and the spiritual world, there is not the same relationship which one finds within nature or within spirit, but rather a relation constituted by the significations of conscious acts which are founded one on another. [3] This "irreal" relationship is elucidated only by transcendental phenomenology. Without it the scientist does not know what he is doing when he establishes the animal on the mineral, localizes the psychic, envelops culture in nature, or vice versa. Consequent upon his failure to constitute this relation "in con-

2. [We translate *esprit* by "spirit" where it is used in the sense of the German *Geist*. The religious and poetic connotations of the English "spirit" are to be kept in the background. *Science de l'esprit* (*Geisteswissenschaft*), however, will be translated by "human science."—Trans.]

3. *Ideas I* uses this structure of *Fundierung* several times: to designate the rooting of the values of things in the objectivity of the thing (§§ 66–67); to characterize the institution of the noemata or thc noeses in the acts composed by collection, explication, relation, etc. (§§ 93 and 118).

sciousness," the scientist is condemned either to build all science on one science (e.g., mathematical physics) or to separate them all according to their different methodologies.

However, this task of constitution, of which we are about to give an account, does not allow us to delve into the hesitations and ambiguities of the idealism of *Ideas I* [4] and to justify the more coherent and radical interpretation of the *Cartesian Meditations*. A curious polarity will be seen to disengage itself progressively from the intentional analysis, one which is reminiscent of the Kantian polarity between transcendental idealism and empirical realism. *Ideas II* does not strive to dissipate the prestige of the Ideas [5] of reality, or of nature, or the prestige of the objective sciences of man. Quite to the contrary, by rooting the Ideas in a performance (*Leistung*) of consciousness, phenomenology justifies and sets them up in contrast to transcendental subjectivity as the objects that make up its sense and save it from the menacing irrationality of a non-concordant flux of consciousness. The object is the possible disharmony overcome. *Ideas II* suggests the image of a vast respiration which produces an alternating inspiration or reflective return to the pure ego of phenomenology, and an expiration or objectification by which consciousness stabilizes itself in the real, in the significations that are unitary and worthy of mention, worthy of λέγειν and of λόγος . Thus, the progression through *Ideas II* is marked by the triple polarity of the transcendental ego and the thing (that stumbling block, the absolutely external), of the ego and the psyche that is itself outside among things, and of the ego and the spirit which is objective in persons and historical groups. Phenomenology shows, to be sure, the relativity of the false absolutes to the consciousness that intends them. Does it not also show what the vanity and folly would be of a consciousness that would not transcend itself into a "sense"? [6]

4. *Ideas I* contends simultaneously that all reality is the "sense" of consciousness and that such a sense (a) rests on intuition, on a seeing, (b) informs a non-intentional matter—a hyle—and (c) envisages beyond itself an object that gives the final mark of "actuality" to this sense and of "reason" to consciousness itself. These themes leave the reader with a certain uneasy feeling echoed by Eugen Fink ("Die phänomenologische Philosophie Edmund Husserls in der gegenwärtigen Kritik," *Kantstudien*, XXXVIII [1933], 319–83).

5. ["Idea" will be written with a capital when used in a Kantian sense to refer to an ideal totality. Ricoeur notes (p. 98 below) that for Husserl, a Kantian Idea is characterized by two properties: totality and openness.—Trans.]

6. The present study devoted to the use of the method of intentional analysis set forth in *Ideas I* is, as I intend it, the counterpart of another study devoted to the idealism of the *Cartesian Meditations* [included next in the present collection]. There I justify the distinction between a methodological idealism implied by transcendental phenomenology and a doctrinal idealism that derives from the philosopher's subsequent interpretation of his method.

[I] "THE CONSTITUTION OF MATERIAL NATURE"

THE STRUCTURE of the first part of *Ideas II* is quite simple. The central study is in Chapter Two and consists in the intentional analysis of the "sense" of the thing. It is preceded, however, by a reflection on the general attitude in which the thing appears as thing. This attitude distinguishes within whatever lies before it, if not a "sense" with its precise characters and strata or levels of signification, at least an "Idea"—the Idea of nature in general. That is to say, it outlines a regulative theme which excludes a priori certain determinations, such as the useful, the beautiful, the good, etc., and prescribes certain theoretical modes of behavior. Thus, the sense of the "thing" adumbrates itself against the background of "nature" (Chapter One). The intentional analysis of thinghood (*choséité*) (Chapter Two) calls, in turn, for a change in perspective. The sense of "the thing itself," such as it is given, is not complete insofar as its interferences with the corporeal and psychic dispositions of the subject are not brought into consideration. On this occasion Husserl develops for the first time his very important interpretation of the perceiving function of the body (Chapter Three). But here this theory is only a step in the direction of the complementary analysis of the objectivity of the thing. In effect, the appearance of individual subjectivity produces a cleavage between the traits and aspects of the thing which remain relative to a single individual and those that are non-relative and true for all. This reference of objectivity to intersubjectivity completes the constitution of the sense of material nature. (We shall emphasize this final turn of the analysis in Chapter Three by separating it from Chapter Four. Chapter Four connects the conclusions reached by the theory of the "perceiving body" to the question of the sense of the thing, such as it is elaborated in Chapter Two, the latter chapter being devoted specifically to the different "strata" of "the sense of the thing as such.")

1. The "Idea" of Nature in General

THE PHENOMENOLOGIST'S FIRST STEP is intended to circumscribe a priori the field of what belongs to nature by the type of interest or attitude that is correlative to it. We do not know which objects belong to nature but only which consciousness they face. In this way we have an Idea of nature, a rule for the regional ontology which will be elaborated.

This attitude—more precisely this doxic-theoretic attitude (*dox-*

isch-theoretisch)—Husserl calls experience (*Erfahrung*).[7] Experience means more than perception in the phenomenologist's language. The sense of perception only appears by the reduction of certain characters of experience, a reduction that uncovers the deficient and incomplete aspect of experience. In experience we are already on the level of a perception shot through with a "thesis," that is to say with a believing that posits its object as being. We live through perception in giving credit to the vehemence of presence, if I may use such language, to the point of forgetting ourselves or losing ourselves in it. This believing (*doxa*) has certitude as its fundamental mode, the correlate of which is the index of actuality. This index is attached to the percept, and in it one can recognize what the ancients designated by the word "manifest" (ἐναργής). In fact, believing is a credence, a crediting, prior to the judgment properly so-called, which takes a position with respect to truth and falsehood. The modality of being which the *doxa* confers on actuality is antecedent to the operation of the *yes* that emphasizes and refers to the believing and also to the operation of the *no* that cancels it.[8] This is the "thetic" or positional character, which once grasped can be neutralized or suspended. Consciousness, instead of being taken in by its world, reconsiders itself with respect to this enveloping power and discovers itself as positing or giving. At the same time the world is reduced to its "sense," unburdened of the weight and opacity of "being" (*étant*). This turn is implicit in the constitution of nature.

But, if in one way experience is richer than simple perception, it is poorer in another. On its theoretical side it proceeds by abstraction from all affective and practical aspects that reality owes to my evaluational and volitional activity. Ignoring, in a positive manner, the good, the beautiful, the useful, and the valuable, I make myself into a pure spectator. With the aspect of value (*Wert*) removed, the aspect of

7. "Das gesamte räumlich-zeitliche Weltall [ist] der Gesamtbereich möglicher Erfahrung" (the whole spatio-temporal world is the complete domain of possible experience).

8. On all of this, cf. I, §§ 103 ff. The modalities of believing (certitude, supposition, conjecture, questioning, doubting) and the modalities of actuality that correspond to it on the side of the object (actual, possible, probable, problematical, doubtful) are themselves on a prejudicative level. I wonder if this remarkable analysis of *doxa* by Husserl is not a good guide for distinguishing between the classic analyses of judgment and belief in the writings of Descartes and Spinoza. Perhaps one could say that since both have completely confused belief and explicit judgment, they are not talking about the same thing and, being on different levels, do not conflict. Descartes is right on the level of genuine judgment which is a responsible, voluntary, and free act. Spinoza is right on the level of prejudicial belief where the positional (*doxisch*) operation is in some way woven into the "representation" itself. It should be added that the critical moment that separates the *doxa* from the judgment is denial, which cancels, and not affirmation, which emphasizes.

thing (*Sache*) remains.[9] "Nature is there for the theoretic subject." Man's evaluations do not interfere with the scientist's concern; they are not constitutive of the Idea of nature.[10]

By an act simultaneously of trust and distrust, by an act of positing and an act of reducing, we become scientists. We concede "what is" (*l'étant*) and withdraw the "valuable." Husserl calls this twofold conscious performance "objectivation." This objectivation, once begun in the area of things, can return upon what it excluded and engage in a conquest of affective, axiological, or practical predicates and then incorporate them in turn into theoretical knowledge. And so the process of objectivation, by which I posit and delimit a nature, goes beyond nature itself, but always according to the model of nature. The nature of things then becomes exemplary for a "naturalistic" psychology, sociology, or aesthetics.

2. The "Sense" of the "Thing" in General

WE KNOW THE ATTITUDE in which the thing as thing appears. Now that we know that the thing is "for" a certain manner of viewing, we can no longer be fearful of interrogating "the thing itself" and taking it for a guide. We shall practice what *Ideas I* calls noematic reflection. It is a reflection since, instead of simply living along, we shall question the sense of what we live through. Yet it is a noematic reflection because it is the cogitatum, not the cogito—the noema and not the noesis—that is elucidated.[11] In the analysis which follows we enter upon the genuinely Husserlian brand of transcendentalism. What interests Husserl in consciousness is not its genius, its power to invent in every sense of the term, but the stable, unified significations into which it moves and becomes established. The "transcendental guide" which must be followed through the labyrinth of intertwined intendings is always the object. If it is true that consciousness is an "I can" (as Husserl repeats in every extended philosophical exposition of his method), then this is why the power of consciousness does not interest him insofar as it is liberating but rather interests him insofar as it is legislative. Phenomenology is a philosophy of "sense" more than a philosophy of freedom. This is perhaps the secret of its greater

9. In Husserl's terminology *Ding* names the thing in opposition to the animate being, while *Sache* names the thing in opposition to the stratum of values.

10. "We assent to an Idea of nature, delimited a priori, where the world is a world of pure things (*Sachen*), we ourselves becoming the purely theoretic subject" (II, p. 25).

11. From this comes the title of Chapter Two: *Die ontische Sinnesschichten des anschaulichen Dinges als solchen* (II, p. 29). With regard to "noema" and "sense," cf. I, §§ 90 and 129 ff.

resemblance to Kant than to the "existential" phenomenologies. These latter are obligated to him for a method and for particular analyses, but their spirit has another source, and their concern is different.

Therefore, let us interrogate the thing itself—the sense of the thing—and let us ask ourselves what distinguishes it from the spiritual order (Geistigheit). Husserl's answer is twofold: extension (Ausdehnung) indicates the thing, but thinghood is its essential attribute. In other words, extension cannot fail without the thing failing also; however, extension as a quality is not yet a thing but only, as it is said, a "phantasm" or "sensible schema" (fantôme).

The study of extension in Ideas II is in no way remarkable in comparison, for example, with the Transcendental Aesthetic. The division of space is a division of the thing itself. Every quality appears or disappears in space, in some way "fills" it. This "filling" differs from one sensorial modality to another: color "covers," odor "spreads," etc. Qualities can only replace one another. There is no absolute lack of quality. On the other hand, an interesting notion for future analyses of the psyche is introduced here. The psyche is not extended, it does not fill a space, and it is not spatially divisible. But it is localized in space, which is not the same thing, or, so to speak, it is ordered to space. This relation of foundation (Fundierung), soon to be clarified, is essential and not accidental.

What makes an extended space a res, a Realität? [12] Let us form a hypothesis. Let us suppress every change in the thing both as to form and as to quality. Let us disconnect it from every context that could bring about a change in relation to the rest of the situation. A "sensible schema" remains, e.g., a painted or sonorous form, etc. Whereas form without quality cannot be thought, the qualified form can be abstracted from all other material determinations by imaginative variation. Now what is lacking in such a phantasm? It lacks the "overflowing" character which leads us to expect something to follow upon it. It is a pure appearance, closed up in itself and incessantly becoming other. It escapes from the question "What is this?" An appearance where something does not appear is beyond discourse.

In suspending all relation to context we have suspended what makes for the reality of the material thing. The sense "thing" is manifest only when we withdraw the parentheses. The relation of the phantasm to circumstances (Umstände) thus appears to be the deci-

---

12. As we have said, it is a matter of separating out an essence, the essence of thinghood, of reading this essence from a well-chosen example, one that can be taken either from memory or from free imagination. The role of imaginative variation in the Husserlian reduction from fact to essence cannot be overestimated. Cf. I, §§ 4 and 23.

sive moment of thinghood. Let us consider one of these circumstances: lighting. Under different lights the phantasm (or pure appearance) of the object continually varies. But we do say that it is the same thing in different lights. Hence we separate out a constancy of quality or form from the flux of variations. At the same time we relate this flux of variations to variations in circumstances. This reference of the variable to variable circumstances is the inverse of the *Dingsetzung* by which we posit a thing as the same thing. Thus, thinghood is that which is presented as independent of circumstances through the variations of the sensible schema. Objective color is what the thing has both at night and in sunlight. Every property draws its objective material reality (*reale*) from a relational operation of the same order, and this reality is as manifold as there are properties that one can treat as "persistent unities in relation to the multiple schemata regulated with respect to correspondent circumstances" (II, p. 43).

This analysis of the reifying apprehension (*realisierende Auffassung*)—which raises the passing appearance to the level of a durable "state" (*Zustand*)—calls for a few remarks. It is as surprising to the "existential" phenomenologists, who find it too intellectualistic, as it is to philosophers accustomed to the analyses of Lagneau and Alain and, even more so, to thinkers molded by Kant's Transcendental Analytic.

From one side, this "positing of the thing" is a relational operation. For, under the name of "circumstances" Husserl refers, if not to the relation of causality, at least to a causal style [13] that would be the root, the original form, of an explicit relation belonging to the higher stratum of thought (*Denken*). At this time, Husserl takes the whole subsequent analysis in a direction deceiving to readers accustomed to the opposition of "existence" and "objectivity," as found, for example, in Gabriel Marcel and Merleau-Ponty. In *Ideas II* there is no question of finding a type of worldly presence beyond the objective relations of the intellectual and scientific level whose significations would be projected by the unfolding of my corporeal powers. Such a design is completely foreign to Husserl, at least in the period of *Ideas II*. On the contrary, he is interested in the progressive determination of objectivity. This interest will be even more manifest at the level of the psyche. There it will be precisely the question of elaborating it as the valid theme of an objective psycho-physiology.

And yet, on the other hand, this analysis is not intellectualistic

---

13. "To understand a thing is to know through experience how it behaves when one presses it, taps it, bends it, breaks it, heats it, cools it, in short, how it behaves in a connection of causal circumstances (*im Zusammenhang seiner Kausalitäten*), through what states it passes, and how it remains the same through these states" (II, p. 45).

because the "causality" under discussion here is not thought. This causality is a dependence seen, something perceived as an aspect of the situation perceived. When the lighting of a colored figure varies, the dependence with regard to the lighting comes to be given originarily. Husserl directs the analysis toward the investigation of relations which may be said to be both concrete and perceived. No doubt he agrees that to pay attention to the constancy of form or of quality and to pay attention to causal dependence are two different directions of interest, though they are rooted in the same "schema." The relation of such a "state" to such a "set of circumstances" is incorporated into the perceptual basis of the phantasm and forms a part of the percept and its sense. In this way, the schema lends itself to many "causal apprehensions" that indicate the possible series of perceptions functionally related to the possible series of circumstances. For example, I attend to such and such an appearance of the same red in sunlight, in blue light, in shadow, etc. Even when Husserl relates "states" to a "substance," he remains on the level of that perceptual *doxa* which we mentioned at the outset, and he speaks of an originary show (*originär . . . aufweist*) (II, p. 44), of real properties in states dependent on circumstances.

The general tendencies of this interpretation are as follows: (1) On the one hand, science does not present absolutely new problems in relation to the perceptual constitution of the thing. It is, rather, this latter entity that the phenomenologist must integrate instead of subordinating the percept to what is scientifically known. Thus, *Ideas II* accentuates the tendency in *Ideas I* to replace the interest in the philosophy of science with interest in the phenomenology of perception (I, §§ 40 ff.). (2) On the other hand, perceptual consciousness stimulates scientific consciousness by its own relational character, for causality as understood plunges its roots into a perceived relation of dependence among intuited properties related to "circumstances" themselves intuitively perceived. (3) The phenomenology of perception is possible because the constitution of the thing includes an "essence" that can be grasped in examples. This point is silently passed over by the modern philosophies of perception that only with difficulty justify their right to speak of perception instead of living through it or their right to speak reflectively of the pre-reflective and to speak rationally of the pre-rational. Husserl justifies himself, rightly or wrongly, by a theory of essences. For him there are a priori significations such as extension, phantasm, relation to circumstances, reality, and substantiality that are read in the things themselves by direct inspection.

On the other hand, this claim to reach the essences of the noemata and to decipher the essence of thinghood by eidetic intuition poses a grave problem which is continuous with the preceding one. For the structures of the thing elaborated by science have a progressive history, and Husserl would not expect the structures disengaged by phenomenology to have just such a history. For this reason it is necessary for him to root the "thing of physics" in the "perceived thing." Thus, the history of the sciences, wherein Brunschvicg studies the sense of reality, does not absorb the perceptual eidos. But after 1930, during the period of the *Crisis,* Husserl seems to have considered this position as a more difficult one to maintain. On the one hand, he was obliged to accentuate the irrational side of the *Lebenswelt,* which is like a matrix of our existence, and in particular to emphasize its pre-relational character. On the other hand, he was obliged to emphasize the rupture introduced into our reading of the things by the Galilean revolution, i.e., the mathematization of reality. Hence, he had again to place in question the continuity between perception and science and to let the scientific vision of the world play the decisive role. At the same time it was necessary for him to integrate the a priori of the apprehension of the thing into a history of culture and to meet the many accompanying difficulties that history introduces into a philosophy of essence.

But *Ideas II* also balances this interpretation of the continuity between the perceptual apprehension of the thing and the scientific apprehension of the thing with a view to their discontinuity. This change of perspective appears when one considers another dimension of the percept, to wit, its relation to the corporeal and psychic dispositions of the process of perceiving. It is from this new angle that the separation between the "subjectivity" of the thing perceived and the "objectivity" of the thing of physics is justified.

3. The Percept Related to the Perceiving Body

HUSSERL ELABORATES his doctrine of the body for the first time in *Ideas II* on the occasion of the movement to the last "constitutive stratum" of the real thing. Why does he have recourse to the body at this stage in the analysis? Because the ultimate elaboration of objectivity supposes that attention is paid to all the allusions and references that the thing offers to a sentient and incarnate subject. Objectivity is abstracted from a subjectivity overlooked until now, a subjectivity which somehow omits itself in going beyond itself into the aspects of the percept. Hence, it is necessary to see that up until now only the aspects of the thing for an isolated subject have been put into place and that we must pass on to the "thing for everyone." Consequently, reflection must first be directed upon the overlooked modes of one's body's implication in the "apprehension of things."

This manner of introducing the body merits emphasis. We move regressively from the percept into which consciousness transcends itself to the perceiving body, from the object to the organ. This procedure deliberately breaks with all "naturalistic" treatment and with all psycho-physiology of sensoriality. Once sensation, like something just come into the world, is located spatially in a part of the world, e.g., in the skin or in an eye, then its signification as conscious correlate of an object (*Gegenstand*) will never be recovered again. On the contrary, the first signification of the body is developed by the movement of reflection which comes upon the "aesthetic" body, as Husserl puts it, *in* the αἰσθητά. Indeed, the omission of the subject and the "aesthetic" body cannot be total. I cannot apprehend the thing without its referring to the subject's "animal" aspect in certain ways.

To begin with, on the level of what we have called the "phantasm" or the "sensible schema," the body is indicated as the center of orientation, the zero point of origin, the *hic et nunc* from which I see all that I see. This reference to the null point (*Nullpunkt*) is grasped in reality itself and includes a concrete relation of orientation, e.g., to the right, to the left, far, near, etc. Likewise, the free mobility of the body is perceived in its "aesthetic" function as a definite dimension of the show of things, because in all perception the body is there-along-with (*mit dabei*), like a freely movable totality of sense organs.

But this free mobility only takes on all of its sense at the level of what we have called "thinghood," or the "reality" of the properties of the thing. Now, on this level of thing-apprehension, it will be remembered, an aspect becomes real when it remains permanent throughout a flowing course of changing "circumstances." This notion of "circumstance" as a concrete, pre-intellectual, category of causality would be, thus, the key to that function of reality. The owned body (*corps propre*) is elaborated as an original dimension of a very general relation of the type "if-then" or "because" (*wenn-so* or *weil-so*).

If kinesthetic sensations are actually considered, e.g., sensations of the eye or the hand, they will be seen to be entirely different from the sensations of color, roughness, or warmth that immediately constitute the aspects of the thing itself. They differ by means of the "apprehensions" or intentive "meanings" that pass through them; hence, the latter sensations are reached only abstractly by an analysis of the intending that terminates at the color of the thing, at the roughness of the thing, etc. But on the other hand, kinesthetic sensations do not go beyond themselves into the thing itself but rather reveal my corporeal existence to me. And yet this revelation of the body still remains a function of the percept, no longer as hyle—as brute matter—it is true, but rather as "motivating" circumstance in the course of perception. The thing can appear to me in this way if I turn my head or my eyes, or if I extend my hand. Thus, the same course of perception refers in a polar manner back to a stream of kinesthetic subjective processes as a typical group of circumstances, for the relation of motivation, the lived-through reference to a motivated order of appearances, still plays a part in the apprehension of "things." And since it is possible for all other sensations to be "motivated" in a spontaneous motion of my body, the totality of sensoriality appears as a unique operation with a double pole. At one end, sensoriality goes beyond itself into the spatial order of the things; at the other end, it is motivated in the free spontaneity of a course of conscious processes.

The importance of this analysis for the "constitution of the psyche" will be seen later. But, if it is true that the psyche is given immediately as "localized" in the special instance of tactile and kinesthetic sensation, we are here holding one of the master roots of the bipolar constitution of the reality of the thing and the reality of the psyche.

Let us pause for a moment at this correlation that subordinates the body to the percept as a "condition" of perception. This correlation in turn leads to a sort of internal cleavage that separates the "normal" from the "abnormal." We have already seen how we attach the "true" quality, the "genuine" color, the "real" form to the "normal" conditions of perception. For example, there is a "good" light under which one sees well, and in this regard the rhythm of day and night, the "day-night" of the ancients, is a structure of perception. The light of day belongs to the percept as its privileged medium. Likewise, there could be a whole phenomenology of the atmospheric "media," of haze, of screens, of transparence and opacity, and in general of all interposed "milieux." On the other hand, there is a "falsity" of perception corresponding to the "anomalies" of the aesthetic body. The body, habitually omitted, refers itself to our attention as an "abnormal circumstance."

The major difference, however, between psycho-physical conditioning and circumstances such as lighting, etc., is that the latter appear to be outside; then the alteration of appearance is perceived as "produced by" the "poor" conditions of its perception. This is why confusion in perception, for example, is given as alteration in normal perception, although as a "true" alteration. Now, it is unusual that the intervention of my body as an "interference" in the percept should be perceived, as when my hand casts a shadow or strikes an object. The ingestion of santonine which alters my perception of colors is not a perceived circumstance. Also, the alteration of the thing does not appear as a "true" alteration but rather as a "simulacrum" (*Schein-veränderung*). I may believe that I see all colors as altered, but since the dependence on these circumstances is not given in the phenomenal field, I have no occasion for relating the alteration of the percept to unfavorable circumstances, hence to take the alteration as "real." It is "as if" another source of light were interfering; still the over-all situation perceived excludes this interference. Also, this "as if" hangs in the air, and the alteration, unattachable to a condition in that which is perceived, is lived through as "irreal." I must change my attitude in order to make the events of the subjective sphere emerge as "conditions" capable of disturbing the course of experience through combination with the "circumstances" of the percept. But, even when it is found, this somatic "conditionality" does not coordinate itself with the perceived situation and remains "irreal" in relation to it.

It is to be noticed that the body which appears in this way is not what French authors, following Gabriel Marcel, have called the *corps propre,* but rather is already a psycho-physiological quasi-reality. Properly speaking, in *Ideas II,* Husserl is careful never to contrast "existence" and "objectivity"; on the contrary, he is careful to follow the progress of objectivation, not on an "existential" basis but on a "transcendental" one. The place held by the notion of "circumstances" in the structure of reality and even in the theory of the body keeps him from such an opposition; but perhaps it also prevents him from pursuing a radical discovery to its end. We will come back to this later when we take up again the analysis of the body as the place of the psyche.

What can be learned from this reflection of "abnormalities" with regard to the constitution of the higher stratum of the thing, a stratum which we have called "reification" (*réalisation, Realisierung*)? By way of contrast, this experience of the "irreal" brings to appearance the silent role of the normal conditionality of the body in our sense of the "real." The real is an orthoaesthetic appearance for an orthoaesthetic body. This prior constitution of normal conditionality is the *Urbestand,* the primal state, in relation to the deviant modifications. When orientation takes part in the constitution of the real appearance and kinesthetic sensations "motivate" the course of the percept, "anomalies" cannot be placed on the same plane. They imply a regular appearance for a "healthy" body. (Usually an "abnormality" is adumbrated against a background of normality. For example, only one hand may have a disaffected sense of touch, only one sense may be disturbed in relation to the remainder of sensoriality which remains normative.) Hence, the constitution of the thing assumes the priority of the normal over the pathological. "Normal constitution constitutes the first reality of the world and my body" (II, p. 68). This normal constitution exposes the "abnormality" as a modification of the "same" thing normally perceived. This reference to normal perception is the other face of the experience of the "irreal" in appearance.

Thus, the anomalies do not cooperate in the apprehension of the thing. They do not induce the appearance of a new level of the thing, but rather they condition the simulacra. In addition, this perceptual falsity is multiple in principle, just as the normality of the concordant perception is unitary.

> There is but one world constituted normally as the true world, as the "norm" of truth, but there is a multiplicity of *Scheine*, simulacra, or perturbations in the mode of givenness which find their "explanation" in the experience of psycho-physical conditionality (II, pp. 73 f.).[14]

Throughout this analysis we have remained true to the phenomenological method which continually turns back from the percept to the perceiving. The already-constituted system of concordant perceptions, which is the orthoaesthetic character of the percept, leads the orthoaesthetic character of the perceiving body to appear concomitantly. The thought of an integrally discordant perception—in no way absurd according to *Ideas I*, § 47—allows us to glimpse the possibility of a radically disturbed perception. But this same hypothesis, which would in fact be correlative to that of a non-world or an a-cosmos, cannot be manipulated to allow one to place the normal and abnormal conditions of perception on the same plane, as relativisms and shallow skepticisms do. The reference from the concordant perception to the orthoaesthetic body belongs to real appearance. Reference to psycho-organic difficulties constitutes nothing real.

Therefore, if this reference of the canonical percept to the orthoaesthetic body is extended to the totality of the psycho-physical subject, the notion of a double relativity of the percept to this subject will be achieved. On the one hand, the relativity to the body and to the orthoaesthetic psyche defines only the "optimal" conditions under which the thing occurs along with the properties that "refer back to it." Far from being synonymous with disturbance, this relativity is just the polarity of the "normal" and the "real." On the other hand, the relativity of the simulacra to abnormalities defines the relativity as disturbance, but its intentional signification (a disturbance of . . .) refers it precisely and subordinates it to that which precedes.

---

14. Once again, one might doubt that a pathology of perception, even in a nascent state, belongs to subjective life. Can the primitive experience of the owned body envelop this minimal physiological cognition without a reversal of attitude?

4. The "Intersubjective" Stratum of the Thing and the Constitution of an "Objective Nature"

THE NEW STEP consists in moving from an identity "relative" to the subject to a "non-relative" identity. Here is where the separation between qualities and quantities functions. The work has been prepared by the elaboration of the "true" thing under "normal" conditions of perception. We must now disentangle the higher stratum of the thing from this relativity to the "normal" body. Why is the geometric rather than the qualitative privileged here? The passage from solipsistic experience to intersubjective experience contains the answer to this question. Moreover, this same distinction depends upon an abstraction that must now be removed.

How does "the relation to a plurality of subjects, who exchange their experience, enter into the constitution of the thing, more precisely into its objective reality"? If it is true that other men are apprehended through their bodies which are parts of my surrounding world, are we not in a circle? But let us rather interrogate the sense of the experience, the sense of the "objectively real" thing. What does it mean? What type of legitimacy is attached to it? We detect an "unfulfilled intention" (*eine unerfüllte Intention*) in the sense "objective thing" which we neglected in the analysis of the manifold levels of the constitution of the thing. The objective thing is a thing for everybody, no matter who. The thing that is constituted in a manifold for one individual subject is only a pure subjective "appearance" of objective reality. Hence, objectivity is contemporaneous with intersubjectivity.

It must be admitted that this turn is taken quite brusquely. Husserl quickly identifies the relation to a community of subjects and the non-relation of the thing of physics to an individual subject on the logico-mathematical level (II, pp. 79 ff.). It is clear that this objectivity implies the possibility of being understood by one or by all. Does, however, this fact imply that the non-relativity of such and such individually enumerated subjects grounds in principle the possibility of being understood by anyone whomsoever? The validity of the rule of subjectivity and the factual condition of intersubjectivity are kept together by Husserl, for his analysis supposes that intersubjectivity is founded in objectivity, since it is the sense of this unfulfilled intention that proposes the enigma. And at the same time the work of constitution tends to discover objectivity again at the confluence of intersubjective intendings. This ambiguity is perhaps essential to an analysis that always takes an object as "transcendental guide," an analysis which sets out from the sense but eventually comes back from the multiplicity of intentive processes to the unitary object. This difficulty, however, must be put aside.

The constitution of objective space is the decisive element in the constitution of the object. The "relation of orientation" from each thing to the *hic et nunc* of my body is dominated by a system of places, true for all, by means of which it is possible to identify all "heres" and all "theres." The "intention" referred to above consists in this "idealization" of the space of orientation as characterizing the higher level of the apprehension of the thing.

All forms, all movements, are ordered to objective space. The day when the scientist decided to challenge all aspects of reality which are not ordered to objective space, he acceded to the physicalistic conception of the world. Husserl brings out this mathematization of reality in the last pages of the first part of *Ideas II;* it becomes the point of departure for the reflections in the *Crisis* on the conflict between the objective attitude and the transcendental attitude. *Ideas II* restricts itself to situating this "intersubjective-objective" determination in relation to the structure of intentional strata; and once again Husserl interprets this determination as the "non-relative and thereby simultaneously the intersubjective" determination of reality.

[II] "THE CONSTITUTION OF ANIMATE NATURE"

THE SECOND PART of *Ideas II* is devoted to the soul (*Seele*). By "soul" we need not understand a metaphysical principle, a *res cogitans* or *pneuma*, but rather a level of reality, the psychic order, which I shall risk translating as "psyche." This new dimension of reality still remains a part of the Idea of nature at the same time that it makes the descriptive structure of the thing exfoliate; hence, its study will be undertaken with the same methodological resources that were just applied to the thing. We shall try to interrogate the sense of this reality just as it announces itself and to explicate the intentions of consciousness that intersect in the sense "psyche." Then we shall carry this sense to the level of eidetic intuition, which is to say that both actual experience and imagination will assist us in elucidating the *summum genus* that regulates the region of the psychic as such.

Husserl's procedure is highly ingenious. The psyche is a very ambiguous order of reality that must be enveloped by two converging approaches: from one side, the psyche is the limit of a movement of objectivation by which the ego places itself outside, makes itself into a thing, "reifies" itself; on the other side, the psyche is the limit of a movement of interiorization by which the body receives a new stratum of signification, "becomes animate." The reification of the pure ego and the animation of the body-object constitute the psyche.

This procedure is very different from that of phenomenologists marked by existentialism who try to situate themselves from the very beginning on a level of experience where the psyche and the owned body might both be given. There is nothing of this sort in Husserl. With him one must first take the rugged path of transcendental reduction, which alone indicates what the ego means, and then introduce the ego into the world. There is no shorter path than this from the constituting ego to the constituted ego. Conversely, one must apprehend the living on the basis of the thing. No short cut is possible in connection with the body-object, for it is just this which must be animated. Existential phenomenology, however, tries to elaborate a direct understanding of an incarnate psyche whose upper and lower limits would be the reflected ego and the body-object. This understanding is to be reached by a secondary operation, reflective in one case, objectivating in the other. Husserl questions the possibility of doing phenomenological work without the dual reference to the pure ego and to the body-thing and of reaching the ambiguity other than by double approximation.

1. "Reification" of the Ego: From the "Pure-Ego" to the "Human-Ego"

THE DISTINCTION between the pure ego, product of the phenomenological reduction, and the human ego, a reality of this world, is a constant in Husserl's thought; it separates phenomenology from psychology. But psychology does not understand itself; it literally strays from the path when it does not lean upon phenomenology. Phenomenology instructs psychology concerning the essence of subjectivity. Psychology does not know what the pure ego is—the constitutor of all reality, that for which and in which things, animals, and men are. Psychology cannot know what the psyche is, a constituted reality woven into the surrounding world of the pure ego. The pure ego and the psychic reality are to be elaborated as poles, the first as the only constituter and the second as one entity constituted among others. And yet the psyche is not one entity constituted like others, for it is the same ego, the same subjectivity, the same stream of subjective life without beginning or end, now, however, "grasped" in a body, interwoven with it so as to form a unique reality. The ego constitutes itself as psyche by this return from itself to the things. Hence, the reification of the ego is understood as a counterpart of the reduction. In reducing things I reduce me, the man, and suddenly it becomes astonishing to be outside, real.

This movement indicates that I cannot make an explication of being-in-the-world without this recoiling, this "abstracting" (II, p. 97) from the body. In this Husserl remains true to Descartes. I understand the union of body and soul from the viewpoint of the cogito which introduces a certain rejection of corporality. Incarnation is now grasped as that which this rejection annuls. In the same way that the heavy thickness of the world is given to me at the limit of the ideal destruction of the world by the method of imaginative variation (I, § 49), just so the bond of the incarnate condition annuls the *epoché,* which nonetheless disputed the pact with my flesh.

1 / *Pure Consciousness and Empirical Consciousness*

THE DIFFICULT THING, however, is thoroughly to understand the pure ego. The variations in Husserl's conceptions of the pure ego from the Fifth Logical Investigation [15] to *Ideas I* (§ 80) and II attest to the fact that it is not easy to elucidate the sense in which every cogitatio is a cogitatio of an ego.

Ideas II groups a progressive series of observations together.

(1) We begin with the image of *Ideas I* whereby all thinking is a "ray from the ego." The ego radiates "through" its acts. *Ideas II* completes the image so that the radiation "from" the ego is indicated by a counter-radiation that issues from the objects. To say that I desire is to say that the object attracts me. I hate means that the hated object repels me. I am saddened by grief; I am carried away by rage, elevated with indignation; I give in, resist, etc. There are many ways for the ego "to behave in relating itself," as *Ideas I* has already remarked. Hence, the ego is neither act nor object but reveals itself as *Ichpol*, the pole of the ego, in a certain "moment" of its acts. Even when passive, inattentive, or obliterated, it is still a manner of being "I." In this way, every cogito lends itself to a "wakeful" (*waches*) modality of the ego, so that "the ego can accompany all of my representations" and penetrate them with its gaze without altering the situation.

(2) The way in which the ego is grasped is reflection, whose function it is to set up the identity of the reflecting and the reflected. This identity is not just of any sort whatsoever; above all in consequence of its temporality, it is not logical. This is why Husserl main-

---

15. Fifth Logical Investigation, § 4, second edition, corrects the "non-egological" conception of consciousness found in the first edition.

tains an auto-constitution of the ego in time (II, pp. 102 f.) just as
certain allusions do in *Ideas I.* The ego is "the unity of immanent time
with which it constitutes itself." It is neither a moment nor a part of it,
for it is the "identity of immanent time."

(3) In this respect, if the ego "occurs," it does not occur like an
event. It does not happen; rather, all that happens happens to it. At the
most, it can stop or initiate reflection; that is to say, it can control
the reflective act of the cogito, but it cannot radiate its acts.[16] This is its
fashion of being *immutable.* Its identity is not that of the object which
I hold the same in a manifold of circumstances, like the true color
under different lights, nor even that of the person who shows himself
as the same in different social situations. The pure ego does not appear
at all; it does not show its face. It is without sides; it is absolute
ipseity.[17]

This ego which is not an object at all, which is in no way an
intended noematic unity, is it, therefore, only a point-like I? Certain
expressions suggest this conviction. It is called the "functional center"
(hence, the image of the center of radiation), the *terminus a quo,* or
counterpole of the object, to which the analogue is the body as center
of orientation and vision. Nevertheless, Husserl tries to go beyond this
abstraction.

(4) What has been said about wakefulness and temporality leads
us to expect that the pure ego, even though "non-real," is still a
subjective life, a "living" (*Erlebnis*). Thus it has "habitualities" which
Husserl knows better than to confuse with the "real" dispositions that
the psychologist sees in the real psyche. What are these "habits" which
play so large a role in the Fourth Cartesian Meditation? It is a structural necessity of immanent time that every operation, opinion, judgment, affection, willing, etc., "should remain" in such a way that its
"theme" can be recognized in its permanence; it is the durable me
myself that I rediscover and recognize. This should be understood:
there is no question of recognizing the same object, a noematic identity; there is a question only of recognizing myself as remaining in the
same intentive process, retained in the retaining of the same "theme."
Thus, this manner of behaving with coherence (II, p. 113) is no more
constituted in the reality of the empirical ego than in the identity of

16. It can neither arise (*entstehen*) nor pass away (*vergehen*), but only enter
(*auftreten*) and withdraw (*abtreten*), for it is capable neither of being born nor
of dying out, but only of "insertion" and "disinsertion."

17. "It is given, rather, in absolute selfhood and in its unadumbratable unity
and is to be grasped adequately in reflection upon itself as a functional center in
an adequate insight. As pure ego it conceals no hidden internal domain; it is
absolutely simple and lies entirely open. All domains lie within the cogito and in
the adequately apprehended manner of its functioning" (II, p. 105).

the object meant. Rather it emerges from the self-constitution of original time (this is in no sense a constitution of transcendence but rather of immanence). This is the permanence not of a content but of an act and of a manner. Habitualities indicate the inclination from being to having (II, p. 119), from the me to the mine, through a sort of inertia in duration. "Every intentive process is an institution (*Stiftung*) that remains the possession of the subject as long as the motivations that imply a change of position-taking do not crop up." (II, p. 113).

The complexity of this doctrine of the pure ego is evident. Husserl wants to do two things at the same time: to go to the extremes of abstraction from the entire human condition in order to ground the real ego in its mundaneity as a pole and also to give a sort of concrete status to this pure ego by conferring upon it the spontaneity of a wakeful or drowsy regard and the permanence of habitualities. Temporality founds this liberty in the instant and this persistence in duration. The *Cartesian Meditations* accentuate this dual tendency, since the pure ego is at once both pole of acts and concrete monad.

2 / *The Reality of the Psyche*

ADJOINING THE PURE EGO is the real ego, and its paradox. "Me—as such—I am an area bounded within the world." This radical affirmation makes the soul external. The psyche is an object (*Gegenstand*) of the subject, as are all "transcendences." And yet its status as object is unusual. It is not outside like things are. To think of man as psyche is to go directly to the ego in him, to the alter ego, to read there a subject pole radiating all of its conscious intendings, marked off within its surrounding world. The pure-ego and the object-ego thus realize a paradoxical coincidence. The pure subject has become object; the *terminus a quo* of all noeses has made itself the *terminus ad quem* of the gaze (*regard*).

In *Ideas I* consciousness is said to be "interlaced" (*verflochten*) with the natural world in a twofold manner, by incarnation and by perception. The style of *Ideas I* requires subordinating the union of consciousness with reality through incarnation to its union with reality through perception.[18] The naturalization of intentionality under the

---

18. § 39. In *Ideas I* the "reduction" of the incarnate character of consciousness is an aspect of the general reduction of the "thesis of the world." This is clear in the case of perception. One cannot suspend the "natural" or "mundane" character of the relation perceiving-perceived without suspending the incarnation of consciousness. In nature the thing acts physically on the body. In order to understand that it is pure percept *for* a consciousness, one must extricate

forms that psycho-physiology understands is the key to this global naturalization of psychological consciousness, rendering it an intra-mundane reality. *Ideas I* devotes two sections to this process of con-sciousness coming to the world (*Hineinkommen*); this process is an abandonment (*Preisgeben*) of immanence by anticipation (*Teil-nahme*) of things. But *Ideas I* does not elucidate the constituting role of the body. Likewise, the "apperception" of consciousness as "reified" remains an enigma. Only the identity of the pure ego and this con-sciousness "linked" (*Anknüpfung*) to the body is emphasized, and yet it "becomes other."

Psychology is, therefore, intra-mundane like its subject matter. It studies the ranking of states (*Zustände*) and constant properties. But unlike physics it has no direct understanding of its subject matter. It does not understand itself if it does not understand its subject matter as a reified non-reality. There is more and not less in psychological phenomena than in phenomenological subjective processes, for there is the subjective process and its signification as natural (*Naturbedeu-tung*).

Ideas I attaches so much importance to this subordination of psychology to phenomenology that it even takes care to note that the imaginative hypothesis of the "destruction of the world," which refers to a consciousness that can have a non-world as its world, is a spiritual discipline for the psychologist himself, since the destruction of the world is also the destruction of bodies, animate beings, and men.[19] This way of annulling oneself as animal in order to find oneself as thinking restores the psyche to us as "relative," "contingent," "tran-scendent." For it then appears that incarnation is not a transcendental structure but only an "empirical regularity" among the phenomena of the world. The twofold "union" of consciousness with the world through incarnation and through perception is thus won as compensa-tion for the phenomenological purification of consciousness and its mundanization. The problem of incarnation emerges as contrast to this act of rejection in which philosophy begins. Before this elabora-tion of pure consciousness by reflection, incarnation was "entirely

---

perceiving from psycho-physiology. The suspension of the empirical ego and its incarnation is, thus, the presupposition of the phenomenology of perception.

19. "It is certain that a consciousness without a body and also, paradoxical as it may seem, without a soul (*seelenloses Bewusstsein*) can be thought. But a consciousness without a person (*nicht personales*), that is to say, a stream of consciousness where the empirical intentional unities named body, soul, and empirical personal subject would not be constituted and where all empirical concepts, including those of subjective life in the psychological sense (so far as this is the life of a person or an animate ego) would lose its base and in any case all being-status" (I, p. 106).

natural." The gesture that rejects nature as "alien," as "another being," isolates the involvement of consciousness in the world.

3 / The Psyche and the Thing

BEFORE RECOUNTING how the subject is reified through the constitution of the body as "animate" body, let us attempt to recognize the type of reality which will serve as the transcendental guide for this job of constitution. Hence, let us take the subject in its animality as a whole and interrogate the experience of encountering an animate being. Let us distinguish its sense from the sense of the thing without taking the relation between its psychic stratum and its corporeal stratum into account. Here the ambiguous character of the psyche thrusts itself into view as something real among realities yet not real like a thing.

Husserl is not trying to introduce innovations into psychology. He accepts it in the state in which he finds it being practiced in German laboratories and institutes at the beginning of the Twentieth Century. That is to say, he accepts it as a department of natural science. The psyche is ordered to reality because it respects the most general characteristics of reality, for instance, a stratification among "states" that persists through a variation of circumstances, "properties," or "dispositions," which coordinate these states in relation to groups of circumstances of the second degree, and a subject of inherence (here a metal, there the electron, and now the psyche). We are talking about man as a substrate which has properties (*Eigenschaften*). These properties are doubtless quite original precisely in the respect in which they are psychic. The analogy is at least complete from the formal point of view, because a psychic property (aptitude, character trait, function) is "announced" bit by bit. An observed unity (*Einheit der Bekundung*) is also tested in the variation of circumstances (e.g., visual acuity, general emotivity, the tenacity of memory, understanding of relations or situations, etc.). Psychology like physics elaborates unities of superposed stages which are not the facts themselves but rather what is announced in the facts. The difference is not in the form of the experience but in the style of the facts themselves. Empirical psychology corresponds integrally to the general criterion of experience: it seeks to attain to properties through states by relating them causally to circumstances.

This analogy between the psyche and the thing which permits speaking of experiences, reality, property, state, or circumstance is based upon the community of the same material ontology which regulates the concepts common to the whole region of nature. However, these determinations must be corrected to such a degree that they are almost annulled by the very style of psychic facts. For if it is true that the reality is in every case a being that persists through variable circumstances, then a psychic "reality" has neither the same persistence nor the same type of dependence on circumstances that the thing has.

It will be remembered that in the case of the thing the first stratum is the "schema" that is adumbrated through variable aspects according to the orientation of the body. And then the schema is realized in constant properties to the extent that a style of behavior is disengaged from the variable play of circumstances. Psychic reality announces "properties" in "states" in a different manner, because these states belong no longer to the order of the schemata but rather to the order of subjective life. The transcendence of man (in the Husserlian sense of the word "transcendence") tends to be annulled. Since the process of mathematizing reality has no initial schema, it lacks a basis at this point. One can no longer speak of the in-itself in the sense of a fixed "index" of the intuitive properties of the thing. It seems that all that was said above should be repudiated. "Because it is not a schematized unity, the soul has neither an 'in-itself' as nature has, nor a mathematical nature such as a thing has in physics, nor a nature like the thing of intuition" (II, p. 132). What takes the place of the being-in-itself of the thing is precisely being-in-flux, and "flux" is contrasted here with "spatial form" or with "schemata." Properties are in flux, the soul is in flux, and a stability comparable to that of the thing will not be found prior to the level of the communal social type whose form of constancy will recall the spatial form of the thing.

Furthermore, the psychic type of "dependence on circumstances" no longer deserves the name "causality." One can speak of a "functionality regulated by laws" (II, p. 132), but its status is particularly equivocal. In effect, the unity of the psychic stream has a coherence of its own through its dependence on the body. In comparison with the unilateral dependence of the thing on circumstances, the psychic flux is quite distinct.

More precisely, several species of dependence overlap in the type of functionality that is appropriate to the psyche. At the lowest level, we find a psycho-physical, or better a "physio-psychic" dependence, since the constitutive apprehension of the psyche attributes real properties to the soul as a function of corporeal "circumstances." This dependence principally concerns sensations and their reproductions, sensual and instinctive affects, but bit by bit it extends to the whole of psychic life. In one sense, we can pursue this physio-psychic interpretation of man indefinitely. But at another level an "ideo-psychic" dependence interferes with this "physio-psychic" dependence, for the soul depends on itself. The soul motivates itself in the associative mode or in the more subtle modes of interconnection (as seen in the case of alteration of intellectual convictions, affective tastes, volitive decisions, etc.). Even more than the first, this second type of dependence overworks the analogy with material nature.

But these two types of dependence that intersect in psychology leave out of consideration a still more essential type of dependence which bursts the limits of psychology. The question concerns the intersubjective dependences that constitute the level of the person. This new dimension is disregarded throughout this second part devoted to the psyche. As the psyche exceeds the nature in which it is ordered, so the person exceeds the psyche which always bears the mark of its dependence on nature by the mediation of the body. The person is announced by traits other than his "natural" or "real" relation to an environment, that is to say, by behavior in the human milieu, in social circumstances (law, morals, religion, etc.).

Rightly speaking, we are changing our "attitude" here, for the "personalistic attitude" and the "naturalistic attitude" (in the broadest sense, including the psyche) are two eidetically different modes of apprehension (*Auffassungsweisen*). In what follows we shall pretend that the person is reabsorbed into the soul, and we shall place the human-scientific apprehension (*Geisteswissenschaft-Auffassung*)—to be studied in the third part—between parentheses in order to remain within the limits of the psychological apprehension (*psychologische Auffassung*) or, perhaps we should say, in order to remain on the level of the union of soul and body or, as Husserl puts it, on the level of organo-psychic (*leiblich-seelisch*) nature.

The consequence is that psychology lends itself to the naturalistic view by omission of the personal stratum, and that it is inserted into nature only by almost repudiating this personal stratum. It has been seen how "ideo-psychic" dependence excludes the entirely external dependence of the thing on causal circumstances and how the historical character of the soul excludes the type of spatial unity of the thing and rejects a priori all mathematization of the psyche. The soul is at the crossroads of a "supernatural" and a "natural" reality, if we may use such language. Its physio-psychic dependence and its ideo-psychic dependence betray this mixed nature. It would be better to speak of "quasi-nature" and of "quasi-causality."

Finally, sight should not be lost of the fact that the "reality" of the soul concerns only the global and massive unity of man in his connection of the psychic with the corporeal. For as we have already said, "What we oppose to material nature as a second species of reality is not the soul but the *concrete unity* of body and soul, the human (or animal) subject" (II, p. 139). The stratum of the animated body and the animating psyche in this quasi-nature of the animal-man remains to be recognized by intentional analysis. At least at this stage of the analysis we have curiously renewed the old notion that the soul is "mixed" (II, pp. 137 f.). The soul is constituted at the point of convergence where the pure ego reifies its body and its psyche in the world and where the nature of physics is bolstered by a stratum of signification that interiorizes it and inclines it towards immanence.

2. The Body and the Psyche

WE SHALL now have to place ourselves at the other pole and see how the psycho-organic (*leiblich-seelichen*) strata are built upon the basis of the material body (*Körper*), though still stopping short of the level of spirit (*Geist*). The movement of Husserl's thought is articulated in two distinct phases. The first phase begins with the analysis of the first part of *Ideas II:* "the percept related to the perceiving body." It is developed within a framework limited by an omission or parenthesizing, for we abstract from mutual understanding, from *Einfühlung*, and more generally from all that we owe to intersubjectivity. Thus, we are voluntarily limited to solipsistic experience in order to extract everything possible from an experience of the owned body. At a later time we shall reintroduce the omitted dimension, for the foregoing abstraction will have allowed the original sense which intersubjectivity confers on the animate body and the psyche to emerge. This distinction between solipsistic experience and intersubjective experience has no "historical" signification; it makes no judgment on the chronological priority of the one over the other; it has only a methodological bearing. This method of abstraction consists in preparing a field of experience by delimiting it in order better to distinguish overlapping significations.

1 / *The Level of Solipsistic Experience*

THUS, WE TAKE our departure from the references which every perceived object makes to my body. We have seen that the constitution of material nature refers to the body with which I perceive. Here Husserl anticipates the investigations of French authors into the owned body (*le corps propre*). But what is remarkable—and what places him in contrast with these French authors—is his concern not to render the sense of the owned body explicit in opposition to objective, scientific, or biological knowledge of the body but on the contrary to show how a "physio-psychic" reality receives sense in correlation with a material nature. Once more we stress the fact that the contrast of existence and objectivity is foreign to Husserl. The problems of constitution do not entail such an opposition. Intentional analysis begins on the level of the owned body and is completed on the level of the object-body when intersubjectivity is brought into play.

Primordial experience is the experience where the body is revealed as an organ of perceiving and as implicated in the percept. To know what this revelation is, let us shift our attention from the thing constituted "through" the organ-function and relate it to the local sensations which the body bears. Here we come upon the psyche just at the point of the organ-function. The case of double contact is the most revelatory: as I touch my left hand with my right, my body appears twice, once as what explores and once as that which I explore.

Now let us interrogate the sensation of contact. It has a very remarkable dual function. The same sensation "presents" the explored thing and reveals the body. Every touch in the broad sense (superficial touch, pressure, warmth, cold, etc.) is open to two "apprehensions" (*Auffassung*) where two sorts of thinghood (*Dinglichkeit*) are constituted. The extension of the thing and the localization of the sensation are elaborated by a kind of superimposition. On one side, adumbrations are elaborated into a flowing sensual schema which in turn moves beyond itself into the identical object. On the other side, sensation announces its belonging to a psyche and simultaneously reveals my body as mine.

The first experience attests to the privileged position of touch in the constitution of an animate body. The eye does not appear visually, and the same color cannot both show the object and appear localized as sensation. The experience of double contact—of "touching-touched"—has no equivalent. There is no "seeing-seen." "Every thing seen can be touched, and on this latter account refers back to an immediate relation to the body, but not, however, by means of its visibility. A purely occular subject could not have a body that appears" (II, p. 150). Such a subject would see his body as a thing. Then the kinesthetic sensations would at most reveal to me my freedom of movement, not the ownness of my body, for "it is as if the ego, indistinguishable from this liberty, could, on the kinesthetic level, move the material thing called 'body' with an immediate freedom" (II, p. 150). Here the kinship and the difference between Husserl and Maine de Biran become evident; it is in struggling with things that I appear to myself as body, but the revelatory role belongs to touch as such and not to effort, for "fundamentally and initially, sensations of movement owe their localization to their constant combination with localized sensations."

The sense of the body revealed by this primary localization of tactile sensations is that of a sentient body which "has" sensations. In short, the psyche shows itself spread out in the lived-through spatiality of the body, and reciprocally the body is lived through as the field of localization for the psyche.

All the other respects in which the body is opposed to the material thing presuppose this initial localization of the psyche. In the first place, there is its property of being an organ of the will, that of being the sole object immediately obedient to my motor spontaneity. Each mechanical movement of a thing is mediated by a non-mechanical, spontaneous, and immediate movement. The role of this spontaneity was seen above in the constitution of the percept. But spontaneity is not used merely in the constitution of things. It is engaged in this present task in order to cooperate with the constitution of the body as countertheme of material nature. This is possible because the body belongs to the ego initially by virtue of being the field of localization of my sensations.

Other sensations, implicated in processes of evaluation, participate in this constitution of the corporeal subject; thus "sensual" feelings (tension and release, pleasure, sadness, agreeableness, disagreeableness, etc.) are the "material" (*stoffliche*) or non-intentive infrastructure—in Husserl's terms, the hyle—of intentive subjective processes where not things but rather values are elaborated. As we saw just now in the instance of tactile sensations, these affective processes are charged with a dual function. They carry an intending towards . . . , and at the same time they exhibit an immediate though diffuse corporeal localization, and thus they reveal their immediately intuitive belonging to the body as owned body (*als seinem Leib selbst*).

The interesting notion in these pages is that the whole hyletic infrastructure of consciousness gives itself as immediately localized. The intentional moment as such is not localized, for "the intentive subjective processes do not form a stratum of the body." Thus, for touch it is not the touching, the formal apprehension, but the tactile sensation which resides in the fingers. The very sense of consciousness—intentionality—is only indirectly localized by its hyle.

2 / The Ambiguity of the Psyche on the Solipsistic Level

AT THIS POINT in our analysis, the question of the "reality" of the psyche is raised again. If the unformed hyle is the localizable face of consciousness, then is not the whole unity to be found on the side of the body-thing that, somehow, is the place of implantation for this strange reverse side of consciousness? We find once more the problem of the quasi-reality of the psychic, which was left aside above, but now we come to it with the resources of a new analysis of the localized psyche.

Husserl presents the problem in the following terms: "How is the content of sensation linked to the constituted thing, and how does the body, which is a material thing, have the contents of sensations in and of itself (*in und auf sich*)?" (II, p. 154). This way of putting the question is striking. The problem is to know what the attribution of psychic qualities to the body understood as a thing signifies. There is no question of recovering and protecting a non-objective "existential" experience of incarnate consciousness, but rather there is a question of taking up the physicalistic understanding of the body in order to attribute sensations to it. In what sense does the body have the property of sensing? In what sense does sensibility belong to the body? Thus, the possibility of psycho-physics and psycho-physiology is in question and not the situating of an irreducible existential experience.

The examples that Husserl gives leave no room for doubt about this. He considers the psycho-physical problem of the concomitant variations of a series of mechanical stimuli and of a series of localized tactile sensations. The example presupposes that the thing perceived is grasped on the most objective level, since the "stimulus" in terms of physics is related to the body as a field of sensations. Under this condition a relation of dependence is instituted between "states" and "circumstances," which is, as we know, the essential thing for objective thought. And since the field of localized sensations is always occupied by sensations, the variations of the stimulus bring about variations of "states," a permanent "property" of being-affected. Thus, "sensoriality (*Empfindsamkeit*) is constituted entirely as a 'conditioned' or psycho-physical property" (II, p. 155).

Thus, to perceive a body as a thing is also "to co-apprehend" (*Mit-auffassung*) its sensoriality, for certain sensorial fields belong to this body-thing. This belonging is not an existential phenomenon external to the series of appearances but rather is an application of the relation of dependence (*wenn-so*). The hand is "apperceived" as a hand with its sensorial field and with its "co-apprehended" sensorial "states." Hence, Husserl sees no opposition between the body as a thing and the body as lived through. To understand an animate body is to grasp a thing impregnated with a new stratum of extra-physical properties that make it a physical-aesthetic (*physisch-aesthesiologische*) unity—a concrete unity in respect to which the physical and the aesthetic are only abstractions.

Hence, we do indeed have a "reality" in the case of the animate body or corporeally localized soul, for there is something that keeps its properties identical through the change of external circumstances. Furthermore, it is always possible to elaborate new properties, new powers (*Vermögen*) as a function of new circumstances. Thus, the relation to intra-mundane (*reale*) circumstances permits our treating the psyche as entirely intra-mundane. At the beginning of this intentional analysis the body was the cooperating member (*Mitglied*) for every perception of things; now it is their counterpart (*Gegenbild*). The body is the thing which "has" localized sensations; in virtue of sensation it is the bearer of the psyche.

This animate body remains the quasi-reality that we were talking about above. The traits that almost cancel its intra-mundane status are undeniable. In the first place, it is the "zero-origin" or center of orientation, the "here" for which all objects are "there," the here which remains and in relation to which everything else changes place. Under the solipsistic perspective (which we still maintain) my body is not somewhere in an objective place; it is the original "here" for every "there." Secondly, it is impossible for me to vary the angle, side, or aspect under which my body appears to me, or to step away from it and have it turn in relation to me. In this sense the organ of perception is an unfinished percept, "a thing constituted in an astonishingly incomplete manner" (II, p. 159).

Thus, we are led to the ambiguity of the psyche. It participates in subjectivity, since it is the soul that has its body, and also in objectivity, since it is the body-thing that has sensations. This body is a part of things, and yet the psyche which inhabits it is the center around which the rest of the world is grouped. The psyche is open to causal relations, and yet it is the point where causality emerges from the physio-psychic order and moves to the ideo-psychic order.

But this reality still lacks those traits which appear when we leave solipsism and return to intersubjectivity. At that point "man" as a natural object will correspond entirely to the natural attitude.

3 / *The Intersubjective Level*

THE UNDERSTANDING of Others, already termed empathy (*Einfühlung*) in *Ideas I*, provides the main way of access to the psyche regarded as a reality of nature. Look! There are men over there, outside, among the things and animals. I understand that they have their psychic lives, that this is the same world for them and for me, and that together we form the psychical world of men.

The intentional analysis that begins here is the first rough sketch of what will be the Fifth Cartesian Meditation. The *Cartesian Meditations* are situated on the level of the idealistic interpretation of the phenomenological method; they attempt to resolve with empathy the paradox of transcendental solipsism to which the reduction of the world to my ego or monad seems to lead. However, *Ideas II* does not use the understanding of Others in order to resolve the entire philosophic problem of objectivity but applies it only to the limited problem of the constitution of the psyche. Likewise, Husserl does not yet insist on the paradox of the constitution of the alter ego itself, the one which is constituted as "alien" even though it is constituted "in me." Here analysis runs on a more descriptive level. To constitute signifies only to interrogate a sense by explicating the significational intentions to which the sense correlates. Hence, this job of constitution remains below the level of philosophical interpretation.

The point of departure is the "original" presence—*Urpräsenz*—of the Other's body. Such is the body of the Other for anyone; it is present like anything else. On the other hand, subjectivity has originary presence only for a single person. It is exhibited only indirectly by the body of the Other. It has not *Urpräsenz* but rather *Appräsenz*. This "appresentation" is constituted on the basis of the resemblance among all bodies considered as things, a phenomenon called "pairing"—*Paarung*—in the Fifth Meditation. By means of resemblance, the direct or indirect "localization" of the psyche in the body is carried over (*überträgt sich*) to all analogous bodies. This is the localization exhibited by the solipsistic experience of my animate body and my embodied soul.

This process of transfer comes to be so extensive that, step by step, I learn to coordinate the psyche with the perceived organism. Thus, an "appresented" localization of the psyche follows from localization lived through on the level of tactile and affective processes. "Cerebral localizations" are of this type. The brain is always the brain of another. Only indirectly do I give a sense to the expression: "The brain is the seat of the psyche." Localization here signifies no more than a purely functional correspondence between two series of changes. This is an empirical correlation elaborated by theoretical consciousness and hence on the same level as the "thing of physics" which structures the percept.

Thus, the "appresentation" of the psyche of the Other has its original reference—its *ursprüngliche Vorlage*—in the solipsistic experience of a total compresence of the psychic and the physical. The unity of man is present only there, or more precisely only in tactile and affective sensations. The "appresence" of the psyche of the Other "in" his body is a transferred compresence (*eine übertragene Kompräsenz*). The Other senses and thinks as I do; his body, too, is a "psychic field," just as mine is an originary sensorial field. But the range of action of this transfer is boundless. All compresence is transmuted into empathy (*geht dann in die Einfühlung über*); the hand of the Other that I see "appresents to me" the solipsistic touching of that hand and all that goes along with this touching. A whole world is born to this hand, a world that I can only presentiate, "render" present to myself (*vergegenwärtigen*), without its being present to me. Thus, bit by bit, an art of signs is formed, a vast grammar of expressions of which the most notable illustration is language. To understand these signs is to constitute man, to apprehend the Other as "analogue of myself" (II, p. 168).[20]

The first consequence of empathy is its return effect upon solipsistic experience. I apply these non-originary, but less limited, empirical correlations between the psychic and the physical to myself, for "the closed (*abgeschlossene*) unity of man is constituted only by empathy and by constant orientation of experiential observation to the psychic life appresented with the body of the Other and constantly grasped objectively along with his body. Subsequently, I apply this unity to myself" (II, p. 167). Thus, I achieve knowledge of the Other.

The second consequence is the quasi-localization of the soul. By virtue of these new correlations of the psychic with the corporeal, the change in the soul is like a codisplacement of the soul (*gleichsam auch seine Seele sich mitbewegt*). To be sure, the soul is nowhere, but yet its connection with the body places it somewhere. It is localized only because it is ordered in relation to a place by an empirical rule (*regelmässig zugeordnet*). In this sense, man moves about, moves away, and moves back. By this quasi-localization a man is incorporated with his subjectivity into my spatial surrounding world. The analogue of myself is over there.

But as a third consequence, by participating in the manner in which Others perceive things, I place myself outside myself. I succeed in objectifying my own body. I anticipate its aspect for Others. Beginning with the other "here," with a "here" appresented as the originary place of the Other, I represent my place to myself as an "over there" for the Other. At this moment everybody is outside, even me, and I can say with Husserl: "Man the object is an external object, transcendent, the object of an external intuition" (II, p. 169). Empathy achieves the "reification" of man, for like other realities he is a unity of appearings,

20. It will be noticed that Husserl eliminates only reasoning by analogy but does not eliminate a certain spontaneous analogical activity, a transfer from the ego to the alter ego. He does not reach a primitive experience of the psyche in the second person. One wonders if the philosophical interpretation of the reduction of the world to the ego has not brought about a sort of inhibition of the descriptive method here by imposing a methodological priority of solipsistic experience over intersubjective experience.

viz., "the identity in a multiplicity of appearings and states which are united under the form of dispositions" (II, p. 169).

Fourth consequence: If one now considers that this objectification of man is situated on the same intersubjective level as the mathematization of the remainder of reality, one glimpses the extent to which it is possible to "reify" consciousness. The mathematization of reality forces the perceived qualities back into the "subjective." The "true being" is then the X thought as the rule of construction for such and such perceptual processes. And thus, mathematized nature becomes an absolute. The "aesthesiological" order is likewise posited absolutely as a dependency of this nature. The subjective life of consciousness becomes a sort of epiphenomenon of such and such a body situated in absolute nature. The physical thing carries the whole edifice as existing in itself.

Thus, whereas the psyche is "reified" by its connection to the physical, the physical is disconnected from the psychic in being mathematized. This process precipitates the complete naturalization of man.

In his reaction to this process, Husserl is not at all concerned with recovering the original experience of the owned body which had been the point of departure for this movement of "reification" or "objectification." To the contrary, what appears to interest him is the progressive shift of accent from the originary subjective life to the psycho-organic reality on the experiential level. Solipsistic experience furnishes the originary sense of the psycho-organic unity; empathy brought about the transfer of this link to the body of the Other which is a true object; physics provided the mathematical and absolute basis of reality.

Husserl's reaction to this process is not existential but transcendental. The more the soul is "objectified," the more the pure ego has to be removed from objectification. Hence, Husserl does not dream of a fusion of the transcendental and the objective within an ambiguous experience which somehow holds them in an irresolvable suspension. Rather, *Ideas II* is constructed on the extreme polarity of an exiled "pure ego" and an objectified "man." This is why the second part ends in the abrupt contrast between the absolute subject for which a physical and animal nature is constituted, a nature regarded as absolute within which the psyche is included.[21] I am at the two extremities: as

21. "But this whole 'apprehension' [of things and men built upon an exact nature] presupposes that which can never be transformed into a simple 'index,' viz., the *absolute subject* with its subjective processes, acts of meaning, its rational acts, etc., *for which* the totality of nature, physical and animal, is constituted" (II, p. 171).

man at the extremity of objectification, as transcendental ego at the extremity of subjectivity.[22]

This analysis recalls the Kantian distinction between transcendental consciousness dealing with the "I think" and empirical consciousness dealing with the psychological ego. It comes closer to this distinction, it seems to me, than do contemporary attempts to grasp experience as lived through and situated on this side of the polarity of the transcendental and empirical.

[III] "THE CONSTITUTION OF SPIRIT (*Geist*)"

THE THIRD PART of *Ideas II* is devoted to *Geist* (spirit). This turn of the analysis may be surprising. *Ideas II* seemed to be oriented towards an antithesis of objective nature and the "last subject" for which reality is. The empirical ego had been included in mathematized reality insofar as it is built up on the body which is itself built up on the thing. The movement of naturalization and the movement of "returning to the ego" do not seem to leave room for another more ambiguous experience where such an antithesis would somehow be suspended.

The first few introductory words warn us that this new reversal of the intentional analysis is suggested by the existence of the *Geisteswissenschaften* (human sciences) in Husserl's time. He borrows the expression and the intention of the human sciences from Dilthey and several others (Windelband, Rickert, Simmel, Münsterberg). Hence at this turn phenomenology draws support from a reaction against the "naturalization" of man arising within the scientific world itself. At the same time Husserl finds a compensation in his study of man which consolidates more than it disturbs the "objective" style of psychophysiology. The constitution of the psyche leaves a "residue" because the "natural" ego is not the equivalent of the real ego. The psyche animating the body is not equivalent to the cultural and communal realizations of man. In reintroducing the dimension of the person and that of community Husserl completes the ego-psyche polarity with a

---

22. "Men are intersubjective objectivities whose bodies are the identical X—the index—of the corporeal appearings of subjects under regulation by laws in the total interconnection of physical nature. As for the soul, it is linked to this objectively determined X and grasped in the net of real-substantial determinations. Thus, it too is objectively determinable. It is a unity which in its dependence on the natural object 'physical body' and in its objectively real connection with this body is a reality in space and time" (II, p. 171). This naturalization of man refers to another domain of being and of research "which is the field of subjectivity and is no longer nature" (II, p. 172).

new schema where spirit (*Geist*) is not the empirical counterpart of the pure subject of phenomenology but is rather a sort of cultural equivalent much more awkward to situate in the phenomenological structure.

Husserl cannot, however, proceed by a simple "repetition" of the *Geisteswissenschaften*. He aims at justifying them by giving them the foundations they lack, that is to say, the constitution of their sense.[23] The scientist practices these sciences specifically as science. Only a phenomenologist can rationally explicate the complex interrelationships of the two groups of sciences. His task is to constitute (1) the sense itself of the opposition between nature and spirit (Chapter One), (2) the sense of the fundamental law of motivation which regulates the world of the spirit, just as the law of causality regulates nature (Chapter Two), and (3) the sense of the "ontological priority of the spiritual world to the natural world" (Chapter Three). This threefold undertaking opens up a possible field of investigation by means of an initial operation of signification. According to what was said at the beginning of *Ideas II*, this operation consists in determining an "Idea." The Idea of spirit will thus serve as our transcendental guide, just as the thing and the animate body served previously.

1. The Opposition between Spirit and Nature

IN PRINCIPLE the possibility of contrasting one attitude with another rests on the more radical possibility of detaching oneself from every attitude, that is to say of performing the phenomenological reduction. This first act shatters the spell of the natural attitude and thus makes another attitude possible. Before ever establishing the priority of one attitude over the other, the phenomenologist renders possible another attitude through the primordial liberty of the "ultimate subject" (*letzte Subjekt*) for which nature is no more than the pure "sense" of the acts constitutive of nature. Thus, he accounts for the difference between the two types of science by the difference between the attitudes in which they are rooted. He shows how to simplify the perspectives on man by means of changing attitudes, the phenomenologist being the disinterested spectator of all attitudes. Under his disinterested gaze, interested practices lose their naïveté and with it their attractive power and hence their exclusive believing in the "being" they consider.

Let us, then, make the sense "person" appear. Will the phenome-

---

23. Dilthey is said to be the first who saw the limits of a natural science of the soul (II, pp. 172 f.). But this man of "brilliant intuition" lacked rigor in the formation of problems and methods and in "scientific theorizing."

nologist create this new Idea by dialectic, or will he draw it by deduction from what has already been said? Not one line in the third part authorizes us to interpret constitution in either of these ways. Husserl always unfolds the complex intentions of consciousness, beginning from a sense already there in which they intersect. Hence, we read the opposition of the naturalistic world and the personalistic world in the appearance of man himself.

It must be said first that the sense of the soul is different from the sense of the person. I see a soul "in" its body, its sense of touch in its hand, its joy in its face. I see the psyche well up and be reabsorbed on the level of bodies which are themselves inserted into the texture of things. Expectations and recollections roll forth and beat their lived time against objective world-time with its coincidences and intervals. Social institutions lend themselves to being grasped as a play of stimuli and responses on the level of the behavior of the animate body. There is nothing in man that cannot be treated in a psycho-physiological fashion. Thus, in the natural attitude man falls back into zoology. Such are the tendencies of a study of sensoriality and localization; to be animate is truly to be an animal (Husserl sometimes speaks of *animalia*). However, we are not in this attitude when we live together, when we speak, when we exchange experiences, or when we live in the family, the state, the church, etc. Here we do not see man as a being of nature but rather as a being of culture. We do not notice the animal when we pay attention to the person. This is why a psychology of sociality, which limits itself to being an interpsychology where man is related to man as a stimulus having psychic functions, is deficient in its relation to man.

The first new trait which is characteristic of *Geist* is that the person is at the center of a surrounding world (*Umwelt*), qualified by its perceived, affective, and practical properties, enriched by culture, science, and art, and, consequently, always in a state of becoming insofar as its sense is remodeled constantly by the history of man. Thus, the "reality of physics," atoms, etc., which was taken just now as an absolute, plays a part in my *Umwelt* only if I "know" it, only if science as cultural activity has modified the look and the conception of the world wherein I live. For the historian and the sociologist, nature is the countryside of a civilization at a certain epoch, just as men see, accept, and value it with its characteristics of utility, desirability, practicability, etc. Thus, the *Umwelt* presents all of the affective and practical characteristics which the theoretic-doxic attitude suspends. In this respect, my surrounding world is more than what the scientist calls nature. The world is this way for the scientist himself outside of the scientific act. We shall better understand this relation to the surrounding world when we shall have grasped it under the law of motivation which takes the place of the law of causality implicit in the psycho-physical notion of stimulus.

The second dividing line between our new reading of man and the reading made by naturalism is the mutual relation of person to person. In principle the "personal connection" exceeds all purely psycho-physiological explanation, which is condemned to relate causally the psychic to the organic and the physical. Now, we are the subjects of a "common surrounding world," because the mutuality of subjectivities and the community of the *Umwelt* constitute one single fact that must be understood by the same relation of motivation. Scientific objectivity is itself subordinated to the common elaboration of a common cultural world. "No ego can become a person in the normal sense for itself and for the Other, a person banded together with other persons (*im Person-enverband*), unless understanding should institute a relation to a common surrounding world" (II, p. 191). Hence, what is implicit in this communal elaboration of a surrounding world is the formation of a "whole" in which each person is a "member" and in which the network of exchanges constitutes a surrounding world of communication (*kommunikative Umwelt*). We understand ourselves "mutually" in order to understand the same world "together." Thus, it is necessary to relate the world to the level of communities as a "social object," e.g., the Greek world, the medieval world, etc. Natural science understands the reciprocities between objects but not the fellow subjects (*Gegensubjekte*) who are capable of instituting "social subjectivities" for which the world is a "social objectivity."

It is worth noting that on pages 190–200 Husserl goes far toward the "collective consciousness" in Durkheim's sense or toward the "objective spirit" in Hegel's sense. Nevertheless, the theme of the individual and of the "primordial individuation" of the spirit will be the final point of emphasis in this book. This last turn of the analysis is prefigured in the explication of social subjectivity, since this same world that we perceive in common is ultimately perceived in an originary manner only by me. The world seen by the Other is apprehended only empathetically (*eingefühlt*) as centered around the consciousness belonging to the Other. Thus, "social subjectivity" is not and cannot be a first or last reality; it is only a sort of derived consciousness. The phenomenologist will continue to have the task of constituting it in the very complex exchanges of intersubjectivity and of subordinating it finally to a unique originary consciousness—my own.

Here is a difficulty which is presented in the opposite way in the Fifth Cartesian Meditation. In *Ideas II* Husserl goes directly to those "communities of persons" which elaborate primitively, so it seems, the senses of things, values, and persons as cultural objects. And he seems to suspect that the phenomenological reduction, applied to the human sciences, would point out the naïveté of any erroneously originary collective consciousness. The "return to the ego" from the human sciences should play the role of Socratic irony or pretended ignorance with respect to the claimed absolute sense of history, or with respect to the collective consciousness, or with respect to class, and so on, and should force a return to the only mental life that I live through originarily, my own, in its "living present." In just the opposite manner, the Fifth Cartesian Meditation immediately opens out from the impasse of transcendental solipsism. It raises the paradoxical question of constituting the Other as "outsider" and yet "in" me. The experience of the Other is only represented to me by transfer on the basis of a "pairing" between the ways in which the body of the Other and my own appear within my sphere of ownness. This is why the Other is "presentiated by sympathetic imagination." Only my mental life is "presented originarily." The intersubjective relations of the ego with the Other who is always "in" me, yet is always escaping from my originary experience, are instituted on this basis.

It is necessary to return to these fundamental grounds in order to understand why transcendental philosophy must remain in tension with any sociology of collective consciousness and any philosophy of history. This philosophy justifies their themes, "social subjectivity" or "objective spirit," on the level of the reality constituted by the same act that destroys their absolute claim.

2. Motivation as the Fundamental Law of the "Spirit"

THE SECOND CHAPTER constitutes the heart of this broad investigation of the "spiritual" order. Leaving behind the opposition of spirit and nature, we initiate an internal explication of this new realm of reality. The nearly one hundred pages devoted to it bear essentially on the categories belonging to this realm. The category of motivation, which corresponds to that of causality in the preceding realm, is at its center.

Husserl places a long reflection on the "ego" and subjectivity at the head of his reflections on motivation in order to situate the new study on a plane inaccessible to naturalization. Rightly speaking, Husserl here takes leave of a strict thematization of the subject matter of the human sciences as they are practiced and develops his own phenomenology of the ego as a presupposition of a true understanding of personal and social reality. Immediately the analysis is brought to bear upon the seat of subjectivity to which the body belongs, which acts and effects its acts and which takes position. Only this ego of acts can be said to be "affected" and "receptive" with respect to its tendencies and its states. First and foremost, therefore, we are invited to read the life of the ego from top to bottom, since it is for the ego of free spontaneity that there is "subjective having" and something "pre-given." This recognition of a subjectivity which is neither act nor spontaneity but which constitutes itself as passivity, affective tendency, or habit, is of the highest interest. It marks Husserl's first effort to institute a total experience of subjectivity where the involuntary and the owned body are not left to a naturalistic explanation but are recovered in their subjectivity as lived through (II, pp. 211–15).

Motivation can be understood by starting out from subjectivity, because first of all it is the style according to which a human ego is related to its surrounding world. Naturalistic thinking is well aware of a relation between psychical circumstances and psychic events, but it does not interpret it as a relation of a "world-for-a-subject" to a "subject-who-behaves-in-relation-to . . ." Now even an illusory object can motivate "behavior in reaction to something." In this first sense motivation covers the whole field of "being incited to . . . , determined to . . ." The motivating world is no longer that which the physicist elaborates but that which I perceive, value, and treat practically as lined with pathways and barred by obstacles. The relation of motivation in its kernel of sense is elaborated phenomenologically, but, on the other hand, it is the use of the motivating world in the sciences of man that alerts the phenomenologist. One can say that in this respect Husserl himself is essentially in debt to it for leading him out of his initial logicism and into a sort of phenomenology of conduct—or if the expressions be preferred, of behavior or praxis—which far outruns a simple theory of knowledge.

Husserl widens this primary sense of motivation step by step, even making it cover the totality of the "spiritual" field. At this point rational and volitional justifications ("I posit this because . . .") are reintroduced in the twofold sense of giving reasons and evoking reasons. All sorts of irrational connections are now added, as well as habitual associations and obscure connections justified by psychoanalysis, etc. (II, p. 222). This point is not negligible, since, as French phenomenologists say, psychoanalysis has sense only if it refers to relations of motivation among significations and not to relations of causality among psychic facts treated like things. Husserl does full justice to "hidden" (*verborgene*) motivations, where consciousness "posits" nothing. For that matter, external experience itself is constituted in passive syntheses; "the operating ego does not need to live in these motivations" (II, p. 225). Hence, motivation designates the law according to which consciousness unfolds, is connected temporally, reacts to the world, and understands the conduct of others in a surrounding world of persons and things. Progress in the understanding of the causal relations involved will in no way advance us in the understanding of the motives for a mode of behavior. Not that causality is suspended and interrupted by the irruption of subjectivity, but the understanding of a course of motivation is not to be had in the attitude in which one apprehends a causal series in nature.

The contrast of causality and motivation cuts almost exactly across the contrast usually recognized between explaining and understanding. Husserl himself makes reference to this contrast, but as a particular case of the opposition between the two major attitudes, natural and spiritual. It serves him as a means for clearing up the new implications of corporeal life in spiritual life. In fact this is the last application that he makes of the law of motivation (II, p. 247). To understand, in his language, applies very precisely to the grasping of a unity of spiritual sense in a diversity of nature. The first application that he makes of the notion is not the understanding of an intent or of the expression of a face, a gesture, or an action; the initial theme is given through the examination of cultural objects animated by a sense: a book, a work of art, or more simply a sentence read or heard. Understanding goes to the unity of a cultural object. It signifies that I am not directed towards the marks that I see when reading, because "I live within the sense through understanding." Somehow the spiritual imprints the physical with its sense to the point of annulling the duality of sense and its vehicle. The book is there in space, in that place. The sense, which is not there, nevertheless animates it with its intention and in some manner absorbs it into its spirituality. Thus, all of the objects of art and culture down to and including the humble utensils of everyday life are transmuted into an objectivity of a new sort which introduces them, along with consciousness, into the world of the spirit. These are the cultural objects which permit our speaking of a "world" of the spirit, for in truth they are the forms of the "objective spirit."

Beyond its own interest, this elucidation of the cultural object has the important function of introducing a new interpretation of the mind-body relation and of bringing out the analysis of the second part again, which did not go beyond the level of psycho-physiology, for the body is imprinted with a sense just like the cultural object, the book, or the temple. I grasp the sense in its unity from the living being in which it is imprinted. As in a sentence, the articulations of the body are founded in the total design of the sense. It is important to notice that Husserl corrects his first interpretation of "animation," which he had carried out in a very naturalistic way in Part Two, by way of a cultural understanding. His language is witness to this shift in levels between a phenomenology of culture and a phenomenology of the psyche. Indeed, the new description emphasizes, somewhat tardily, the extent to which an interpretation of the soul which took its departure from localized sensations had remained naturalistic. *Geist* proclaims the limits of psycho-logy.

This movement of reflection clearly points to the passage from objectification to the existential understanding of Husserl's successors, but it is not conducted as these successors conduct it. Husserl first consolidates the naturalistic interpretation of the psyche on the level of ordinary perception. He recaptures the sense of human "expression" on the level of a phenomenology of culture rather than on that of a phenomenology of perception. The man for whom a face is spiritual, for whom an action can mean something, is he for whom language has a cultural sense, for whom cultural objects are already constituted in the unity of a spiritual sense and a physical support. Thus, the classical problem of consciousness and body is reduplicated by Husserl in a naturalistic theory of "animation" and a cultural theory of "expression." The first does not get much further than the localization of sensorial fields in corporeal extension, since the body is the term of reference. The second takes the sense of the body from its conscious intentions; the body is here effaced entirely, just as the pronounced sound or the printed word in dialogue or reading is reabsorbed in the sense understood.

At the end of this reflection the ego is no longer an appendage of its body. On the contrary, the person becomes the body's reference point; it is he who sustains it, leads it, and expresses himself through it, yielding to or resisting it. Everything in the sciences of the spirit is a "performance" of the spirit. It is through relation to this free spontaneity that receptivity and passivity themselves have a sense and that the being of the ego may be extended into a possessing which brings it down to the point of an endured necessity.

3. The Relation of Nature to Spirit

AT THE END of *Ideas II* Husserl raises the question which the reader has been waiting for since the elucidation of *Geist* introduced a new turning point into the problem of the constitution of reality. If spirit is different from nature, what relations between these two realities can be thought? The question is open only to an answer beginning from *Geist*, not vice versa, for the human spirit, as we have seen, has a "lower level," an "underside," which is nature. This underside is open to naturalistic treatment. The psycho-organic complex, treated in the natural sciences of man, is the objectivistic commentary or naturalistic index for this naturalized side of spirit.

Voluntary action is a good example of this passage from spirit to nature. Spirit "works" (*œuvre*) in the world only so far as people understand and approve it. But what are "works" in relation to spirit are also "things" in relation to nature. The bodily "organ" of this "work" is also the body that physics knows and the place where psycho-physiology localizes the psyche. The psyche itself is at once the bundle of tendencies through which spirit moves its own body and the natural reality which depends upon the body-object.[24]

These two interpretations intersect in the body. In the course of the investigation of spirit and person (Part Three of *Ideas II*), the notion of "owned body" is justified, whereas Part Two dealt with the psyche and the organism in naturalistic language. The relation that the body institutes between spirit and nature in no way merits the name of causality. At the most one can speak of conditions, never of causes. And this relation has no sense outside of the dual status of the body as locus of sensation naturalistically considered and as organ of the will personalistically considered (*aesthesiologische Leib und Willensleib*) (II, p. 284). One could just as well say that nature and spirit are mediated by the double status of the psyche, or one can read by turns a mundane phenomenon conditioned by the thing-body and a spiritual lower level or "basement" by which spirit sustains and acts on the world. The ambiguity does not extend to the extremes of thing and spirit but is rather in the mediating complex of animate body or incarnate psyche. For a naturalistic view everything becomes a thing bit by bit, even spirit which only has its works as its witness. For a spiritualistic view everything becomes spirit bit by bit, even things such as the scene and point of impact of action and passion. On the level of soul-body, motivation is twisted into causality, or causality is turned back into motivation.

Does this mean that the possibility of passing from one reading to the other confers an equal dignity on both? At this point Husserl means to affirm the "ontological priority of spirit over nature" (this is approximately the title of Chapter Three of Part Three). As we are going to see, this pre-eminence itself is what poses the most embarrassing question of *Ideas II*: that of situating exactly what in this work Husserl calls spirit (*Geist*) in relation to that which his works generally call "consciousness," the subjective life of consciousness reached by the phenomenological reduction.

24. The pages devoted to tendencies understood as the intermediary subjective processes between intending and corporeal movement are astonishingly perspicacious and have great importance for a phenomenology of the will (II, pp. 283–88).

The priority of spirit over nature appears fully if one approaches the question from the theory generally accepted in the time of *Ideas II*, the theory of "psycho-physical parallelism." This parallelism has two postulates which the theory of spirit challenges: first, every reality of consciousness corresponds to a physical event; in addition, the physical event plays the explanatory role. Now, exactly the contrary must be said: the elucidation of spirit supplies the reasons which in principle exclude a generalization to the whole of conscious life of such notions as the explanation of sensation through the organization of the nervous system. Besides, the type of intelligibility that belongs to spirit dominates psycho-physical explanation in principle. Let us consider these two points separately.

In the second part, Husserl presented as a fact and without justification that only the "hyletic" aspect of consciousness is open for an explanation with reference to the body. He meant by "hyle" the non-intentive or non-"noetic" side of consciousness (sensations, affections, impulses). Why so? Because the interconnection of intentive moments into a consciousness which continues itself by "retaining" its recent moments and in "protending" toward its imminent moments obeys a priori laws of compatibility (*Verträglichkeit*) among the subjective processes of consciousness. The phenomenologist lays bare these a priori laws by reduction of the world of things, bodies, and souls. This consciousness remains a monad which implies itself in a closed temporal system. This possibility in principle of suspending the absolute claim of things—of one thing in particular, the brain—to being the carrier of consciousness, attests to the fact that the noetic side of consciousness cannot without absurdity be dependent on the organism. These "eidetic a priori laws of consciousness" which prescribe the style of the temporal interconnection of consciousness limit the extension of psycho-physical explanation to the "regulations of fact" permitted by this auto-constitution or, as Husserl says, are "left open" by it ("only that can be empirically conditioned which is left *open* by the essential connections").[25] Thus, it is up to experience and to experimentation to establish the dependence in fact of the hyletic aspect upon the organism, within the limits opened up by the internal connection of consciousness.

Husserl thinks, consequently, that he can radically refute parallelism without getting caught up in the deceptive alternative of either "parallelism" or "reciprocal influence between the mental and the organic." At the same time his refutation contains among its motifs

---

25. "Empirisch bedingt sein kann nur das, was die Wesenszusammenhänge *offen* lassen" (II, p. 293).

the cardinal affirmation with which the book ends: "Nature is relative to absolute spirit." Strike out nature, and there remains the ego that strikes things out by the reductive act. Strike out spirit, and nature collapses for lack of a consciousness for which and in which its sense is articulated.

The argument leads us to the root of Husserlian idealism. The spirit in question here has no sense out of context with the famous phenomenological reduction and can only be upheld by the *ego meditans* which would continue to think even without a world. We shall return to this enigma of the relations between the *Geist* of the *Geisteswissenschaften* and the *Bewusstsein* (consciousness) of phenomenology in a moment. Husserl says nothing about it and terminates his book on another note.

The study of spirit is brought to its culmination with the notion of the individual and individuation. A reality regulated by an internal law of motivation, a reality which interconnects itself according to its own law of compatibility among subjective processes of consciousness— such a reality is, par excellence, an "individual." The fashion in which it individualizes itself is exactly contrary to the fashion in which a thing is individualized, for a thing is always only a case of a general rule, of a *quid* drawn from innumerable examples; each individual thing has its reason external to it in the order of the world, in the totality of its external relations. Each spirit, on the contrary, is unique by its style of motivation and by the coherence of its history. It only happens once (*einmaliges*). Can we say that to be a "this" (*Dies*) is a particular case of ecceity, thisness, *Diesheit*? The fallacy is clear; ecceity is a pure form and not a common genus. "The form of a This is not a What, and in this sense it is not an essence. It is general in the sense of a [pure] form." [26] This meditation on individuation, rediscovered by beginning from the theme of motivation and from the succession of a consciousness with itself—and which, it should be mentioned in passing, is very much in line with a Leibnizian philosophy of individuality—this meditation confirms and seals "the ontological priority of spirit over nature," because spirit realizes primordial and absolute individuation. A thing acquires individuality only for a consciousness which claims it in a course of appearances. Its own individuation is "the secondary individuation of something-over-against" (*des Gegenüber*) (II, p. 301). In other words, a unity of appearances—that of the thing—is relative to the absolute unity which consciousness primordially forms with itself. In their ambiguity the soul and the body participate in both the one and the other form

26. "Die Form des Dies is keine Washeit und in diesem Sinn kein Wesen. Es ist allgemein im Sinne der Form" (II, p. 301).

of individuation. As naturalizations of spirit they illuminate its primary individuality. As subject matter of the natural sciences they are a mode of unity in appearings.

Thus ends *Ideas II*. The reader is surprised at the difference in tone between Part Two and Part Three. In the second part, an isolated object, the psyche, firmly anchored in nature, immersed in the body-thing, slowly emerges over and against the ego. The analysis ended with a sharp contrast between the ego, radically purified by the transcendental reduction, and the empirical reality of man, vigorously polarized by a nature which is mathematized to the extreme. We were able to compare this polarity with that of the transcendental "I" and the empirical "me" of Kant. The great difficulty lies in locating the explication of spirit in relation to this polarity. To begin with, the latter analysis does not really follow the preceding one. Spirit is not grounded in the psyche as the latter is grounded in the things. Its study constitutes a new departure and calls for a sort of conversion which brings attention back to this side of the final state of objectification reached by the preceding study. The surrounding world which motivates my personal life with its trees and books, its lakes and temples, should rather be seized upon at the initial stage of thing-apprehension (*Dingauffassung*), when the body is still the "aesthetic" body implied in the percept and when the percept is not yet reformed by the scientific view of the universe. The world of culture is implanted not in the scientific universe but in the percept that precedes all scientific objectification. The strange structure of *Ideas II* stems from this fact. At the end of Part Two, the analysis is pushed in a first direction toward the naturalistic conception of man and of things. Then the analysis is reversed in order to set off in another direction, toward the account of absolute consciousness at the end of Part Three. Basically, this way of going about the matter recalls the contrast which was in the air at that time between explaining and understanding: the psyche is explained, the spirit is understood.

But then it is no longer possible—not in the same way at least—to contrast the "reality" of spirit to the transcendental ego. Spirit is not like a thing, nor even like the animate body and the psyche, its empirical counterpole. All the categories of the person and of sociality summed up under the title of motivation are fundamentally the phenomenological categories and are found in *Ideas I* or in the *Cartesian Meditations*. Yet "spirit" was introduced at the beginning of *Ideas II* as a sector of total reality, as something constituted facing the process of constitution. How can it be dignified at the end of the same book as the absolute to which all nature is relative?

There is, evidently, an enigma in the architecture of *Ideas II* which up to this point has been simple. Perhaps the enigma can be explicated in this way. Husserl finds a movement in the human sciences of his time reacting against the reigning naturalism. He integrates these sciences of the spirit into his articulated system of reality by superimposing a new theme, spirit, on the series thing-body-psyche. This series has its own coherence in the natural attitude. Husserl organizes the new sciences under the title of a new attitude that remains within reality. The new sciences are born on the margin of the transcendental reduction and remain on the "naïve" side of every science that posits its object as being. But on the other hand, in order to integrate this new object into reality, it is necessary to constitute its Idea, that is to say, to deploy the intentive processes whose correlates are the basic concepts of the *Geisteswissenschaften*. Thereupon, these basic acts are uncovered as identical with the reflective operations which the phenomenologist uses. Thus, *Geist* is nothing other than the ego of phenomenology, but without the light of the phenomenological reduction. It is a reality, the reality of the person in his relations to his surrounding world, to social groups, and to other persons. But the sense, the directive Idea, which permits thematizing the categories of the human sciences is the pure ego of phenomenology.

Husserl himself recognizes the ambiguous status of *Geist* on several important pages.[27] The "personal ego," while different from the "pure ego," is still a species of object, even though non-natural. I can stand back with respect to it as with respect to all "experience," to all experience relative to a "reality." Should I define the person as the source of his acts, as he who has his body, as the substrate of the properties of his character, as the unity of a course of development, as an "organism with powers," as a responsible and reasonable being—in every case the person is found (*vorgefundene*) or discovered as a pre-existing reality. The adherence of a zone of shadow, of passivity, or of hidden motivation, to the spontaneity of the "I can" emphasizes even more this prior character of the pre-given, of the pre-reflective, in the discovery of the person. As Husserl says emphatically, the *personales Ich* (personal I) is a *Mich* (me), an "I" in the accusative and not in the nominative (II, p. 253), an "I-object for me." This is clearly why in *Ideas I* it falls to the phenomenological reduction along with the world. But that does not prevent it from playing the role of analogon of a phenomenological revealer for the pure ego.

Thereupon, the very Kantian schema, reached at the end of the

---

27. *Reines Ich und persönliches Ich als Objekt der reflexiven Selbstapperzeption* [pure ego and personal ego as the object of reflective self-apperception], pp. 247–51, and *Konstitution des persönlichen Ich vor der Reflexion* [constitution of the personal ego prior to reflection], pp. 251–53.

second part, is overthrown. The third part introduces an intermediary term between the pure ego and the psyche in its body (there we were able to recognize something like an echo of the [Kantian] transcendental "I" and the empirical self). Just such an intermediary term is the person in his surrounding world of things and persons. (Such intermediary terms are alien to the critical mentality.) Thus, Husserl is at one of the sources of those philosophies of the person, of existence, of the concrete subject, etc., which try to fill in the hiatus left by Kant between transcendental reflection and empirical psychology. But at the same time that Husserl initiates the understanding-psychology of the person, he shows its limits, for the person does not have the purity of the transcendental subject. He is not the ultimate ego. He is still in the world of "experience." He is involved there by all of his motivations. His precritical "naïveté" is precisely that of defining himself by his behavior in an *Umwelt*. The proof of this is the reversible character of the ego-world relation; I understand a person by his motives, the influences that he undergoes, etc. Beyond infatuation with the person and with existence, Husserl maintains his ideal of philosophy, which is the emergence of an *ego meditans* having no part in his own praxis.

At least this theme, intermediary between the empirical and the transcendental, between naturalism and pure phenomenology, teaches the scientist to step up his notion of reality and to enrich it with as many voices as there are methodological styles. On his side, the philosopher finds a real manifestation of the consciousness which he seeks and which depicts cultural objects for him (monuments, works, institutions) by concerning himself with understanding-psychology, with the history of culture, and with the field of the sciences. Familiarity with this consciousness inclines him to effect the return to the pure ego which is, according to Husserl, the ever imminent beginning of philosophy.

4 / A Study of Husserl's *Cartesian Meditations*, I–IV

To Professor S. Strasser,
the excellent editor of *Husserliana I*.

[I] HUSSERL AND DESCARTES

THE INITIAL AIM of the *Cartesian Meditations* [1] is to locate the transcendental motif of phenomenology, gradually elaborated since about 1905, within the history of philosophy. This concern, with which the lectures of 1929 begin, introduces the historical manner of becoming aware of the task of phenomenology which later prevailed in the *Crisis* of 1935. The *Crisis* discerns a mode of philosophizing within transcendental reflection which has its own history and which traverses the history of "naïveté." By naïveté we mean, broadly speaking, the history of the sciences, technologies, and objectivistic philosophies which continue to be fascinated by scientific naturalism. To be sure, this former history does culminate in the phenomenological philosophy. Yet, in the renewal of the Cartesian theme of the cogito, the *Cartesian Meditations* envisages a radicalization which puts aside the historical error. The fact that there is a history after Descartes, who claimed to put an end to the wanderings of thought and to begin philosophy anew, occurs because Descartes was not sufficiently radical or sufficiently true to his own radicalism. Philosophy could triumph over its own history and could realize its "eternal sense" if it would

1. First presented in Paris as a lecture series in German in 1929. [French translation by Gabrielle Peiffer and Emmanuel Levinas, *Meditations cartésiennes*, 1st ed. (Paris, 1931); 2d ed. (Paris, 1947); German edition by Prof. S. Strasser, *Cartesianische Meditationen und Pariser Vorträge*, *Husserliana I* (The Hague, 1950); English translation by Dorion Cairns, *Cartesian Meditations* (The Hague, 1960). The English translation contains the pagination of *Husserliana I* in the margin, to which this and the next essay refer by numbers in parentheses, preceded by the letters *CM*.—Trans.]

follow its task through to the end. The *Cartesian Meditations* suggests the notion that the history of philosophy has a sense insofar as it proceeds toward the suppression of its own history by progress in the direction of the true beginning.

It can be said that every philosophy is an interpretation of the history of philosophy, an explication of its contradictions, and a justification of its possible unity by the suprahistorical sense of the philosophical activity or the philosophical intention. Husserl, following Descartes, investigated this sense in the notion of a radical beginning, but he followed it further than Descartes. From this "eternal sense"—from this *Urbild*—flows the very "enterprise" of philosophizing. The *Crisis*, in contrast to the *Cartesian Meditations*, shows that this eternal sense, which is a task, an obligation to philosophize, specifically engenders a history on the reflective level, a history of signification, because it is the development of its own sense.

Why must the cogito be radicalized? Husserl's Descartes is not Gilson's, Laporte's, or Alquié's; it is rather a Descartes read by a Neo-Kantian, for the greatness of Descartes, according to Husserl, lies in his having produced the project of a philosophy which is at the same time a science and the ground of all sciences within the system of one universal science. By rights the cogito is the transcendental subject. But Descartes betrayed his own radicalism, for the doubt should have put an end to all objective externality and should have disengaged a subjectivity without an absolute external world. However, the cogito is grasped by Descartes as the first link of a deductive chain whose successive links are the *res cogitans*, the existence of God, and through the services of the divine veracity, the existence of objective nature.

Before taking another step, we must stop to consider this interpretation of Descartes, for it completely fails to recognize the polarity which supports the whole Cartesian philosophy. This is the polarity between the cogito which in itself absorbs all objectivity as its sense (the "ideas" of physics and mathematics are the sense of the cogito) and, on the other hand, the existence of God from which every being as created depends. These two requirements intersect again in the idea of infinity, an idea which belongs at once to the cycle of the cogito, insofar as it is an idea like others, and to the cycle of being, in the respect in which it is the mark of the infinite being in my thought.

One can certainly contest the possibility of a philosophy with two sources—the cogito and God. That is to say, one can deny the possibility of holding at one and the same time a philosophy where subjectivity is the reference pole of all that can be thought and a philosophy where being is the reference pole of all that exists. However, to fail to recognize this structure of Cartesianism is to produce a philosophy other than Descartes's and not to radicalize Cartesianism.

Perhaps the best introduction to the sense of Husserl's *Cartesian Meditations* is this destruction of the original sense of Cartesianism according to which the cogito is itself a being situated between being and nothingness, a lesser being, inhabited and invested with an idea which makes it burst forth. This is the idea of infinity. This idea, having more being than the ego which thinks it, provokes a displacement of the center of gravity of subjectivity toward the infinite being. Husserl's whole advance omits this polarity. I speak of omission, since there is nothing which warrants our saying that Husserl understood his transcendental philosophy as atheistic in principle. At least the transcendental ego is sufficient for all of the tasks of a *philosophia prima* (CM, § 3). And this is the very term that Descartes applied to his own meditations (*Meditationes de Prima Philosophia*).

Transcendental philosophy courageously comes to grips with the very great difficulties, to which we shall come in due course, of a philosophy which is to be only an egology, never an ontology. This is a philosophy where being not only never gives the force of reality to the object, but above all never founds the reality of the ego itself. Thus, as an egology it is a cogito without *res cogitans*, a cogito without the absolute measure of the idea of infinity, without the unique cogitatum which would be the mark of an entirely different foundational subjectivity.

Husserl accepted all of the difficulties of such an egology. These difficulties come to a head at the end of the Fourth Meditation in the objection termed "transcendental solipsism." In consequence, the Fifth Meditation, which replies to this objection, can be considered as Husserl's substitute for the ontology introduced by Descartes into his Third Meditation by means of the idea of infinity and by the recognition of being (*être*) in the very presence of this idea. Whereas Descartes transcends the cogito by means of God, Husserl transcends the ego by the alter ego. Thus, Husserl sought a more sound foundation for objectivity in a philosophy of intersubjectivity than Descartes had sought in the divine veracity. Hence the importance of the Fifth Meditation. After his Paris Lectures, Husserl elaborated this Meditation to the point of giving it almost the length of the other four together. These *Cartesian Meditations* should be considered as a progressive ascension towards a certain critical point—which is almost a breakdown—viz., the *solus ipse* of an egology without ontology. The constitution of the transcendence of the Other in the immanence of the sphere of my ownness (*ma sphère propre*) has the same decisive signification as the passage from the Idea of the infinite "within" the Cartesian cogito to the very being "of" the infinite outside of the cogito.

One may wonder whether Husserl escaped what might be called the "Husserlian circle" any better than Descartes escaped his own famous "circle." In the same way that Descartes can be criticized for basing all truth on the divine truth and this on the idea of infinity, we may question whether Husserl succeeded in getting the originary ego, "in" which the alter ego is constituted, back "into" intersubjectivity. Just as there may be a problem in Cartesianism where the two-source structure is primitive, so there is room for wonder whether Husserl, who accepted no original polarity between the ego and being, succeeded in accounting for the otherness of the Other and the otherness of the whole of nature which the Other draws out and centers around itself.

[II] THE DIFFICULTY OF THE RADICAL "POINT OF DEPARTURE" (First Meditation)

IT IS INTERESTING to observe carefully the mechanism of thought which, at the end of the First Meditation, leads to making the ego cogito the "actual" principle, the "actual" point of departure of philosophy (*einen wirklichen Anfang*). Since one can set out neither from an absence of thought nor from a science accepted as a cultural fact (Descartes too quickly took for granted the scientific ideal of mathematical physics), one must set out from the guiding idea (*Zweckidee*) of universal science, from the attempt to give an absolute foundation to the sciences. Hence, before the transcendental "experience" of the Second Meditation, there is a prior point of departure which is a sort of obligation. Here one is to abandon oneself (*sich hingeben*) to the assumption or claim that animates the sciences, to "live in" (*einleben*) their impulse and intention and thus to regrasp the idea of science as the correlate—the "noema"—of this "intending" which animates the scientific effort.

This is to say that phenomenology must reach its point of departure by initially situating itself as a secondary activity in relation to the primary activity of the sciences. Thus, something is already decided before the point of departure. For, in contradistinction to the Heidegger of *Being and Time*, this philosophy situates its philosophical activity in relation to an activity already rendered theoretical and not in relation to a more primitive power or action. To some extent the

Crisis will correct this epistemological limitation of the pre-beginning by rethinking the sciences themselves as a cultural activity and even as a species of theoretical praxis.

This is not all. The guiding Idea (*Zweckidee*) would be sterile if it were not "differentiated" (as the matter is expressed in CM, §§ 4 and 5) by a theory of evidence which "repeats" the fundamental themes of the *Logical Investigations*. It is necessary not only to assent to the guiding Idea of universal science before beginning and in order to begin, but it is also necessary to document this Idea in a theory of true judgment according to which the being-status (*valeur d'être*) of the judgment consists in the fact that an "empty" significational intending is fulfilled by the "fullness" of an evidence, be it empirical or be it essential (the latter is the famous categorial intuition of the Sixth Logical Investigation).

To this notion of evidence we must add the notion of apodicticity, which is not exactly that of adequate evidence, i.e., complete fulfillment. As we shall see, the cogito has adequate evidence only in its present moment and not without its indefinite horizons of recency and imminence. Apodicticity characterizes what is primary. It is that to which all mediate evidence refers, viz., the inconceivability of the non-being of the evident thing or state of affairs. Hence, apodicticity is the resistance offered by the evidence of essence to the critical test of imaginative variation (a test to which too much importance cannot be accorded in Husserl's eidetic method). By means of this test apodictic evidence excludes doubting and can refer back to itself reflectively without self-destruction. This notion of apodicticity accentuates the character of vision belonging to evidence. We shall return to this matter of light and vision in Husserl, for, as the Third Meditation will demonstrate, it is not easy to bring phenomenology's intuitionistic tendency into accord with its effort to "constitute" the structures of consciousness. In effect, this effort is on the order of "producing" (*Leistung*) rather than of "seeing" (*voir*).

Thus, the beginning philosophy is preceded not by a presence but (1) by a principle: the obligation to accept the Idea of truth, and (2) by a definition: the definition of truth by evidence. The initial obligation requires us to judge truth only by evidence. Descartes had already admitted that the cogito presupposed "common notions": being, thought, idea, etc. The notions of truth, evidence, etc., elaborated in the *Logical Investigations* play the same role in relation to the radical beginning of the Husserlian *Meditations*. Before putting ourselves in the presence of a primary evidence, we must know what "evidence" is and what is "primary," and we must accept the obligation to seek such evidence.

The problem,[2] then, is to pass from the Idea of evidence to a primary actual evidence. "Of what use would this principle and the preceding meditation be to us, if they did not furnish the means for taking an actual (*Wirklich*) point of departure, which would allow us to actualize (*verwirklichen*) the genuine Idea of science?" Hence, it is necessary for us to find a truth which of itself bears the mark (*Stempel*) of a first truth.

The remainder of the First Meditation is lucid. It involves shifting the privilege of primary evidence from the presence of the world to the presence of the ego. This challenge to the pseudo-evidence (*Selbstverständlichkeit*) attaching to the presence of the world is the transcendental *epoché* itself. The *epoché* is performed very rapidly in the *Cartesian Meditations* and does not require the interminable preparations and precautions of *Ideas I*. But its motive is not easy to come upon. Experience, Husserl says, does not exclude the possibility that the world does not exist. Hence, the critical effort is brought to bear upon the apodicticity of the experience of the world. And here an application of the method of imaginative variation may be recognized; nothing resists the metaphysical fiction that the world is not.

No longer is there any trace of the skeptical anxiety and vertigo to be found in the writings of 1905–7. Indeed, the certainty attaching to the primary character of the ego cogito supports this methodical proof by means of the hypothesis of non-being. This certainty destroys the illusion attaching to the pre-given (*vorgegeben*) presence of the world. The certainty of the apodictic character of the ego cogito is already at work in this challenge thrown to the familiar and enveloping presence of the world always-already-there. What presents itself as "ontological basis" (*Seinsboden*) collapses; and the "believing in being" (*Seinsglauben*) which was accorded it is dispelled, leaving nothing more than the phenomenon-of-the-world-for-my-consciousness; that is, it leaves a world-perceived—in reflective life.

Although this procedure is reported briefly here, it nevertheless removes an equivocation in *Ideas I*. The latter work presented consciousness as a "residue," as what "remains" when one places the existence of things between parentheses. The *Cartesian Meditations* emphasizes the positive character of this operation. "When I regard

2. The "Paris Lectures" (*Husserliana I*, pp. 3–39) sum up this first movement of thought in an emphatic manner: what counts is what is "founded," "legitimated," "by recourse to the things themselves and to the 'states of affairs' (*Sachverhalte*) in original experience and evidence (*Einsicht*)" (CM, p. 6). Husserl soberly specifies the relation between evidence and apodicticity: "Judge only with evidence, and test the evidence critically; once again, do so only with reference to evidence" (CM, p. 6). The summary in French is even more striking (CM, p. 195).

my life exclusively as consciousness of this world, I gain myself as the pure ego with the pure flux of my cogitations." I gain myself, that is to say, I appropriate for myself what is my "own" (*eigen*), namely, the for-me-ness of the world; "the world is for me only what exists and has status for my consciousness in such a cogito" (CM, p. 60). In fact, the *epoché* is not a placing between parentheses, as *Ideas I* has it, for there is nothing in the parentheses. The world is retained with all of its modalities (actual, probable, possible, true, false, attentively noticed, not noticed, etc.), but it is transformed into a "phenomenon of being."

The kinship is evident between the Cartesian doubt and this suspending of the "belief in being" which we apply to the world. Contrary to Descartes's Sixth Meditation, however, no world will be found again. The *epoché* does not consist in stretching an ontological bond in order to be more assured of it; rather, it claims to dispel irrevocably the realistic illusion of the in-itself. Only the intersubjective perception of the Fifth Cartesian Meditation will change the "for me" of the First Cartesian Meditation into a "for others," a "for us," and a "for all."

The intention of the *Meditations* of Descartes is quite different. It is striking that Descartes goes directly from the *dubito* to the *sum* well before the appearance of the idea of infinity in the Third Meditation (though this is not the case in the *Discourse*). The concern of the *Meditations* is not so much epistemological or transcendental as ontological. Descartes seeks a being, quite as much as a ground of validity; perhaps even more so. If the ego has in fact more being than its objects, it has less being in its *esse objectivum* than the idea of infinity. The Cartesian cogito, intermediary between being and nothingness, manifests both the greater being which consists in thinking and the lesser being which reveals the wandering and precarious character of the *dubito*.

Such an evaluation of the grandeur of the being of the cogito is absolutely foreign to Husserl and his Neo-Kantian interpretation of Descartes. This concern for ontological evaluation, beginning with the Second Meditation of Descartes, renders the second Copernican Revolution possible, which, unlike the first one, subordinates the being of the doubting-thinking subject to the perfect being and does so despite the first Copernican Revolution, which centered everything thinkable upon thinking. This ontological interest even leads Descartes to treat the cogito as "*res cogitans*," its status as "*res*" being nothing other than its ontological status. This is why the problem of the being of the world is not governed by doubt and can be presented again in the Sixth Meditation without bringing back into question the inherence of the ideas of the things in the cogito.

In Husserl there is nothing like this. His epistemological concern is not tied in with another concern which moves beyond it after having roused and animated it. In the texts which describe the inherence of the world in consciousness I would explain Husserl's rather disconcerting glide from the "for me" (*für mich*) into the "from me" (*aus mir*) by the absence of a genuine set of ontological problems. "I cannot act and make a value judgment in any world other than the one which finds in me and draws from me (*aus mir*) its sense and its status." "All of its universal and particular sense, all of its being-status (*valeur existentielle, Seinsgeltung*), it draws (*schöpft*) exclusively out (*aus*) of such cogitationes" (CM, p. 65). "The objective world which exists for me (*für mich*), which has existed or will exist for me, this objective world with all of its objects in me, draws from me (*aus mir selbst*) all of its sense and all of the existential status that it has for me" (CM, p. 65). This oscillation between the *für* and the *aus* (the "*in mir*" bringing the two relations together) is characteristic of the whole procedure of the *Cartesian Meditations*. It includes a non-thematized decision which may well be called a "metaphysical" [3] decision, one which is merged with a genuinely "critical" and, we believe, irrefutable and fertile movement of the transcendental *epoché*. This decision consists in saying that there is no other dimension of the being of the world than the dimension of its being for me, and there is no other set of problems than the transcendental one. Whereas Descartes would limit the being of the world in two ways (by the cogito which supports the thinkable and by God who supports the created), Husserl decides that there is but one possible system of limitation and that the ontological question is the epistemological question.

Husserl's transcendental philosophy will be, therefore, a philosophy of "sense"—giving this term the broadest possible extension, one much beyond any narrow intellectualism. It should include perceived sense, imagined sense, willed sense, sense affectively experienced, sense judged and told, and logical sense. The world *for* me is the sense of the world *in* me, the sense inherent *in* my existence, and, finally, the sense *of* my life; the Fourth Cartesian Meditation will say that the world is the concrete life of my monad.

3. In his "Remarks," Roman Ingarden has already objected to Husserl on this score (Dr. Strasser has happily joined Ingarden's "Remarks" to the Husserlian text in *Husserliana I*, pp. 205–18): "Within the framework of the *epoché* I have the right to bring judgments to bear only on myself, not on the world" (CM, p. 208). By this objection Ingarden merely means that a judgment of this kind about the world is premature and can only be the result of transcendental constitution; it cannot be an initial and introductory proposition. Ingarden is making no mistake, for such a judgment about the world includes a "metaphysical decision . . . which is equivalent to a categorial thesis about something which is not an element of transcendental subjectivity" (CM, p. 210).

There remains to be understood the "pre-given" quality of this world, which is the snare of philosophical "naïveté." Why is this pre-given world, which becomes "secondary" from the transcendental viewpoint and in relation to the "meditating," "disinterested" ego (which we shall consider later), why is it first with respect to "Life"? Descartes avoids this problem in his Sixth Meditation. The same problem, renewed in the *Crisis* under the name of *Lebenswelt* (life-world), remains unsolved in the *Cartesian Meditations*. We shall see that the theme of originary evidence in the Third Cartesian Meditation answers in part to this difficulty, after putting aside a much graver problem in the very heart of the notion of "sense."

At the end of this First Meditation, one wonders what remains of the *sum* of the cogito. Husserl gets it back in another way. Though he eliminates or at least omits the ontological and ultimately theological dimension (the cogito as *ens creatum*), still the cogito disengaged by the phenomenological reduction is a *sum* in that it is a "field of experience," the terminus of an originary intuiting, for the reflection which apprehends it is a seeing, a seeing "fulfilled by the self-presentedness (*Selbstgegebenheit*) of consciousness."

Reflection on the *sum* of the cogito is, therefore, entirely contained within the notion of apodictic evidence attached to the cogito. For the being of the cogito is entailed by the apodicticity of reflective evidence, even though, to repeat, transcendental experience is not an adequate experience owing to its "open horizonal structure," which is involved in the discovery of the ego (CM, § 9). This experience is not adequate, but it is apodictic. This is sufficient in order for the *I-think* to give itself in its "I am."

We are now at a new critical juncture which allows us to pass on to the Second Meditation. This juncture is produced by treating the cogito, bearer of the sense of the world, as a "field of experience" and by treating transcendental reflection as a "transcendental experience."

[III] TRANSCENDENTAL EXPERIENCE AND EGOLOGY
(Second Meditation)

THE INITIAL PROBLEM of the *Cartesian Meditations* was to find a beginning for science and, more specifically, a beginning which is an "actual" principle. This principle is the cogito. How shall we continue beyond this "first" step? Here the course of the *Meditations* passes through a point of inflection. One might expect a specifically epistemological attempt to ground the sciences on the principle of the cogito, following the line of the First Meditation. But none of this for Husserl. "To continue" is, for him, to elaborate an experience of the cogito which is, at the same time, a science. This turn is of primary importance, for it decides the very existence of phenomenology. The "Critical" philosophy does not develop an experience of the cogito. To it the very idea of transcendental experience would appear monstrous, something like an empiricism of the transcendental. Husserl refers not to Kant but to Descartes in the *Cartesian Meditations;* nevertheless, he is especially careful to establish against the latter that what follows from the cogito is not outside the cogito but rather still is the cogito. Phenomenology's great discovery is that the "I think" is not only referred to by the sciences but is for itself a "sphere of being" (*ein Seinssphäre*) which is subject to an articulated and structured experience. The two words "experience" and "structure" are the passwords for entering the Second Meditation, whose title is, in detail: "The Field of Transcendental Experience and Its Universal Structures."

Phenomenology is the visualization of the first principle, set up in transcendental "reality." It is an exercise of intuiting applied to what Kant calls merely the conditions of possibility.[4]

I believe that the key to a difficulty of Husserlian thought is to be sought in this situation. It is not easy to situate the transcendental reduction, which suspends believing in the independence or in-itself of the world, in relation to the eidetic reduction, which goes from fact to essence. The transcendental reduction entails the eidetic reduction, beginning from the point where consciousness is treated as the field for a seeing, for an intuitive experiencing. If this entailment is not followed up, phenomenology, in effect, becomes only a transcendental empiricism. If the transcendental can be looked at, seen, and described, then this intuiting must grasp the transcendental fact in essence, unless it is to founder in a description of contingencies. This is why it brings the "fiction" into play, causes the datum of consciousness to vary imaginatively, and develops experience in the mode of "as if." The "fiction" is the path from the fact to the eidos of the experienced "reality," and it permits our grasping a consciousness as an a priori possibility.

Husserl recognizes the considerable difficulties in this statement of

4. In Kant there is no thematization of the evidence of the transcendental; that is, there is no thematized intuiting of the transcendental. And yet, when he does not follow the regressive method, as he does in the *Prolegomena*, but directly interrogates the mind (*Gemüt*), does he not carry out an intuiting of the structures of subjectivity?

the phenomenological problem. If phenomenology is an experience and if it is true that all experience forgets itself in the terminus of its seeing, then phenomenology introduces a new naïveté.

At first we are going to abandon ourselves purely and simply to the evidence belonging to the concordant flow of this experience. Hence, we reserve for the future the problems of a critique of the bearing of the apodictic principles. This first step is not yet philosophical in the full sense of the term. We will proceed here in the manner of the naturalist who abandons himself to natural experience and who, as naturalist, excludes from the theme of his investigations questions relating to a general critique of this experience (CM, p. 68).

There develops from this new naïveté the anomaly of a transcendental experience which will be, in its first moment, pre-Critical. The very notion of transcendental experience implies this kind of difficulty. And this is not all, for the treatment of the cogito as a *Seinssphäre*, as a "field of experience," cuts through the ambiguity of the Cartesian cogito, at least in the sense in which the Kantian tradition understands it. Is this cogito personal or impersonal? Husserl unequivocally opts the personal character of the ego cogito. This option is consistent with the method itself; for if the cogito is a field of experience, this cogito is mine, even when elevated to its eidos. The Fourth Meditation, as we shall see, leaves no doubt about this point. The eidos ego is not the self-function in general; it is not the power which you, I, and all men have to say "I." It is the purity of myself reached through imaginative variations on my own life. This is just why the problem of the other self is so seriously posed in Husserl's philosophy. I do not get away from myself through the eidos ego. Nor by way of the reduction of conscious experience do I secure any access to a self in general which would be "anybody" and from which I might get back into the plurality of consciousnesses. I have no access to the plural by way of the universal. At the beginning phenomenology accepts all the difficulties of an egology, for which I myself alone am I.[5]

The Fifth Meditation teaches us that transcendental solipsism is not an impasse but a strait through which philosophy must pass. "It is necessary to develop it as such for methodological reasons, notably in order to present the problems of transcendental intersubjectivity in a suitable manner" (CM, p. 69).

5. "Without a doubt it is in conformity with the sense of the transcendental reduction not to be able in the beginning to posit any being other than the ego and what is inherent in it and this together with a horizon of possible, but not yet actualized, determinations. Certainly such a science will begin as pure egology, and consequently it seems to condemn us to solipsism, at least to transcendental solipsism" (CM, p. 69).

Hence, in accepting all the difficulties of an experience of the transcendental, which at the same time is an experience of the *solus ipse*, Husserl initiates the explication of the ego by itself. Therefore, between the cogito as principle of the sciences and the sciences themselves is inserted the explication of the "I am," for this egology is phenomenology itself.

[IV]   INVESTIGATION OF THE "COGITATIO": INTENTIONALITY (Second Meditation, Continued)

AND YET the Second Meditation does not directly initiate this egology. At the beginning of § 14 Husserl announces a "shift of the center of gravity of transcendental evidence." One would expect an elucidation of the "I am"—of the ego in its unity—but in reality we now turn to an explication of the multiple cogitationes. Why this shift in accent? This shift is a necessary detour which will take on its full sense only within the Fourth Meditation, the only meditation which is truly "egological."

The ego is the pole of its own cogitationes. Also, it is much more than this, as we shall see. It is the monad which concretely develops the sense of the world for itself. To do egology is to integrate the cogitationes into the ego. Hence, it is necessary to enter the cogito by the many (the cogitationes) and not by the one (the ego), leaving this perspective on the manifold of consciousness to be corrected later by an inquiry into the law of the synthesis of this manifold, i.e., into time (CM, §§ 17 ff.). Yet his shift in accent is still somewhat brusque. Rapidly, and without giving justification, Husserl posits that the multiplicity is a flux (*Strom*), that this flux is the life of the identical ego, that reflection on the self is reflection on life, and that such reflection is possible at any moment.

Besides the advantage of entering the difficult problem of the ego of the cogito indirectly, this detour through the cogitationes permits conducting experience as an articulated experience, as the experiencing of a structure, There are two reasons why phenomenology is not only an "experience" but also an "analysis." First, because it distinguishes types of cogitationes (perceiving, imagining, willing, etc.), and second, because it distinguishes an intending and a terminus intended within each cogitatio, a cogitatio and a cogitatum. Here in fact, analysis is intentional analysis.

Upon recognition of the theme of intentionality transcendental phenomenology becomes specified as a philosophy of sense. The exclusion of the world does not suppress the relation to the world but specifically makes it emerge as a movement beyond the ego towards a sense "which it carries in itself." Reciprocally, the transcendental reduction interprets intentionality as the intending of a sense and not as some sort of contact with an absolute external world.

At the same time "reflection" takes on its broad sense, for to reflect on oneself is not just to fold oneself up into a philosophical solitude cut off from the world; it is also and principally to reflect upon the cogitatum of the cogito, on the world for me, on the noema of the world. Reflection does not sever the cogito from the cogitatum, but it does sever the meant world from the world existing absolutely. Reflection frees the world as intended from a certain opaque power of absolute existence which impregnates (hindurchgeht) experience at the same time that it devours me, its witness. But in ceasing to sink into and to lose itself (hineinerfahren, hineinleben) in lived and living experience, the ego splits itself correlatively: an "uninterested" impartial spectator wrenches itself away from "interest in life." At this point the triumph of phenomenological "seeing" over vital and everyday "doing" is complete.

It is difficult not to compare this elevation of the meditating ego with the Platonic conversion by which the psyche, "captivated" by reality, draws closer to the νοῦς from which it came. Thus, does Husserl not attest to the permanence of certain metaphysical acts and to the survival of a sort of philosophical archetype, even within a completely disontologized philosophy?

One can always ask what motivates such a rupture and such an elevation at the core of the ego in a philosophy which does not refer, as Descartes's did, to the absolute measure of infinite being. One may also ask what the authority is for speaking of the world as a universe of cogitata. Husserl clearly saw this difficulty, but he resolves it a bit too quickly at the end of § 15. He admits that all reality appears against the background of the world, that this background is known-along-with (mit-bewusst), that it is "the existent background which persists through the fluctuation of consciousness." Properly speaking, this "background of the whole of natural life" is not the ground for a figure, for the Gestaltist experience of ground always applies only to fragments of the world and never to a total background.

This difficulty which Heidegger's philosophy explicates radically is not without an answer in the Cartesian Meditations, but its solution presupposes analyses that have yet to be made. It presupposes that the life of the cogito is not an anarchistic outburst but rather is always guided by permanences of signification (cf. the object as transcendental guide, to be considered later) and that the correlate of the unity of the ego is the Idea of a total and unique signification which includes all significations into an infinite system. This Idea, which continues to be an ideal and a task for cognition, is presupposed by the notion of the world (in the singular) over against the cogitationes (in the plural). The "rationalistic" implications of this presupposition of the unity of the world will have to be emphasized at a later time.

However, if Husserl anticipates this analysis, it is doubtless because the *epoché* already has a unifying power with regard to the world. The *epoché* is a break en bloc with the world-belief (*Weltglaube*). The world is implicated as an unenumerated totality by this act which brings it together, strips it of absolute existence, and refers it globally to the cogito. Hence, it is the unity of an act of rupturing which permits anticipating the unity of an act of constituting.

At the point we have reached, the "revelation of myself" will be investigated from the side of an inquiry bearing on objects "in" the acts which mean them. The full concretion of the ego will be reached by the full investigation of the noema-world; that is to say that the concreteness of my existence is itself also a limiting Idea.

[V] SYNTHESIS AS THE FUNDAMENTAL FORM OF
CONSCIOUSNESS: TIME
(Second Meditation, Conclusion)

IN ORDER that an "analytic" examination of the cogito considered in its multiple and discontinuous cogitationes can lead to an investigation of the ego as such, it is necessary that this "analysis" be compensated for by a short account of the "synthesis" which makes it into a cogito. Thus, time appears twice in the *Cartesian Meditations*, once in the Second Meditation, along the return route from the many to the one, and a second time in the Fourth Meditation, through a direct examination of the pluralization of the ego. The way to time in the Fourth Meditation is direct, for Husserl attempts to treat a priori time as the form of compossibility of subjective processes with one unique monad. But the Second Meditation gets to time by the indirect means of a description of perception. This introduces the notion of a synthesis of identification, for every intended "sense" is already the product of the unifying of a manifold. We recognize the celebrated analysis of perception which discloses a multiplicity of "adumbrations" within the object which are re-grasped into the unity of a sense (the cube, the tree, the book, etc.). This anticipated sense is confirmed or disconfirmed by the subsequent course of perception.

This analysis, which is of a great interest in itself, has considerable philosophical bearing, since it is a stage in the reintegration of the world into consciousness. It is necessary to undo the object into "adumbrations," into variable "modes" of appearing, in order to destroy its prestige. In particular, this work of taking apart clarifies Hume's procedure and constitutes the truth of his "atomism." When we are sunk in objectivity, the prejudice of the world draws its force not from the fact that we are quite lost in the many but rather from the fact that we are still devoted to the one. The trap set by the actual is that it yields us too soon the one, the same, the identical. Once dissolved into the multiple appearings, the identity of the object can still be recaptured on the side of consciousness. Since every sense is a synthesis of identification, the notion of synthesis can emerge. By way of a continuing synthesis, consciousness means the same in the different and identifies it in truth; its unity is always presumptive, claimed. At this point we have acquired the notion of synthesis as the "form of connection belonging exclusively to consciousness."

At the same stroke, since the appearing of the object through "adumbrations" occurs within a flux of appearances, the phenomenology of perception implies a phenomenology of time. Hence, from the first the synthesis of the object is temporal. An object supposed to be immutable in nature is in flux in consciousness. Thus discovered, time is always the time of consciousness. It is worth remarking that on this occasion for the first time in his *Meditations* Husserl uses the term "constitution": the unity of an intentional object is constituted in a temporal synthesis. Hence, the notion of constitution signifies: (1) inherence in consciousness or intentional inclusion (2) of an identifiable sense (3) issuing from the synthesis of a manifold of modes of appearing and (4) flowing passively within the unifying form of time. This notion is equivalent to the developed formula of intentionality as it is reached through the phenomenological reduction.

This mode of approach to temporality has only one inconvenience, that of implying a passage to the limit. For how can one move from the synthesis of identification initiated by this or that object, by this or that sense, to the total temporal synthesis of one ego? "The whole of philosophical life in its totality is unified in a synthetic manner." Here we encounter a difficulty analogous to that involved in the notion of world; in fact, this is one and the same difficulty approached on each of its two sides, for "this life is a universal cogito which in a synthetic manner embraces all the individual states of consciousness able to emerge from this life and which has its universal cogitatum founded in quite different ways in multiple particular cogitata" (CM, p. 80). In the same way that each sense stands out against the ground of the world, each cogitatio presupposes the unity of consciousness as a totality which serves it as background. It must be admitted that this notion of the whole of my life is not prepared by the preceding analysis. And we know how Heidegger will render problematic this notion of the totality of my *Dasein*. Husserl holds that the total unity appears and that one can observe and thematize it in a universal consciousness.[6] This is the key to the problem of time, for the consciousness of time is the form of universal synthesis which renders all conscious synthesis possible.

Here a new difficulty presents itself: Husserl says that temporality (*Zeitlichkeit*) is not the immanent consciousness of time (*Zeitbewusstsein*) but its correlate. Not temporality but the consciousness whose noema is temporality is what Husserl names the *Grundform der Synthesis*. Hence, time is a noesis which is a form. As for temporality as noema, it is that which brings about order in all subjective processes; it brings about commencement or termination, succession or simultaneity.

There are two closely related and poorly resolved difficulties here: (1) How can one pass on from this or that subjective process, which flows according to the universal form of subjective life, to the total consciousness? (2) What does this total consciousness signify as a form for which temporality would be the correlate? It is curious that one form of totality should have a correlate and that an inclusive form is itself intentional, is a consciousness of . . . time. Husserl himself was astonished at this, since if temporality is a cogitatum, it is instituted within a diversity of appearing, in a flux, and this leads to an infinite regress. I grasp time within time. Husserl admits that this makes for an extraordinary difficulty, but he does not emphasize it and sees it rather as an aspect of the "wonder" of consciousness (CM, p. 81).

If we do not understand very well what makes consciousness a totality, in any case we do know that the field of consciousness is open, that it has an unlimited horizon. In order to be assured of this it is sufficient to return to the experience of a present cogitatio: it implies something virtual or potential. Every situation of thought, be it perceived, imagined, willed, etc., implies a possibility of continuing to perceive, to imagine, to will, in certain motivational directions. Every situation calls for an investigation where the potentialities involved prescribe the style of their own actualization.

To tell the truth, this analysis is badly connected to the preceding one. We pass from such and such a subjective process to the whole of

---

6. "The universal cogito is the universal life itself in its indefinite and unlimited unity and totality. Because it always appears as a totality one can 'observe' it in the pre-eminent manner within the perceptive acts of attention and one can make it the theme of a universal cognition" (CM, p. 81).

consciousness; also we have the consciousness of time posited as a particular whole. Now we start again from such and such a subjective process in order to spread out its past, future, and simultaneous horizons. Here time is not a totality but the indefinite horizon open forward, backward, and simultaneously. Hence, the analysis begins from the present in which I always am. For Husserl the two procedures should be superposed upon each other, since this temporal form is an open totality. Nevertheless, these two procedures are not the same. The first of them moves straight to the totality; the other remains in the present and discovers indefinite horizons in it. Does not the first presuppose an overview and a totalization which the second forbids? Husserl intends to bring these two analyses together by using the notion of totality as a Kantian Idea which simultaneously implies the two aspects: totality and openness.

In any case, the introduction of one potentiality or possibility of consciousness, which is not a logical possibility but rather a virtuality of existence, is of considerable importance for the Husserlian interpretation of synthesis. It even permits us to come upon one of the fundamental springs of Husserl's thought, the latent rationalism to which we alluded previously.

Indeed, the discovery of this virtuality could serve to celebrate the power of consciousness and, to employ a word which is particularly un-Husserlian, the genius of consciousness. Certainly Husserl emphasizes the view that consciousness reveals itself through the "horizonal structure" of an "I think." I can rotate an object, I can see it from the other side, I can see other things in following the lateral motivations, pretraced and prescribed by the field of perception. I can act differently. I can do and be otherwise. In brief, the horizonal structure is the index of my liberty.

And yet this is not the line of analysis that Husserl exploits. What interests him is not the indetermination, the exuberance of consciousness, the gratuitousness of the "I think." And even less is he interested in the negativity or destructive power of the ego with regard to every positing of things, even with regard to its works and its acts petrified in custom. Rather, Husserl places this discovery within the perspective of constitutional problems. His concern is for the "sense" which is gradually determined, the "sense" which is not in process, which was pre-intended and which is consolidated by a progressive determination of the indeterminate, and which in turn gives rise to indetermination. In short, the horizonal structure is the most important aspect of intentionality in its function as synthesis of identification.

The methodological and epistemological use of this potential structure of consciousness elicits an entirely different concern. Husserl introduces the theme of the open flux not as a Bergsonian or as an existentialist would, but rather with care for specifying the style of the intentional analysis of identities, the permanences of signification into which consciousness moves beyond itself. Husserl always spreads out the horizons of consciousness under the guidance of a "sense" to be constituted. An object must first be proposed as an "index," as a "transcendental guide."

Thus, the theme of the potentiality of intentional life is subordinated to the analysis of "sense" (CM, § 20). Phenomenology moves from a claimed "sense" to the power of consciousness. And it is in this respect that it is an analysis, for to analyze is to explicate the implicit, the potential, which overflows the actually intended. This is to release the superadded intentive processes, the *Mehrmeinungen*, which "encroach on" (*transgresser; übergreifen*) all intentive processes (*visées*). Evidently, the connection between the method of analysis of phenomenology and the horizonal structure of consciousness is close.

We are here both very near and very far from the existentialist notion of consciousness as transcendence, as movement beyond self. We are very close, since prior to existentialism Husserl defines consciousness by this power to go beyond itself, by *über-sich-hinaus-meinen*, and we are very far, since Husserl never undertakes to consider the creativity of consciousness unless led by a "transcendental guide," the object. This guide ties creativity and binds its genius to a "something" which can be expressed at a higher level of consciousness. Language is possible a priori because for consciousness self-transcendence is anticipating the same in the different, claiming a unifying sense in otherness. Consciousness is the father of the logos in that it moves beyond itself into the identical. The problem of the "same" keeps Husserl from leaving the rationalistic framework of his investigations. The Idea of "sense" is the restraining discipline of Husserlian phenomenology. This is why his intentional analysis of "sense" is not an existential analysis of the "project." [7] The "wonder," for Husserl, is precisely the fact that through the flowing and potential there can be a "sense" at all.

Husserl does not push much further beyond this astonishment when confronted by "an intentional synthesis, which, in every con-

7. "Only in this manner can the phenomenologist explain to himself how and in what determinate modes of this current of consciousness the fixed and permanent objective unities (the objects) can become conscious. In particular, it is only thus that he can understand how this marvelous operation (*diese wunderbare Leistung*), viz., the 'constitution' of identical objects, is realized for each category of objects . . ." (CM, p. 85).

sciousness, creates unity and noetically and noematically constitutes the unity of the objective sense" (CM, p. 86). He halts before that which *Ideas I* calls the teleology of consciousness. The hypothesis of the destruction of the world—that is, the hypothesis of a consciousness which is not unified, which "explodes" into a chaos of discordant appearances—appears to be irresistible from the side of the object. It is all the more admirable that consciousness can create unity. If we return to the parallel with Descartes, we would have to place the problem of the teleology of consciousness in the light of the Cartesian problem of the divine creation of the eternal truths which corresponds to the same astonishment before the contingency of the necessary, of the "sense."

We now understand better why an egology must make a detour through a theory of the cogitatum. The flux of consciousness would submerge us without the transcendental guide of the intentional object, for this is what presents the true problems of subjectivity. These are problems concerning the types of intentionality (perceiving, imagining, etc.), problems concerning the regions of the object and their noetico-noematic structure (nature, animate body, man, culture, etc.). Ultimately one can say that the Idea of the world is the transcendental guide of egology. This Idea structures the ego and assures us that transcendental subjectivity is not a chaos of intentive subjective processes (CM, § 21). This problem of the whole of the world and of the whole of time with which we were just occupied finds its solution less in a datum than in the credit which the phenomenologist extends to the final unity of the cogito. Totality is an Idea in the Kantian sense; that is to say, still using the language of Kant, it is reason itself extended beyond the understanding. Though Husserl is not an intellectualist, he is a rationalist by this prior credit which he extends to the possibility of system; from this credit proceeds a task and, so to speak, an ethic of phenomenology. Husserlian phenomenology is not a descriptive game, even less a salve for troubles for conscience; rather it is the "immense" (*ungeheure*) obligation to constitute the system "within the unity of a systematic and universal order, and by taking as mobile guide the system of all the objects of a consciousness . . . , to carry out all phenomenological investigations as constitutional investigations, ordering them strictly and systematically with respect to each other" (CM, p. 90).

This infinite regulative Idea, this obligation, paradoxically makes the system the proper task of intentional analysis. Without this obligation the analysis would dissolve into curiosity and lose itself in the interminable ramifications of description.

[VI] THE SITUATION OF EVIDENCE WITHIN PHENOMENOLOGICAL IDEALISM (Third Meditation)

IT SEEMS that the moment has come at the end of the Second Cartesian Meditation for converting this explication of the constitution of the objective sense in consciousness into an egology and for carrying the solipsistic interpretation of the ego to its severest extreme. But Husserl again introduces an analysis intermediary between this exaltation of "the Idea of the universal unity of all objects" and the ego, which is the bearer of this immense Idea. In many respects this analysis brings the idealism achieved in the Second Meditation into question again.

The notion of constitution is not sufficiently "differentiated" or "pregnant," says Husserl (CM, § 23), since we have not yet integrated it with the explication of evidence. It is evidence which adds the dimension of being to the cogitatum and the dimension of truth or reason to the cogito.

The reading of this Third Meditation, it must be admitted, gives the reader a rather uncomfortable feeling. He has the impression that the re-emergence of the theme of the constitution of objects in the subject marks both the culmination and the disintegration of this idealism. On the one hand, idealism would be established if, in effect, one could show that the philosophy of "sense" omits no question concerning being, for thus being would be a function of sense. The *epoché* should suspend all questions about the being or non-being of the world; and in fact this distinction is recovered again within consciousness as the correlate of reason (*Vernunft*), as an original dimension of sense. If this move were to succeed, one could truly say that there is nothing left between the parentheses, hence that phenomenology gives an account not only of a structure or an outline of the existence of the world, but also of its fullness. The being of the world, not just its schematic sense, would be "in" consciousness. The Third Meditation does tend toward the culmination of presence, just as the Second tended toward the culmination of the order, the unity, the totalization of the system.

What, though, does this aspiration cost?

Evidence, according to Husserl, is the presence of the thing itself in the original (in contrast to the presentiation, memory, portrait, image, symbol, sign, concept, word); one would be tempted to say presence in flesh and blood. This is the self-givenness (*Selbstgegebenheit*) which Husserl calls "originary."

Now if the object is constituted by "touches," "adumbrations," "sketches," "perspectives," what is the originary? How can the unity of the object be anything other than a claimed unity? Is the originary, the adumbration, presented at each instant? The notion of presence in flesh and blood seems to introduce a disparate factor, a Self (*Selbst*) of the object (be this object a thing, a value, a state of relation), which "fulfills" a void, keeps a promise. The thing is present itself. Has not the idealistic interpretation of "sense" destroyed the possibility of there being a "*Selbst*" of the thing? Does this immediacy not lead from the transcendental to the transcendent?

It must be admitted that Husserl's phenomenology labors under two requirements which this Meditation attempts to harmonize. First, there is an idealistic exigency which expresses itself in the theme of constitution and which recognizes only one process of "verification" always going on. This is the work (*Leistung*), the "doing" of consciousness. Secondly, there is an intuitionistic requirement antedating the phenomenological reduction which is expressed in the dictum of the *Logical Investigations, "zu den Sachen selbst,"* and which terminates the work of understanding with a seeing: here the thing itself is given. On one side the object is the index of a never-completed process of identification, or an open synthesis. On the other side the "fullness" of presence completes the sense (*Endmodus*); the meant dies away within the confines of the datum. Thus, we have on one hand the synthesis of identification whose object is the index and on the other hand the fulfillment by the originary. After this point, two possible senses of constitution intermingle throughout Husserl's work: first, to constitute is to unfold the implicit claimings, to spread out the actual and potential intendings; and second, to constitute is to recognize and distinguish the irreducible types of "seeing," of fulfillment by the originary: sensuous intuiting, categorial intuiting, empathy, etc. A phenomenology which would be content to balance the two tendencies is imaginable. This is what most phenomenologists have done who have not accepted Husserl's radical idealism. The notion of the synthesis of identification is not the source of trouble. Though there is no obligation upon synthesis to be some one given type rather than another, still synthesis must be oriented by fullness. Verification can only be recourse to the immediate. Hence, we can understand the matter in this way: the unity of a sense is in part "claimed," and this is the work of anticipatory consciousness; also the unity is "confirmed," and this is the sanction of presence.

The notion of the originary does not resist this adjustment, for the originary need not be adequate. In other words, the presence of the thing perceived is given only in adumbration and hence allows for a possible subsequent discord; it is also in process, just as the unifying performance is within consciousness. It is a fullness which has a history, while, on the other hand, the performance of consciousness participates in the instantaneous character of the fullness of consciousness which is there now. Hence, one could interpret the performance of cognition as a dialectic of claiming in flux and of presence in the instant.

This moderate interpretation of Husserlian phenomenology is possible, though in fact it sacrifices the radical idealism of the *Cartesian Meditations*. It secretly institutes a bipolar interpretation of truth which leads us back to the Descartes of the *Meditationes de Prima Philosophia* and his duality of being and the thinkable.

The task of the Third Meditation is less one of bringing these two perspectives together than of subordinating the one to the other by reabsorbing so far as possible the notion of originarity into the transcendental idealism reached in the Second Meditation.

Husserl begins by saying: "The cogitata could not even 'have status' for us, if a synthesis of evident identity were to lead us into a contradiction with an evident datum." He even adds: "We can only be assured of actual being by the synthesis of verification, evidence which from itself gives the exact or true reality." Immediately afterwards Husserl alters the interpretation of this evident datum—a datum which might be held to be a sanction exceeding the working of consciousness—to the sense of a "presence for us." "Every justification proceeds from evidence, has its source in our transcendental subjectivity itself; every imaginable adequation is produced as our verification, is our synthesis, has in us its ultimate transcendental basis" (CM, p. 95).

This turn in the theory of evidence is decisive, for all attempts to identify intentionality with some sort of contact with being are avoided. But at the same time evidence, reintegrated into me as a moment of my monad (Husserl says "our" synthesis, our "verification"), falls under the solipsistic objection towards which the first four meditations are deliberately directed.

The end of the Third Meditation continues this modification of the theory of evidence on the transcendental level. There is something of the constituted in the evidence itself (CM, § 27). Evidence is in the instant, presence is the originary present; this is the theme of the manuscripts of Group C, which are devoted to time. Now the slightest evidence surpasses this passing actuality of presence. It is elaborated as a lasting having. I can come back to it if I want to. By this dialectic of presence and having, evidence re-enters my sphere of "I can." Thus, the in-itself of evidence is consolidated by a sort of sedimentation, as the *Crisis* will say. But this in-itself is only the correlate of an "I can return to it." The in-itself answers to habitual evidence. The in-itself exceeds the for-me, just as having exceeds present presence.

> The isolated evidence does not produce abiding being. The in-itself refers to the "potential" (I can always return to it), which, therefore, is a dimension of my transcendental life. The in-itself is the correspondent of an infinity of intendings and an infinity of verifyings; thus, it refers to potential evidences which, like facts lived through, are repeatable to infinity (CM, p. 96).

In this way, by relating evidence to what the Fourth Meditation calls the habitus (habituality), Husserl adjusts evidence to the requirements of an egology.

This procedure is particularly promising for a "phenomenology of perception." The Third Meditation does not permit us to say how this conception of potential evidence could account for the famous "categorial intuition" discussed in the *Logical Investigations*. No doubt such a consideration would necessitate an entire history of culture such as the *Crisis* envisages. On the other hand, it is successfully applied to perception and, indeed, seems to have been made for this application. The case of perceptual evidence in effect introduces indefiniteness into what initially appeared to be instantaneous, and hence it introduces openness into the power of fully satisfying us. *Ideas I* had already tried to hold the two characters of originarity and inadequacy together on the level of perception. Perceptual evidence is always unilateral; that is, it is subject to subsequent breakdown, even though it alone gives the *Selbst da* of the thing. The character of performing synthesis and that of originary fulfillment are balanced in the ambiguous status of perception which fully satisfies us and yet always provides us with more work.

Can this ambiguity be interpreted in the one way allowed by idealism? As it seems to me, Husserl's descriptive analyses suggest rather that the *Selbst da*—the reduction of the present moment included in every presence—is what consciousness finally does not make. Also these analyses suggest that the transcendent is constituted by a double movement of bursting forth: on one side the presence which fulfills is always a superabundance of presence in comparison to the anticipations of empty consciousness, and on the other side, consciousness leads the dance because it is the superabundance of sense—the *Mehrmeinung*—in comparison to the presence in the instant as yet without signification. The double analysis of the "potential" character of evidence in general and of the horizontal structure of perceptual evidence in particular tends to "demystify" the absolute, dumb, and gaping aspect of "seeing" and place it back into the movement of the whole of consciousness in the continual working of "evident verification." Consequently, the notion of a complete synthesis within a total presence is only an Idea (CM, § 28); the world is the correlate, the correspondent of the Idea of a perfect empirical evidence. The Idea of a total datum is, then, no longer an "initial" but rather a "final" Idea; such an Idea is the limit of a history of the spirit.

On the other hand, it is difficult to see how this reduction of the Idea of total evidence removes the enigma involved in the present of consciousness as presence "in flesh and blood" of something. *Ideas I,* an even more ambiguous book, oscillates among several possible philosophical systematizations and in its fourth part (I, pp. 128 f.) represents the reference to the object as an arrow which traverses the sense like an intending from the "sense," the "sense" transcending somehow into the reality. In the final analysis *Ideas I* undertakes the task of constituting the "relation" of the noema as "sense-intending-a-being." This task would also culminate in an explication of seeing (Part Four, Chapter Two). Thus, *Ideas I* is clearer than the *Cartesian Meditations* in presenting the central difficulty of the Husserlian notion of constitution, the difficulty of bringing the theme of sense-giving (*Sinngebung*) into coincidence with the theme of self-givenness (*Selbstgegebenheit*). Consciousness gives sense, but the thing gives itself.

The *Cartesian Meditations* are silent about this initial seeing. Nevertheless, the end of the Third Meditation allows us to suppose that Husserl regarded this initial seeing as no extraordinary thing in the life of consciousness, if consciousness is considered not as presence of the Other but as presence of oneself. The transcendental solution to the enigma of evidence is the reduction of presence to the present, to a temporal datum. The last instance:

> The role of the objective basis of the most fundamental sort—is always held by immanent temporality, the life which flows on, constituting itself in itself and for itself. The elucidation of its constitution is the theme of the original consciousness of time, a consciousness which constitutes in itself the temporal data (CM, p. 99).

At the cost of the final sacrifice of the *Selbst da* of the *Selbstgegebenheit,* the theory of evidence re-enters into egology. The future importance of the Fifth Meditation emerges now as even greater than before, for if evidence does not make us get beyond ourselves, the whole burden of otherness rests on the otherness of the Other. There is no primitive otherness in the evidence given to me alone. Only the alter ego draws the world out of me. In the solitude—not social, but transcendental—of my ego, the otherness which is not yet alter ego, but *altera res,* "thing," is but an instantaneous slice of my own life. This conviction is not thematized in the Third Meditation, but it stands out after the reduction of the Fifth Meditation, the reduction of all presence to my sphere of ownness, and this reduction is implicitly at work in the transcendental treatment of evidence. In other words, the Third Meditation already develops a solipsistic theory of evidence.

[VII] THE EGO OF THE COGITO, OR PHENOMENOLOGY AS EGOLOGY (Fourth Meditation)

1. The Monad

THE FOURTH MEDITATION compensates for the displacement of the center of gravity by which at the beginning of the Second Meditation the project of egology was set aside in favor of an explication of the cogitatio. We have now only to insert the acts of the ego back into the ego. The task of the Fourth Meditation is to gather all of the preceding intentional analyses up into the ego. The for-me-ness of the world does not exhaust the for-itself of the ego: "The ego exists for itself; . . . it continually constitutes itself as existing" (CM, p. 100). This constitution takes place in three steps. Not until the third step does the constitution of the ego for itself come to include the constitution of the world for the ego.

According to a first approximation, the ego is the identical pole of the multiplicity of acts, of the manifold of cogitationes. *Ideas I* stops with this analysis. Husserl admits without discussion that the ego presents a problem analogous to that of the object, yet also quite opposite to the object. Like the object, it is an identity in a multiplicity. The flux of subjective processes would then lend itself to two syntheses, polar opposites of each other: that of the object and that of the ego. The ego is regarded as "the identical ego which lives actively or passively in the subjective processes of consciousness and through them relates to object poles" (CM, p. 100). Thanks to this "through," even though highly enigmatic, the cogitata are the correlates not only of the multiple cogitationes but of the identical ego as well.

But the ego is more than this; it is the ego of the habitus, of retained and abbreviated convictions. This analysis, new in relation to *Ideas I,* has a double function: in the first place, it confirms the constituted character of the ego. The ego is not only the reference pole but also the "substrate of its permanent properties." That is, it has a style which is the character of a person. *Ideas II* clarifies this extension, for the ego has permanent properties, just as the thing does when the thing is subjected to a relation of the type "if-then" (*Wenn-so*) between determined circumstances and a regular behavior of the thing. Thus, the notion of permanent property is situated midway between the variable states of the thing and the substantivized "X" which bears the determinations of the thing.

But the analysis of the habitus upsets the rather factitious symmetry between the thing-properties and the character-properties of the person by introducing an original dialectic of being and having into the ego. The ego gives itself coherence by this manner of "retaining," of "maintaining its position-takings." This theory of the habitus provides a framework for the remarks on potential evidence, for the in-itself of evidence was the correspondent of the possibility of returning to the evidences which we have retained. In fact, getting beyond the otherness of every presence is the second function of the notion of habitus, for the world is "mine" through familiarity; it enters into my sphere of ownness through habitual frequentation. Thus, having is not a spiritual downfall but rather an original structure of transcendental experience. By habit, I would say, I inhabit my world. One should not underestimate the importance of this notion, since it sets the scene for the entrance of the more important notion of monad.

The notion of monad indicates the complete integration of the presences into their "senses," of each "sense" into the cogitationes which intend it, and of each cogitatio into its ego. Everything is the life of the ego. The "for"-me is unfolded "from" the ego. Now we understand the mediating role of the habitus, for it joins the world to my life in an organic manner. Even what is alien—the alien par excellence being the Other—is cut out like an exotic enterprise within the familiar countryside of my existence. The complete ego, the "concretion of the ego" as Husserl says, is I, as identical pole, plus my habitus, plus my world. Such is the sense of the notion of monad as taken over from the Leibnizian dynamism. It marks the total triumph of interiority over exteriority and of the transcendental over the transcendent. Ultimately, to do phenomenology of the ego is to do phenomenology itself.

2. The Eidos Ego

HERE MORE THAN EVER Husserl runs the risk of a sort of transcendental empiricism to which we have been pointing ever since the notion of transcendental experience was introduced at the beginning of the Second Meditation, for if the ego is the integral experience, are we not transporting the contingent (the *faktisch*) into the transcendental (CM, § 34)? I, so far as I am this ego (*Ich als deises Ego*), am alone and unique. After evoking for the second time an irruption of brute fact into the transcendental field, the field which should be the principle of all science, Husserl has to secure the transcendental reduction by the eidetic reduction (CM, §§ 34–35). Since the ego is a monad and not the impersonal subject of Critical and neo-Critical philosophy, the transcendental reduction disengages a "factual ego," and phenomenology appears condemned to recounting the "factual events of the factual transcendental ego" (*faktische Vorkomnisse des faktischen transcendentalen Ego*) (CM, p. 104).

But phenomenology is also a victory over brute fact by the method of imaginative variation. It is a victory in the direction of the eidos accomplished in such a way that the fact is no longer anything but an example of a pure possibility. Hence, phenomenology will be the theory of the possible ego, of the eidos ego, secured by the example of my transcendental ego on the *empirisch-faktisch* level. Thus, even the ego must be "imagined" in order to separate it from brute fact. This backing away from my own contingency is essential to the birth of the *ego meditans*, just as much as the suspension of belief in the world is. The *ego meditans* is born from a double reduction: the transcendental reduction of the being of the world and the eidetic reduction of the factual ego. This movement of thought does not proceed without difficulty. The remarkable and strange thing is that this passage to the eidos ego brings into play only variations on my own ego (*Selbstvariation meiner Ego*) and has no reference to the Other in the second person. Thus, I imagine myself as other without imagining an Other. This is quite necessary, since before constituting the Other, my ego is the only ego.

What, however, is this eidos ego which is not a generalization from me and from the Other and which bridges over the disparity between the positing of myself and the positing of the Other within a subjectivity in general? In short, what is the eidos ego, if it is not my fellow man? The similarity of egos will in fact not appear until the Fifth Meditation, where it occurs by way of a relation of pairing between me and Others. However extraordinary it may be, Husserl is obliged to assume an eidos of the sole and unique ego, an essence which is illustrated only in the variations of my own existence and in the style of "if I were another . . ." The essence is the sense "myself" which resists the circumstantial variations of my factual existence. It requires no reference to a couple or to a community. In this way the eidetic ego definitely has no reference to the similarity between the first and second person and works its variations on the solipsistic plane. Thinking this matter through to its end is not easy; yet the course of Husserlian reflection requires it.

At least, when the hold of the contingent is loosened by means of variations on oneself, one reaches a species of a priori, an eidetic form (*Wesensform*) "which contains an infinity of forms, of a priori types of actualities and potentialities of life" (CM, p. 108). Hence the self-constitution of the ego is not a construction (whether dialectical or not). It halts before the structures which bring an end to the freedom of the imagination, and thus intuition is transported into the very core of the transcendental field, a fact which the notion of transcendental experience led us to foresee from the start. Likewise, perhaps this is the only way of resolving the difficulties presented by the synthetic exposition of the *Critique of Pure Reason*. If this synthetic exposition is not an *inspectio mentis,* I do not see what the method could be which fails to proceed in a regressive manner from the works of the mind to their conditions of possibility.

By reference to this *Wesensform* we can restate the problem of time in more radical terms than previously used. It is no longer a question of generalizing the remarks already made concerning the temporal synthesis of a particular object. We grasp time in its totality directly by inspection of the eidetic ego. It is sufficient to formulate the question: Under what conditions of compossibility is the ego a possible ego? The test of imaginative variation brings out an immutable style of compossibility; this is the universal form of temporality. Time is not constructed (as Hamelin would have it) on a basis of relation and number; rather, it is recognized in essence in the eidos ego as that which implies the "universal essential lawfulness of temporal egological coexistence and succession." [8] This law of compossibility is so fundamental that by means of the science of the forms of universal temporality, egology is par excellence a system with which any imaginable ego constitutes itself.

How does Husserl pass from the notion of egological compossibility to that of time (CM, § 37)? By the intermediary notion of motivation, which is the kind of causality for consciousness; it is the if-then (*wenn-so*) structure of the interconnectedness of consciousness. Rather than being a flux (*Strom*), this motivation presents the universal form of unification. Hence, there is an equivalence of the three notions: formal legislation of a universal genesis, motivation, form in flux. "The ego constitutes itself so to speak in the unity of a history." Husserl preserves time as a form by means of this Idea of totality, for all particular constitutions are made within the "framework" of formal genesis. But what does this mean? No doubt it means this: if by imagination I make all the factual motivations vary, then the universal

8. . . . *universalen Wesensgesetzlichkeiten der egologisch—zeitlichen Koexistenz und Sukzession* (CM, p. 108).

genetic form remains, and this is the temporal style of every synthesis which is the condition of possibility for my ego in general.

Now we perceive the sense in which time is constituted; this is the sense in which it is regarded in the essence of the ego. The constitution of transcendences was a reduction to the ego; the constitution of time is not a reduction to anything, unless it be from fact to essence. But the eidetic reduction is ultimately only an observation (*constat*) sublimated into an essence, the observation of the flowing character of the life of consciousness. It will be objected that there is just one constitution of time beginning from the present and going through the intermediary of the horizonal structure of any subjective process. This is true. But that the present has such past and future horizons is an irreducible fact which no a priori law of compossibility can bring into being.

Moreover, if there is a constitution of time in the sense of a performance by consciousness which is no longer an observation and if this constitution of time has the originary present as its source, as the manuscripts on temporality develop it, then the difficulty of passing from a continuous present to a total form of time continues to be considerable. How can we make the totality of time appear in an experience which is always a present experience opening onto indefinite temporal horizons? Thus, I wonder if Husserl has truly overcome the weakness of his philosophy of time by this somewhat artificial notion of the law of compossibility in which time is at once the horizon of a continual present and a total form.

That temporality is an ascertained or observed structure before being a law of the compossibility of the ego is amply verified by the subsequent distinction between the two geneses, active genesis and passive genesis. Active genesis designates the maintenance of former acts of the ego in new acts. It is encountered in acts of the higher level such as acquired conviction, habitual evidence, and habitus in general. Now this constitution is not sufficient in itself: "But in any case, construction by activity always and necessarily presupposes as a lower stratum a passivity which receives the object and finds it as if ready-made, for in analyzing it we run into constitution as passive genesis" (CM, p. 112). This passive genesis is effective on the level of the perception of things, in those syntheses of identification where analysis has discerned a moving diversity of "adumbrations." To be sure, one can undo the perceptible unity of the thing by "intentional analysis," yet the object continues to appear as "completely made." Without us its history shrinks into an imperious datum which, in turn, affects us and inclines us to act.

In order to account for this passive genesis, Husserl calls upon something similar to Hume's laws of association (CM, § 39). Here phenomenology executes a sort of regrasping of empirical laws whose observational character cannot be disguised. This is why Husserl is led by this passive genesis to a sort of irrational residue or precipitate which excludes the active constitution of the ego in the habitus.

> In all of these considerations, the fact is irrational, but it is only possible as integrated into the system of a priori forms which belong to it as egological fact. On this point it is necessary not to overlook that the fact (*Faktum*) itself together with its irrationality is a structural concept within the system of the concrete a priori (CM, p. 114).[9]

One could not say more clearly that the constitution of time is not integrally a performance (*Leistung*) of consciousness, even if it is always a genesis of things.

At least this analysis has the virtue of placing the ego and time on the same level. Time is not only, as with Kant, an intuition a priori, that is, a mode of representation; it is rather a style of existence. Husserl is at the source of a new interpretation of time as the very advance of the existent which I am. By way of this theme of "egological genesis," of the temporal constitution of oneself, Husserl leads back from represented time to originary time, in a manner quite different from, yet ultimately convergent with, that of Bergson.

The notion of habitus seems to have mediated between the notion of a constitution of transcendences (that is to say, of things external to or outside of consciousness) and the notion of a constitution of the ego. One can even say that the two constitutions finally coincide in the habitus. The in-itself is to be unfolded temporally as the stratified, the sedimented. Thus, Husserl's phenomenology is at the root of the greatly increased importance of habit in contemporary phenomenology of perception, for it is the weight of the acquired, of the settled, which must be equivalent to the objective, at least insofar as one remains below the level of intersubjectivity. The reduction of presence to the present, which we discovered at the end of the Third Meditation, would imply this maturation of considerations referring to time in the theory of objectivity.

Husserl's originality on this point lies in having discovered the dynamic temporal constitution of our familiar world by the eidetic reduction, by the reduction to the eidos ego, and not only by the transcendental reduction which is confined within the factual ego. The imaginative variations on my ego remove the limitations of an empirical ego which already has its world of nature and culture. In short, our

---

9. Husserl says *Faktum*, and not *Tatsache*, in order to emphasize not only the empirical but also the contingent character of the fact.

fascination by what is already there is destroyed by the method of imaginative variation. The empirical ego faces the already-constituted, and this situation condemns it to a static phenomenology which can only be an art of classification comparable to that of the natural sciences, in short, a typology. One must rise to the universal structure of genesis in order to conceive "that the world whose ontological structure is familiar to us is constituted by the ego." Static phenomenology halts before a familiar world which is correlative to our habitus. The eidetic reduction leads us to accept the phenomenology of the habitus by proceeding in the manner of a systematic removal from the natural sphere. It places us below what is already constituted and by that very act gives a sense to the "already," which is perceived at the imaginary border of the "not yet." The possible ego illuminates the actual ego as one of its variants, and thus the unnaturalized consciousness understands the habitual consciousness, and the disengaged consciousness understands the engaged consciousness. This is the sense in which I understand the connection in Husserl between "the ultimate genetic problems" and the reduction to the eidos ego.

This manner of temporally interpreting the constitution of transcendences and from there swinging back to the constitution of the ego renders even more troublesome the enigma of the originary present with which we ended the study of evidence. For it is ultimately the right to bring the presence of the Other back to the present of myself which founds the right to constitute transcendence on the temporality of the ego and this temporality itself in the originary present. To the enigma of the originary present is added the enigma of passive genesis which, in Husserl's opinion, specifically limits the role of the habitus and of the whole of the active genesis of the subjective processes of consciousness.

The reaffirmation of transcendental idealism which the Fourth Meditation reaches marks the high point of the first four meditations. Sections 40–41, which contain the most striking formulas of Husserlian idealism, are not a pure and simple repetition of the reduction of the world to "sense" and "sense" to the cogito; rather they are a radicalization of this idealism as a function of the notion of the monad introduced at the beginning of the Fourth Meditation. Section 33 concludes:

> Since the concrete monadic ego contains the totality of conscious life, actual and potential, it is clear that the phenomenological explication of this monadic ego—the problem of its constitution for itself—must in general include all problems of constitution. And in the final accounting this constitution of the self for the self coincides with phenomenology as a whole (CM, pp. 102 f.).

This sentence is the key to §§ 40–41, for if all transcendental reality is the life of the ego, the problem of its constitution coincides with the self-constitution of the ego, and phenomenology is a *Selbstauslegung* (an explication of the self), even when it is the constitution of the thing, the body, the psyche, and culture. The ego is no longer simply the subject pole in contrast to the object pole (CM, § 31); it is the all-embracing, for all is produced (*Gebilde*) from transcendental subjectivity, produced from its producing (*Leistung*). Phenomenology is the "self-explication of my ego, as subject of every possible cognition." [10] Hense, phenomenology and idealism are inseparably linked in the doctrine of the ego and of its temporal constitution.

Here the realistic imagery of the absolute exterior, which a misunderstanding about intentionality might maintain and renew, is definitely removed. "Transcendental subjectivity is the universe of possible sense" (CM, p. 117).

The turning point introduced by the contrast between empty intending and full presence in the Third Meditation is entirely reabsorbed: "All proof and all justification of truth and being are accomplished wholly in me, and their result is a character of the cogitatum of my cogito" (CM, p. 115). The whole puzzle of a being which in manifesting itself as itself would go beyond consciousness is reduced to the very power of consciousness to go beyond itself into its implicit horizons. All of the false interpretations of being come from the naïve blindness to the horizons which determine the being-sense and to the corresponding problems concerning the elucidation of intentionality. When these horizons are disengaged and pursued, a universal phenomenology of the ego by itself results which is explicitly concrete and evident.

Now we understand the extent to which the interpretation of presence as present at the end of the Third Meditation was decisive. This interpretation now permits making the whole weight of the problems of constitution rest upon a theory of temporality. Husserlian phenomenology then appears as a struggle between two tendencies: (1) As description restricted to the things just as they are given, phenomenology is a generous effort to respect the diversity of appearing and to restore to each of its modes (perceived, desired, willed, loved, hated, judged, etc.) its quota of strangeness, and, if I may say so, of otherness; (2) In its capacity as an idealistic interpretation of its own descriptive activity, Husserlian phenomenology is a radical

---

10. . . . *Selbstauslegung meines Ego, als Subjektes jeder möglichen Erkenntnis* (CM, p. 118).

effort to reduce all otherness to the monadic life of the ego, to ipseity. From this comes the discomfort which Husserl's writings produce in his readers. On the one hand, no contemporary thinker has contributed more than he has to giving us the full and unexpected presence of reality. Yet none has pushed the reduction of the presence of the Other to my present so far as he has, nor the dissolution of otherness into self-explication.

The Fourth Meditation has thus brought the fundamental difficulty of the *Cartesian Meditations* to its culmination with complete clarity. This is the difficulty of transcendental solipsism. If phenomenology is "elucidation of myself"—"egology"—how will the otherness of Others be justified? How, in consequence, will the genuine objectivity of the world common to all of us be constituted? The Fifth Meditation must answer these questions which the first four have patiently rendered all but insoluble.

5 / Husserl's Fifth Cartesian Meditation

A WORLD OF THOUGHT is constituted in Husserl's Fifth Cartesian Meditation. It alone is nearly as long as the first four meditations together. This disproportion is more than the accidental result of the reworkings which this text underwent; [1] it attests to the fundamental importance of the problem of the Other in Husserl's philosophy. This problem is the touchstone of transcendental phenomenology and extends very much further than the merely psychological question of the way in which we know other men. We must consider how a philosophy whose principle and ground is the ego of *ego cogito cogitatum* takes account of that which is other than I and of all that depends upon this fundamental difference, viz., (1) the objectivity of the world insofar as it is the object of a plurality of subjects, and (2) the reality of the historical communities built upon the network of exchanges going on among real men. In this respect, the problem of the Other plays the same role in Husserl that the divine veracity plays in Descartes, for it grounds every truth and reality which goes beyond the simple reflection of the subject on itself.

We shall examine successively:

I. The setting up of the problem, beginning with the solipsistic objection

II. The methodological decision to reduce all transcendence to the sphere of ownness

III. The explication of the existence of the Other by means of analogy

IV. The explication of nature as correlate of the community of monads

1. In *Husserliana I, Cartesianische Meditationen und Pariser Vorträge,* the Paris Lectures occupy pp. 3–39; what became the Fifth Meditation occupies only pp. 34–39 [cf. n. 1, p. 82].

V. The explication of history as monadic community of the higher level

The whole problem will be to know how the primacy of the ego, sole *originary* principle of transcendental phenomenology, can be maintained throughout this progression toward the Other, toward the world of Others, and toward the Others as world.

[I] Exposition of the Problem, Beginning with the Solipsistic Objection (CM, §§ 42–43)

The problem of the Other is presented in a very abrupt manner by way of an objection interrupting the course of a meditation directed by the ego into itself. This objection is well-known to us; it is solipsism. The Fifth Meditation arises from the transformation of this objection received from without into a challenge accepted by transcendental phenomenology entirely from within. Solipsism has always been the common-sense objection to idealistic philosophies, since according to common sense the other egos are not reducible to the representation one has of them. They are not even represented objects, unities of sense, which one can verify in a concordant course of experience. Others are other than I; they are other egos. Transcendental phenomenology is obliged to recognize this objection as a difficulty undermining it from within. As the logical consequence of the reduction, more precisely of the reduction as understood in the Fourth Meditation, not only is all being reduced to being-sense, but all sense is furthermore incorporated into the intentional life of the concrete ego. The consequence in the Fourth Meditation is that the sense of the world is only the explication of the ego, the exegesis of its concrete life. This is the monadism which makes of solipsism an internal difficulty to the extent that monadism absorbs all differences, all other being, into my own ego. Hereafter, all sense must have birth *in* (*dans, in*) and *arising from* (*à partir de, aus*) me.

Confronted with this difficulty, Husserlian phenomenology is drawn between two seemingly opposed requirements: on the one hand, it must follow the reduction through to the end and maintain its wager on the constitution of the sense of the alter ego "in" and "arising from" the ego; on the other hand, it must account for the originality, the specificity, of the experience of the Other, precisely as the experience of someone other than I. The whole Fifth Meditation will undergo the tension between the two requirements of constituting the Other *in* me and constituting him as *Other*. This challenging paradox was latent in the other four meditations. Already the "thing" was torn out of my life as something other than I, as object of my ego, even though it was only an intentional synthesis, a claimed unity of sense. But the latent conflict between the requirement of reduction and the requirement of description becomes an open conflict from the moment that the Other is no longer a thing but another ego, someone other than I.

In order to sharpen this paradox, Husserl begins by making up a balance sheet for what is ordinarily called "the experience of the Other" and takes the "modes of givenness" of the Other as his "guiding thread." Let us get a clear understanding of what is in question here. We have already encountered this matter of a "guiding thread" in connection with the constitution of the thing. For how is the experience of the thing to be explicated except by thematizing the unity of sense which allows us to name the thing, to designate it as terminus of a synthesis? No description, no explication, no constitution would be possible if the terminal-sense of the experience were not taken as a guide, viz., the positing of a transcendence over against me, especially when this other is the Other. The "vehicle of sense" [2] of what is called the Other presents itself as a strange paradox, even as a threefold paradox.[3]

The *first paradox:* although, speaking absolutely, only one is subject, I, the Other is not given simply as psycho-physical object situated in nature but is also a subject of experience by the same right as I and as such perceives me as belonging to the world of his experience. *Second paradox:* the world is not simply a private scene but a public property. This is not so easy to understand, for on the one hand there is the "world-phenomenon" for each and on the other hand there is the "world-phenomenon" opposite to (*gegenüber*) all subjects of experience and to all their "world-phenomena." The sense of what we call the objectivity of the world plays upon this second paradox. *Third paradox:* the constitution of objects of a new type attaches to the experience of the Other. Cultural objects—books, tools, works of all sort—which

2. Husserl's expression is *noematisch-ontisch Gehalt* (CM, p. 112:35). [The numbers following the colon refer to lines of the text as numbered in Strasser's German edition of *Husserliana I.*] We translate it [into French] as *teneur de sens.* Husserl ordinarily means by it a content of thinking open to eidetic or essential analysis. [Cairns translates this phrase as "noematic-ontic content." Ricoeur, however, evidently has in mind another aspect of the etymological antecedents of *Gehalt.* He thinks of it as referring to the holder, that which grasps the contents, thus the *teneur* of the sense or content. Hence, we translate *Gehalt* or *teneur* as "vehicle."—Trans.]

3. After § 48 these three paradoxes provide the framework of the Fifth Meditation, and we adopt the same articulation in our study: our third, fourth, and fifth parts correspond to the first, second, and third paradoxes.

specifically refer back to an active constitution on the part of alien subjects, these cultural objects are "there for everybody," more precisely for every member of a particular cultural community.

This, then, is what is given, what is found, in the "vehicle of sense." But this datum of common sense is taken up as a problem by phenomenology, for phenomenology becomes astonished at what goes without saying and submits matters to clarification that initially appear as clear as day.[4] Certainly there are problems for a philosophy which has undertaken the task of understanding everything, of constituting all "in" and "arising from" my intentional life.

[II] REDUCTION TO THE SPHERE OF OWNNESS (CM, §§ 44–47)

HERE HUSSERL INSERTS an audacious methodological decision even more paradoxical than the problem to be solved. In order to clarify the sense of the Other, we are going to subject him to a special reduction. Since the Other figures as a special transcendence, the temptation to hypostatize this transcendence must be thrust aside through an abstention appropriate to this temptation. This Husserl calls "reduction to the sphere of ownness." What does a move like this signify? Essentially, it is a question of transforming the objection of solipsism into an argument. I decide to abstract from all that is given to me as alien. This does not mean that I remain alone in the ordinary and non-phenomenological sense, as if the empirical solitude of an isolated or solitary man did not already assume association with other men. In the transcendental sense this means, rather, that I decide to take into consideration only "what is my own" (das mir Eigene). Henceforth, according to the ego requirement asserted in the Fifth Meditation, all events are only monadic events.[5]

---

4. "How can this be understood? (Wie klärt sich das auf?) In every case I must maintain this as absolute truth: that every sense which can have a 'whatness' and 'the fact of actual existence' for me is not and cannot be except in and by my intentional life; it only exists in and through its constitutive syntheses, being clarified and discovered for me in systems of concordant verification" (CM, p. 123:26–31).

5. It could be objected from the standpoint of the reductive technique that this reduction has already been carried out. In suspending the thesis of the world has not the Other also been reduced (Ideas I)? It has, but the reduction in question here is of a second degree. It presupposes the suspension of the general thesis of the world and consists in delimiting or circumscribing within the reduced sphere of sense an intentional nexus of the experiences which constitute myself, me, as an ego. This is why Husserl speaks of abstraction, for I abstract from the constitutive operations bearing reference to the Other.

The reader is sure to wonder whether this abstraction is possible, that is, whether anything remains that merits being called "ownness sphere." Actually, if one considers that everything in my experience bespeaks Others, that the world is a world of culture, that the least object is loaded with all the glances which are brought to bear upon it, then one can wonder whether there is an owned world (*un monde propre*) deserving to be termed a world prior to intersubjectivity. Do only my ego and the intentive processes of meaning belonging to my own being make up a world?

This is a weighty objection. But what Husserl does here must be carefully understood. In no way is it a question of genesis in the chronological sense of the word, as if the experience of myself could temporally precede the experience of the Other. Rather, it is a question of a parentage of sense, for the sense "Other" is drawn from the sense "me" because one must first give sense to "me" and to "my own" in order then to give sense to the "Other" and to the "world of the Other." There is something "alien" (*étranger*) because there is something "own" (*propre*), and not conversely. The sense "ego" is transferred from me to the Other if it is true that the Other is "alter ego." This is just why reduction to the sphere of ownness constitutes in no way a dissolution of the Other into me but rather the recognition of the paradox as a paradox: "In this very specific intentionality there is constituted a new being-sense that encroaches on the own being of my monadic ego. There is constituted an ego, not as 'I-myself,' but as mirroring itself in my own ego, in my monad" (CM, p. 125:28–32). The two key words "encroaches on" (*überschreitet*) [6] and "mirroring" (*Spiegelung*) bear witness to the paradox of the wresting (*arrachement*) of another existence from my existence at the very moment that I posit the latter as unique. Here one cannot fail to think of the Hegelian problem of the doubling of consciousness, for in the experience of only myself there is every sign of an encroachment in the direction of another ego. The entire remainder of the Fifth Meditation consists

6. [Cairns translates *überschreitet* in the passage referred to above by the phrase "goes beyond." Ricoeur's French here and occasionally elsewhere in this essay is *transgresser*, for which "goes beyond" is too weak a translation. Also, the moral tone of the English "to transgress" forbids its use here. The paradoxical fact to which our attention is being directed is that the Other is not "outside" me, yet is opposed to me (cf. p. 123 f. below). *Transgresser* seems to emphasize the sense of opposition or contrast. On p. 99 above, *transgresser* is used to translate the German *übergreiffen*, which may mean "to encroach on." The reference to Hegel in the next sentence of the text and the general emphasis of the discussion suggest this latter as a reasonable interpretation. However, care must be taken to avoid thinking of the Other as a natural something already there which somehow moves toward, approaches, or invades me—or vice versa. Cf. pp. 130 f. below.— Trans.]

in tracing the lines of sense by which the experience of ownness refers to the alien Other.

A public brought up to respect sensory experience and science can be brought to understand the intent which animates Husserl in the following manner. In the natural attitude men are there, and they communicate with each other. These men are all equally real, but I am not one of them. They are all Others. This is true, however, only for an observer who does not take part in the field of experience. In this sense they are not even Others, the ego not being thematized. There is neither I nor Others. There are only real men. With the emergence of philosophical questioning there concurrently emerges a subject who gives orientation to the whole field of experience; thereafter "the" world becomes *world-for-me*. But with this reorientation of the world into a world for me, an asymmetrical situation also obtains within the field of experience; there is I, and there is the Other. Whereas in an experience without a subject one man is just as real as another, in reflective experience only one is I, and all the rest are Others; the I-Other relationship is born as a philosophical problem. Then, to constitute the Other as Other, in and through myself, is to show how the sense "ego," born with reflective coming to awareness of my existence as an entry way for all sense, is communicated to these Others and permits me to say that those Others over there are also selves, egos. But they are egos only in a derivative, secondary sense, because the sense "ego" is initially constituted in me and for me. This parentage is in no way chronological; rather, it follows the logical order of sense.[7] Thus, the reduction to the ownness sphere has no psychological or anthropological signification. If I should withdraw from the content of my experience what it owes to commerce with Others, undoubtedly there would remain no content worthy of being called mine; but I can make abstraction from the sense "alien" which is attached to such and such a content and doubtless to all experiential contents. Thus, I first constitute the sense "ego," and then I transfer the sense "alter ego" to the Other.

The ownness sphere is clearly, in this sense, a product of abstraction. But this abstraction is methodologically necessary because it allows us to place in correct order a primary sense of the word "me"

7. "With this stratum we have reached the final limit to which the phenomenological reduction can be taken. It is clear that one must reach the experience of this 'sphere of ownness' belonging to the ego in order to be able to constitute the Idea of the experience of 'someone other than I.' Without this latter Idea I cannot have the experience of an 'objective world.' But I do not need the experience of the objective world, nor that of the Other, to have that of my own 'sphere of ownness'" (CM, p. 127:18–23). [Professor Ricoeur quotes from the French translation, p. 80.—Trans.]

and a secondary sense which attaches to whosoever is an Other for me. Hence, it is useless to try to make what Husserl calls "the sphere of ownness" correspond to some "stage" which child psychology or psychoanalysis allows us to distinguish. It would be just as useless to foist over onto Husserl some experience of isolation or solitude, for the Other would still be present there, by way of disputation, deception, or nostalgia. The ownness sphere is actually the residue of an abstractive operation. But this residue is at the same time the first link of a chain of significations following along which the ego can first say "my" ego and then the ego of the "Other."

Does this mean that the residue, the product of abstraction, can in no way be elucidated? Husserl recognizes in this "stratum" a "unitary coherence" (CM, p. 127:12) and even a "concrete unity" (CM, p. 129:21). How can the product of an abstraction be "concrete"? There is no contradiction here if one recalls that in Husserl "concrete" always designates a self-sufficient or independent totality (cf. Fourth Logical Investigation, "Whole and Part"). As for "abstraction," it is a matter not of an Aristotelian or Lockean abstraction of a general idea but of the methodical separation of an intentional nexus. Hence, there is no contradiction in reaching a concretum through abstraction, for this only means that an isolable totality corresponds to the abstraction of the ownness sphere.

This isolable totality is the owned body (*corps propre* or *Leib*), the body which I move, with which I perceive, by which I express myself. This body serves as reference pole for all physical bodies (*Körper*) which, under this second degree reduction, no longer make up an objective world but rather a primordial nature, an owned nature. This is the totality—owned body, owned nature—which receives the name of "ownness sphere": "consequent upon this abstractive elimination of all that is alien to me, a sort of world remains with me, a nature reduced to what belongs to me (*à mon appartenance*)—a psychophysical ego with body, soul, and a personal ego integrated into this nature, thanks to its body" (CM, p. 129:8).

It will be objected that this experience of the owned body is not in fact an immediate datum. I think we must grant the point to the objectors: this experience is the result of an abstraction, and in the same way the ego itself is an abstraction on the analogy to which I transfer the sense "ego" to Others. Husserl employs a remarkable expression at this point. He says that by this abstractive reduction I "make my body reduced to my ownness *stand out* . . ." (CM, p. 128:28). This *Herausstellung*, it seems to me, signifies that the primordial always remains the end aimed at by a "questioning back" (*Rückfrage*). Thanks to this *Rückfrage*, reflection reaches back through the successive constituted strata and grasps within the breadth of its experience what Husserl calls a "primordial institution" (*Urstiftung*), back to which these superposed strata refer. Hence, what is primordial is itself the intentional terminus of such a searching back. Therefore, there is a need to seek, under the title of ownness sphere, not some sort of inchoate experience conserved within my cultural experience, but rather something prior, never given, the limit of a purification (*Reinigung*) (CM, p. 128:39) of everything which does not belong [to me]. This is why, despite its intuitive core, this "experience" remains an interpretation, an explication (*Auslegung*).

Even if this experience is not immediate, still, to the extent that it results from an abstraction and remains derivative from an explication or from an interpretation, it is a positive experience; ownness is not defined here in negative terms simply as non-alien. To grasp the owned body, owned nature, and the whole ownness sphere as an autonomous positive totality means to provide the subsequent constitution of the Other with an antecedent foundation. This primordial sphere must be understood to be at once the terminus of a purification and the departure point for a constitutional performance. It is a something pre-given which, by reason of its charge of potentiality and the stretch of its horizons, has the density of an *I am* which always precedes the *I think*. In this way all that one can say against the immediacy of this experience pleads in favor of its fullness. All of this potential, the ballast of the actual, gives breadth to the experience of the primordial and the owned. This endless coming to awareness of the "owned" penetrates a life whose wealth exceeds reflection. Thus, the reduction to the ownness sphere, far from impoverishing experience, leads it from the cogito to the *sum* and fulfills the promise, expressed in the Fourth Meditation, of an egology which would set up the ego as a monad. By way of an astonishing detour, the transcendental, once reduced, reveals being (*être*) as superabundant.

At the end of this first movement it becomes clear that the abstraction which reveals the owned body and owned nature is definitely more than a didactic fiction. Likewise, and above all, it reaches the sense of incarnation. This nature which is my own is a nature centered in my body. When this nature becomes the sphere for the exercise of my powers, it is what I can see, touch, and hear. Thus, the reduction to the ownness sphere makes the body as body stand out (*herausstellen*). Until now my body remained the unnoticed organ, the organ traversed by my acts, which terminated at things. Thenceforth, the "own" is my flesh (*ma chair*), to use Merleau-Ponty's term.

Not only is the abstraction not a didactic fiction, but it is instead the contrary of an impoverishment of experience. The world is reduced to the horizon of my body, but I coincide with this reduced world; I flow directly down into this world of my flesh; the world is my own; but as for me, I am mundanized by means of this flesh which I immediately am.[8] The abstractive operation, begun in the manner of a subtraction, is revealed as a movement toward the fullness of the ego. This latter, moving from the pole of its acts had become center of its habitualities, and then a monad. Now it is my flesh.[9] Correlatively, nature, which until now was only something to behold, becomes the surrounding world of my flesh. Sunk into the midst of this nature, I experience myself as a "member of . . ." (*Glied*) this totality of things "outside me" (CM, p. 129:36). From this dialectic of the "outside me" and the "in me," which my body has instituted, proceeds the whole constitution of the alien "in" and "outside of" ownness.[10]

[III]   THE "ANALOGICAL" GRASPING OF THE OTHER (CM, §§ 48–54)

HOW DO WE GET from this admitted and accepted solipsism to the constitution of the *Other*? The whole problem is now to discover within the sphere of ownness the motives for an encroachment which posits an "Other," an "alien."

It might be said that in raising this question after the reduction to the owned sphere Husserl limits himself to repeating the initial problem (CM, § 42) and that the reduction to the sphere of "ownness" has only rendered the problem more insoluble. In a sense this is true. Does Husserl himself not say that the experience of the Other is "contrasted" (CM, p. 135:20) with the experience of ownness? Does he not say for the ego reduced to its ownness that the being-sense attaching to the Other "wholly transcends its own being" (CM, p. 135:32)? Do we not come upon the experience of the Other as an irreducible "factum" (CM, p. 136:7)? Do we not erect this experience as an additional stratum, one erected upon primordial experience? Then it seems that the primordial experience has served only to bring a higher

---

8. "We now can say this: while I, this ego, have constituted and have continued to constitute this world existing for me as a (correlative) phenomenon, I have carried out, by means of corresponding constitutive syntheses, an apperception of myself (as 'me' in the habitual sense of a human personality immersed within the totality of the constituted world) which transforms me into a being of the world (*eine verweltlichende Selbstapperzeption*)" (CM, p. 130:19–26).

9. "All of what the transcendental ego constitutes in the first stratum as 'non-alien,' as 'what belongs to it,' is, in fact, its own by virtue of being an element in its own, concrete being . . ." (CM, p. 131:10–14).

10. ". . . *toute constitution de l'étranger 'dans' et 'hors du' propre.*"

level transcendence "into relief" (*Abhebung*) (CM, p. 136:12), and nothing else remains but to inquire into the experience that gives sense to this new transcendence.[11] The program that can be discerned at the beginning of this investigation seems definitely to have been limited to deciphering an irreducible experience and to unfolding (*déployer*) the three superposed strata corresponding to the three problems stated at the beginning: the grasping of the Other as Other, the constitution of an objective world common to all subjects, and the elaboration of the various communities of persons.[12]

But if the experience of "ownness" only served to sharpen the contrast of the same and the other and to emphasize the irreducibility of a transcendence that is excluded from the sphere of ownness, the whole effort up until now would be for naught. Moreover, only one of the two phenomenological requirements would be satisfied, that of correctly describing original experiences; the second requirement would not be satisfied, that of constituting the sense of all transcendence "in" the immanence of the ego. What Husserl calls "intentional explication" (*intentionale Auslegung*) comprises both of these requirements. Hence, the excess of sense attaching to the experience of the Other must have roots in my own experience.

Here the decisive theme arises: the analogical grasping of the Other as another ego. This theme is the center of the Fifth Meditation. Balanced in it are the two requirements of phenomenology: respect for the otherness of the Other and the rooting of this experience of transcendence "in" primordial experience. This theory of analogical apprehension is, therefore, of considerable weight. Thanks to it solipsism should be overcome without the sacrifice of egology. In other words, the encroachment beyond the sphere of ownness is to be accounted for, while at the same time the primacy of the originary experience of the ego is confirmed.

Is this the squaring of the circle? It would seem so, if a certain mediation were not suggested on the one hand by the experience of the Other and on the other hand by the experience of myself. The remarkable thing is that in the experience I have of the Other, the Other is

11. "It is a question of examining this experience itself, of elucidating through the analysis of intentionality the manner in which it 'confers sense,' the manner in which it can appear as experience and be justified as evidence of an actual being having its own explicable essence, as evidence of a being which is not my own being and is not an integral part of it, even though it cannot take on sense or justification except by beginning from my own being" (CM, p. 136:30–36).

12. "What we have just presented is an anticipation of the results of the intentional explication which we must carry out level by level if we are to solve the transcendental problem and truly elaborate the transcendental idealism of phenomenology" (CM, p. 138:24–28).

announced as being there, in person, "in flesh and blood," though nevertheless without being given in the original. I do not see the life of the Other. If I did he would be an extension of my own life: he would be I. The Other is not "presented" directly, immediately, but "appresented" through his body, which alone is "presented," since it appears in my primordial sphere just as other bodies do. Hence, the key to the problem is to be sought in connection with the body of the Other. For only his body can *be given* to my perception while at the same time *giving* the Other. Now the experience I have of my own body contains another suggestion which the preceding observation brings to mind. This experience speaks to me of a reification, of a mundanization of the ego, which, in a certain way which we shall explain, can motivate the constitution of the Other. In *Ideas I* Husserl already noted that consciousness maintained two intermingled sorts of relationships with the world: a relationship of perception—the world is there, facing me, offering a spectacle—and a relationship of incarnation. By means of my body I identify myself with one of the things of nature, with a physical thing (*Körper*), which becomes my owned body (*Leib*), at the same time that I myself am incorporated into nature. Thanks to this *Verflechtung*, to this "interlacing" (*entrelacs*, as Merleau-Ponty says), I apperceive myself as a mundane reality. With striking terseness Husserl calls this grasping of consciousness as a thing of the world, "mundanizing self-apperception" (*Verweltlichende Selbstapperzeption*).

Now our task is getting on. How are we to relate this "appresentation," or mediate grasping of the Other, to his body, and this "apperception," or reified consciousness, to myself? Husserl's reply comes in three stages, and each of these stages, as well as the movement through them, is important.

First stage: By virtue of a sort of analogy that works from body to body, the signification "ego" moves from my body, apperceived in the world, to the body of the Other, which appresents another life to me. Thanks to this analogy the sense "ego" is transferred from my body to the body perceived over there.

> Let us assume that another man enters our perceptual field. Under the primordial reduction this means that in the perceptual field of my primordial nature there appears a body (*Körper*) which, so far as primordial, can only be a determining element of myself (an immanent transcendence). Since in this nature and in this world my owned body (*Leib*) is the only body (*Körper*) that is or can be constituted originally as an organism (*Leib*) (a functioning organ), that other body (*Körper*) over there—which, however, is also given as an organism (*Leib*)—must have derived it in such a way as to exclude a truly direct and primordial

justification (that is, by a perception in the strict sense of the term) of the specific predicates belonging to the organism (*Leiblichkeit*). From this point on, it is clear that only a resemblance connecting the other body (*Körper*) with my body within my primordial sphere can provide the foundation and the motive for conceiving "by analogy" that body as another organism (*Leib*). (CM, p. 140:23–29)

This is perhaps the most important passage in the whole Fifth Meditation, for it marks the meeting point of the two requirements, descriptive and constitutive, that dominate the whole of phenomenology. This "apperceptive transfer" (or "analogizing apperception") must at once respect the originality of the experience of the Other and root it in the experience of the owned body which "motivates" this "transfer." But recourse to analogy creates as many problems as it solves, for this analogy is not a type of reasoning. It is not a question of a reasoning by analogy through which we conclude from the similarity of bodily expressions the similarity of living experiences. Rather, the question concerns an analogy which functions on the level of "passive genesis," as when we understand a new reality by analogy with one already known: the new understanding proceeds from an antecedent experience which furnishes a sort of originary institution (*Urstiftung*). Hence, analogy is a very general process of pre-reflective, antepredicative, experience. It is encountered in every reference to an originary experience by a new experience which finds its model or its type in the former. That which specifies the analogical transfer brought into play in the experience of the Other is what Husserl boldly terms "pairing" (*Paarung*) (Title of CM, § 51, also *passim*). All other analogies go from object to object in the same sphere of experience, but here the analogy goes from the "own" to the "alien." Hence, a species of analogy must be found which brings into play this encroachment from the originary towards the non-originary. Such is the paired configuration of ego and alter ego—the consequence of their bodily similarities. This "pairing" brings it about that the sense of the one refers to the sense of the other, is transposed or transferred to the second. In the bodily presence of the Other I recognize the analogue of my own reification, and I extend to the Other the sense "ego," even though only my living experience has the originary quality. The "pairing" thus furnishes the associative support of the analogy and brings into play the most primitive passive synthesis by which I pass from ego to alter ego.

Nevertheless, Husserl does not conclude the analysis here. Still lacking is a decisive trait introduced by him by way of an objection which seems to bring everything back into question: "Is the structure of the apperception truly transparent at this point? Or is it a simple apperception by transfer like any other? What makes this body the body of another and not a second example of my own body?" (CM, p. 143:16–19) That Husserl himself should have formulated this question is understandable, for his analysis is much less oriented toward the pulsing, carnal, even sexual, sense of the paired formation than toward its logical sense. Like analogy, the paired configuration is a universal structure, the initiation of a multiplicity or of a totality. In this respect it is an originary form of all passive synthesis. Contrary to what one would expect, "pairing" is a relation which lacks the fullness of a living experience. This is why Husserl now turns toward what he has called "appresentation" to seek in it the fulfillment and concrete verification of what so far is only the intending of the Other. Analogy only furnishes the supposition, the empty anticipation, of an alien life. This intending of transfer has yet to be confirmed by the concordant signs which confer fulfillment and being-status (*valeur existentielle, Seinsgeltung*) upon it.

This will be our second stage, since from now on our analysis takes place at the precise point where the presentation of the body of the Other in my own sphere of experience becomes appresentation, "outside" of me, of the subjective life of the Other. This specific moment of transcendence must now be encircled. This experience corresponds to the precise question: How is it that the (apperceived) Other is one with his (presented) body?

What we are to take into consideration here is the manner in which the supposition of an alien life is verified. This verification corresponds, in the order of the experience of the Other, to what the Third Meditation has already described within the framework of the constitution of the thing. There verification consisted in the "concordance" of aspects or adumbrations. An intending is confirmed or disconfirmed by this play of concordances or discordances. In an analogous way, the supposition or anticipation of an alien subjective process (e.g., joy) is confirmed by the concordance of expressions, gestures, behavior: "The body of the Other announces itself in the succession of experience as truly being an animate body in the unique way of its changing but ever concordant behavior" (CM, p. 144:14–16). The concordance of behavior illustrates quite well the theory of signs with which the First Logical Investigation begins. It will be remembered that Husserl distinguishes two species of signs: those that indicate, which he calls indices, and those that signify and are properly the signs of language. Concordant behavior falls into the first category of signs, since it is the index of an alien life. It indicates the subjective life of the Other by its harmonious interconnection. Thus, it gives a "verifiable accessibility" to what is not "originarily verifiable" (CM, p. 21).

At first glance, the relationship between the argument from analogy and that of behavior is not easy to grasp. Our first inclination would be to oppose one of these two interpretations to the other. Is not the analogy an indirect grasping of the alien life beginning from my own? Does not the concordance of behavior offer a direct reading of this alien life? Nevertheless, Husserl uses the two arguments successively. Actually, it must be understood that they do not have the same function. Even taken alone, analogy attests to the Other's also being an ego; no theory of expression could render it superfluous. The concordance of expression comes to fulfill my anticipation only on the condition that this anticipation should be able to intend another ego, that is to say, an ego similar to me.

It could be objected, it is true, that Husserl gives precedence to analogy and to pairing—despite the general and even formal character of this relation—because this relation gives the constitution of the Other a more idealistic turn, the direct interpretation of behavior in psychological terms having a more realistic accent. There is no doubt of this, as a text like the following sufficiently demonstrates:

> From the phenomenological point of view the Other is a modification of my ego (which, for its part, takes on this character of being "mine" owing to the necessary pairing which sets them into opposition). Clearly, and for the same reason, all that belongs to the concrete being of this other ego is appresented in the same way within an analogous modification. It is appresented thus first as a function of its primordial world and then as a function of the fully concrete ego. In other words, the other monad is constituted through appresentation in my own. (CM, p. 144: 30–32)

Also, in another way there is a progression from the empty sense to the fulfilled sense when there is a passage from the analogical grasping to the concordance of expressive signs. Then the same text can be read in a different way; insofar as the Other remains an analogue of my ego, the Other is only a modification of my ego; but, in showing himself as addressed toward me in concordant behavior, he truly becomes "Other."

The third stage of constitution marks a new step in the direction of the liberation of the Other from my primordial sphere. This time it is imagination which starts up reflection. While the whole preceding analysis took place within the circle of perception—pairing and the interpretation of behavior are actually perceptual experiences—the new analysis develops in the setting of "free variations" on the following theme: I am "here" (*hic*), the Other is "there" (*illic*), but "there" (*illic*) is where I could be if I were to move. From "over there" (*illic*) I would see the same things but under another perspective. Hence, through imagination I can coordinate the *other places,* the *other* perspectives, to *my* place and to *my* perspective. *Illic,* that is where I can go. Hence, it is my potential *hic.*

Thus, the pairing appears less enigmatic, for I pair the Other not only to my actual experience but to my potential experience as well; by imagining what I would see from over there, I advance further into the analogous existence of the Other. Hence, imagination serves to "illustrate" or "presentiate" the associative link which the first stage of the constitution of the Other provides. But instead of fulfilling this analogical intending by perception of behavior, I fulfill it by free creations of the imagination, and thus I give the associative transfer from me to the Other not only the vivacity of the image but also independence with regard to my present perspective. The fiction is this liberation from my perspective and this movement into another point of view. By means of it I can understand the *illic* for me as a *hic* for him. What I have called "appresentation"—and which initially was nothing more than a species of logical analogy and a sort of doubling—now becomes a transfer into another life in imagination and in sympathy.

To be sure, this life is not given to me in an "original production" but in a "reproduction" in the mode of "if I were there." This "assimilative apperception," whose explication or interpretation we are patiently following, receives a concrete sense from this fiction, without, however, the life of the Other ever becoming for me the equivalent of the one life of which I have originary experience, my own.[13]

Recapitulating the three moments of the constitution of the Other, we can say that the first moment draws its force from a universal law, association, specified by an even more determinate transcendental called pairing. Thus, the movement of encroachment by which the sense "ego" is transferred from the original to the analogue is rendered intelligible. The second moment brings the help of a perceptual decipherment of the expression of behavior by which I fulfill the intending of another life. The third moment adds to this reading of the concordances of behavior the fiction "if I were over there." Thus, the intending of an alien life progresses from empty to full, without, however, this

13. "Hence, there is an ego appresented as Other. The coexistence, incompatible within the primordial sphere, becomes compatible through the following fact: my primordial *ego,* which constitutes other *egos* for itself, does so by means of the appresentative apperception which, conforming to its specific sense, never requires or admits its confirmation through a presentation" (CM, p. 148:18–23).

transgression of my ownness sphere giving me the subjective life of the other in the original.

Is this to say that we have succeeded in constituting the Other? The remarkable thing here is that Husserl himself—with his admirable scrupulousness—puts us on our guard against his own explication. If it is true that the pairing of my *hic* with the *illic* of the Other is rendered less incomprehensible through the mediation of my potential experience ("if I were over there"), this pairing remains essentially an enigma, for the *hic* of the Other, just as it is for him, differs essentially from the *hic* which would be mine if I went over there. This "over there"—insofar as it is a "here" for the Other—does not belong, even potentially, to my own sphere. The "as if I, myself, I were over there" does not permit introducing the here of the Other into my sphere. My here and the over there of the Other are mutually exclusive.

In the end it is just this moment of exclusion at the heart of the analogical transfer which, as the following formula expresses perfectly, brings idealism up short:

> Because of the constitution of its sense, the Other appears in a necessary fashion as an intentional modification of my ego, initially objectivated. . . . In other words, another monad is constituted by appresentation in mine. (CM, p. 144:28–37)

Right up to the end the descriptive spirit and the requirement of constitution tend to meet but fail to blend into each other, for according to the idealistic requirement of constitution, the Other must be a modification of my ego and according to the realistic character of description, the Other never ceases to exclude himself from the sphere of "my monad."

Perhaps the attempt at a further unification of Husserl's enterprise must be renounced. Husserl is his most admirable self when he brings out anew a difficulty which he seemed to have resolved.

[IV] INTERSUBJECTIVE NATURE (CM, § 55)

THE THEORY OF ANALOGY—with its three stages—is only the first step of an enterprise of considerable proportions which we marked out at the beginning. To the recognition of the Other as Other is added the constitution of a nature held in common and then of a cultural world where characteristic objects—books, institutions, monuments—are correlative to genuine communities of persons.

What makes for the difficulty between the first and second stages?

The construction of a common (*gemein*) objective nature already presents the problem of "communalization" (*Vergemeinschaftung*). This is difficult because the analogical grasping of the Other does not account for the reciprocity among egos which the entire subsequent analysis requires. The me-Other relation is essentially asymmetrical or non-reciprocal. The Other is a projected ego and as such a modified ego. Pairing is oriented in one way only, from the primordial ego to the analogous ego. Yet the constitution of an objective nature, prior even to that of cultural communities, requires that the experience of the ego should enter into composition with the experience of the Other on a basis of reciprocity, although the latter draws his sense of *alter ego* from my own experience as *ego*.

This problem, more than any other, embarrassed Husserl, as is evident in the manuscripts on "intentional sociology." [14] These manuscripts complicate the difficulty by accentuating the reflexive character of the experience of the Other. *Cogito alterum cogitatum* should be the formula for the recognition of the Other in a resolutely egological philosophy. For such a philosophy there is but one ego, which is multiplied associatively. The apodicticity of the existence of the Other remains derivative from mine. Only one ego is presented; all Others are appresented. Upon this asymmetrical relation, then, all communities must be constructed—first those of intending, then those of willing and working. From this point forward we are assured that however real these "communities" may be, they are never absolute in the sense that the ego alone is real in reflection. Hence, we must learn to coordinate empirical realism, for which communities are real beings, with transcendental idealism, for which all being-sense is drawn from the ego.

Here again we can follow the traces of the conflict between the two requirements within Husserl's work of constitution. The one demands respect for novel significations which the progress of analysis uncovers; the other requires derivation of the being-status of communities from the being-status of the ego.

Thus, the constitution of a world held in common within the intersubjective network of experience will be our first problem. For the phenomenologist this constitution should be carried forward from an initial constitutional kernel. The center of radiation of the whole analysis is the identity which must be recognized to hold between the signification of the body of the Other for him and the signification

---

14. Cf. René Toulemont, *L'Essence de la société selon Husserl* (Paris, 1962). Among the more important manuscripts referred to in this work, note F I–33, M III, 3 IX, 1 (*Gemeinschaft* II). On the reflexive character of all appresentation, cf. Toulemont, *op. cit.*, pp. 88–96.

which it has for me. How is the body of the Other the same for him who lives it as his "here" and for me who perceives it as my "there"?

Let us first try to understand the place of this question within the sequence of analyses which are going to lead us to the notion of a common nature. At first glance, the chasm between my experiential sphere and that of the Other is unbridgeable. Speaking absolutely, there are as many worlds as there are appresented subjects. But if the enigma of the identity of spheres of experience cannot be resolved directly, perhaps one can resolve it indirectly by passing through the stage of the body of the Other. For if I do not understand how two subjects can intend the same object, that is to say, how an object can be the same in a plurality of subjective lives, perhaps I can understand how this body perceived "over there" by me is lived through "here" by the Other. The experience of the Other brings it about that the body "over there" indicates another subjective life. It is appresentation which brings about the identification of the "over there" for me with the "here" for him, for it presents us with the first object that tears itself out of my solitude and begins to gravitate about a pole other than I. To us this polarity may appear obscure because we situate ourselves at a moment where the experience of the Other has already done its work and has already, in a way, doubled the world. But one can come upon the moment when the presented element (the body seen there) and the appresented element (the Other who announces himself there) are still indivisible. At this moment where the same and the different are undivided, it is one and the same reality that pertains to my *own* sphere and indicates an *alien* existence. Hence, there are not two realities separated by a hiatus—for, on the one hand, this body is present with (*chez*) me (it belongs to my ownness sphere insofar as perceived), and, on the other hand, this presence is the presence of the Other.

This undivided experience contains in abridged form the solutions to all the subsequent difficulties. The body present to me reveals another; in return the Other renders this presence alien to me. Likewise, since the body over there for me and the body here for the Other are not only two analogous bodies but the same body, a nature in common is possible: "This is the same body; it is given to me as *illic*, to him as *hic*, and the totality of my nature is the same as that of the Other" (CM, p. 152:2–4).

By what intermediary have we passed from the identity of the body to that of nature? In what sense is the totality of nature for me the same as the totality of nature for the Other? The intermediary notion that must be introduced here is that of perspective, for my body is the zero-origin (*Nullpunkt*) of a point of view, of a perspective which gives a determinate orientation to the system of my experience. I understand that the Other has another perspective which orients his experience differently. The body of the Other belongs to my system and to his, and this allows me to understand that the same object can be perceived under different perspectives.

This recourse to the notion of perspective may seem very Leibnizian. But in Leibniz all perspectives are integrated into a higher point of view, that of God, by an operation of over-viewing (*survol*) which allows passing from the monad to the monadology. No such view from above is permitted in Husserl. It is always from the side, and not from above, that each of us discovers that the same world is grasped from different points of view. For the other perspectives are appresented within one originary perspective, mine, as being different perspectives upon the same object and the same world.[15]

Thus, monadic idealism is safeguarded against monadological realism. The sense "world perceived by an Other" is erected within my ownness sphere. "But that specifically does not forbid its intentionality from transcending my ownness, and consequently my ego from constituting in itself an Other and constituting him as existent" (CM, p. 152:38, p. 153:3). Thus, the existential index analogically conferred upon the body of the Other—by virtue of paired constitution—comes closer and closer to covering all that appears to that Other. There are definitely two strata but not two worlds: one stratum lived through in the original and another appresented as his. This is what happens when I complete my experience of the world with that of travelers and geographers who have seen places that I have not visited and which I shall undoubtedly never see. These two strata are strata of one and the same object, of which I say that I perceive it and that the Other perceives it also. But this "also," which proceeds from the doubling of consciousness, does not bring about a double world.[16]

15. "I do not initially have an appresented second original sphere with a second nature and a second bodily organism (the organism of the Other) in this nature, so that I must then ask how it happens that the two spheres come to be conceived as a mode of presentation of the same objective nature. But by the very fact of appresentation and its necessary unity with the presentation which accompanies it, the identity of my primordial nature and of the nature represented by the Others is necessarily established, and in general by reason of this (appresentation) another and in consequence his concrete ego can be there for me" (CM, p. 152:24–32).

16. "After these clarifications it is in no way enigmatic that I can constitute another ego in my ego or, to speak in an even more radical fashion, that I can constitute another monad in my monad and, once constituted, grasp it specifically as Other. We also understand this fact, inseparable from the preceding, that I can identify the nature constituted by me with the nature constituted by the Other or, to speak with all the precision necessary, with a nature constituted as constituted by Others" (CM, p. 154:35, p. 155:3). In passing Husserl examines two corollaries

Thus, the reciprocity of consciousnesses, brought into play by the communal experience of nature, is firmly kept within the strict framework of appresentation and monadic idealism. Rather than fear that the initial hypothesis of the primordial constitution of the ego should be sacrificed, one may fear that the reality and diversity of human experiences are sacrificed to the rigor of this egological primacy. The identity of the world, to the degree that an identical world is perceived by two consciousnesses, is ultimately driven home by Husserl on the model of the identification synthesis, as it is performed by a single consciousness. In the end the identification of a presented world and an appresented world is no more enigmatic than the identification of a world presented and a world presentiated, for example, in portraiture or memory. The possibility of "coming back to the same object" gives the entire series of successive perceptions the character of intending the same. Again, this identifying synthesis between my experience and that of the Other can be brought together with another variety of identifying synthesis, that which is introduced by ideal objects. Actually it is said that these objects are atemporal, which means simply that "I can find again" or "reproduce" the same identifying evidence at different moments of my life. The supratemporal reveals itself as omnitemporal. These two comparisons give an approximate notion of what the synthesis of identification can be when it relates two mutually alien experiential spheres.

But is it true that the identifying synthesis between the alien and the own belongs to the same genus? Has it not been said (CM, § 51) that there are two syntheses, the synthesis of association and the synthesis of identification? Can one really compare association between the own and the alien with the association of a perceiving and a remembering within the same flux of subjective life? Do not all of these comparisons obscure the specificity of the doubling of consciousness? The demand that Husserl wants to meet is easy to understand: there are two consciousnesses but not two worlds. Remembering this, it is legitimate to compare the associative synthesis of flesh to flesh to the identification synthesis which, within a single flux of subjective life, maintains the identity of a single sense. But does not idealism also fail to provide an account of the analogy between the own and the alien when it reduces this analogy to a simple variant of the identifying synthesis?

---

which are treated at much greater length in *Ideas II* and in the manuscripts on community: the problem of anomalies (the world of the blind, the deaf, the pathological world, etc.) and that of non-adult perception: infants, primitives, animals. These problems are broached by phenomenology insofar as they insidiously reintroduce a duplication of the world. On these problems, cf. Toulemont, *op. cit.*, pp. 78–88 ("*Modifications du type d'autrui*").

There is at least one point where this comparison is fruitful. It concerns the coordination of all particular durations into one unique "temporal community." If time is to be the form of coexistence for several monads, an account must indeed be given of the fact that it cannot be multiple. In the end, there is but one time, as there is but one world. Private time, that of each monad, is ordered in relation to a common objective time of which it is a "mode of appearing." If this is how the matter does stand, then the reason is that objective mundane time has the same character of identity as intersubjectively constituted "realities." But things do stand with objective time as with objective nature: *the internal consciousness of time of the primordial monad* is the origin (1) of the time appresented in the Other, and (2) of the common objective time, the time of the world.

[V] THE INTERMONADIC COMMUNITY (CM, §§ 56–58)

COMMUNITIES properly so-called are communities of persons, and specific cultural objects correspond to them. Nevertheless, it is possible to term the entire preceding process, ending in the constitution of an objective nature, a "formation of community" (*Vergemeinschaftung*). The constitution of a common (*gemein*) world is the first step to and foundation for all other intersubjective communities. By a sort of reaction, the common project of men—the world, time— cements the union of men and transforms the association of their bodies into an indissoluble connection. In all truth I can say that "what is (*l'étant*) is in intentional community with what is" (CM, p. 157:17).

It seems to me that Husserl's originality lies in this methodical progression from solipsism to community. Whereas the sociologist begins from the group as a fact, Husserl grounds the possibility of the human relationship (*le lien humain*) upon a first stratum of processes creative of community, viz., the intentional community whose correlate is objective nature. In its turn this intentional community proceeds from what is called "pairing" of body to body, which represents the first encroachment beyond the sphere of ownness.[17] Hence, what is important in Husserl is not what he says *about* community but how his analysis advances step by step *toward* community. This is why that which is first for the sociologist or anthropologist is last for the phenom-

---

17. The principal stages of the itinerary that leads from the monadic reduction to the collective life are summed up perfectly in a passage from the *Crisis*, Part Two, pp. 307–8, cited by Toulemont at the head of his chapter on "*La Societé humaine*," *op. cit.*, p. 97.

enologist. One can even say, for Husserl, that the goal is too quickly reached. In consequence the calculated slowness of his last sections multiply the preceding steps to the point of fatigue.

Thus, at the moment when one expects to see him speak of historical communities, he introduces yet another intermediary analysis, that of the reciprocity of standpoints and the "objectifying equalizations" that the latter implies. Why this new turning point? Because that which is a matter of course for common sense must become astonishing for reflection. If it is true that only one is I, and that Others are other, this objectifying equalization by which I become an Other for these Others, an Other among these Others, must be accounted for. It is an equalization in the sense that reciprocity abolishes the privilege of the single ego, and it is an objectification in the sense that this reciprocity brings it about that there are only Others. I am an Other among Others. Thus, a community of real (*réels*) men is possible.

The paradox is apparent. On the one hand, one must say that the sense of the Other, of the psycho-physical man, hence also of me insofar as I am an Other among Others, is constituted "purely in me, the meditating ego" (CM, p. 158:21); this latter is against any hypostasis of society into an absolute being. On the other hand, it is legitimate to profess a realism of reciprocity which at its limit makes me an Other among Others.

Here the transcendental idealism undergoes a severe test. The existential index which attaches to the Other as "being" (*étant, seiend*), then to me as equally "being" (*seiend*) Other, finally to separation and fusion as really immanent separation (*reelle Trennung*) and really immanent unification (*reelle Verbindung*), appears quite incompatible with the idealistic thesis whereby the Other is constituted "in" me. The difficulty is all the greater since Husserl during the same epoch took the specificity of social relations very seriously.[18] He even speaks here of communities of the higher level as realities distinct from the nature upon which they are constructed. For good or bad, it seems sure that one must renounce the asymmetry of the relationship me-Other required by the monadic idealism in order to account for this objectifying equalization required by sociological realism.

Such is the fundamental difficulty attaching to the notion of transcendental intersubjectivity after it becomes a question of interpreting

18. In Chapter Three of Toulemont's book, one finds detailed studies of communication, working together, the birth of a collective spirit, and the diversity of "cultural predicates" (*op. cit.*, pp. 97–140). Chapters Four and Five deal with animal sociability, custom and tradition, language, the family, the familiar and the strange worlds, the nation and the race, cultural Europe, and the community of philosophers and scientists.

it in realistic terms as the reciprocal relation of Others within a "world of men." To resolve this difficulty Husserl has recourse to the constitution of the psyche (elaborated in *Ideas II*) as he had recourse to the owned body at the beginning of the Fifth Meditation. The psyche, like the owned body, is a naturalization and a reification of the ego. On the basis of this naturalization something like a "reciprocity of Others" can be instituted. I see myself within the world as psyche among psyches, as psyche equalized with, separated from, and tied to the other psyches. Each man appears to each other man in an intra-psychic (*innerpsychisch*) manner, that is to say, "in systems of intentionality, which, as psychic lives, are themselves already constituted as existing in a mundane manner" (CM, p. 158:31–33).

Hence, the notion of the "psychic constitution of the objective world" (CM, p. 158:34) must be introduced in order to realize, in the emphatic sense of "realize," this "objectifying equalization" which is the condition for all higher levels of communalization. Thus, it follows that the "ego" must appear in the world not only as flesh but also as psyche. At this level the Others are also realized as psyches, separated and reciprocal. In the world of men intersubjectivity is a psychic reality. Now we hold the key to the relation between monadic or egological idealism and psychological (or sociological) realism. This key is the self-objectification of the monad as psyche. In this way the "naturalism" practiced in the human sciences is motivated and justified.

The end of the Fifth Meditation consists in a rapidly presented program of studies that can be carried out under the aegis of this parallelism between sociological realism and egological idealism. For example, it can be shown that exchanges among men culminate in genuine "objectivities," viz., communities that can be considered as personalities of a higher order. These higher-level persons correspond to "cultural surrounding worlds" which are limited objectivities, just as the group which "has" each of these surrounding worlds is limited or closed.

In the manuscripts an investigation is undertaken into the unlimited, universal community, the community of scientists and philosophers.[19] It will be the problem of the *Crisis* to locate the historical emergence of this unlimited community. Beyond the delimited cultures, it corresponds to that other universal community spoken of in the Fifth Meditation; this community is situated rather on this side of cultural communities and represents the possibility of every normally constituted man to reach the same objective nature.

19. On the "archontic" or "transcendental" society, the privilege of Europe and crisis of cultural Europe, cf. Toulemont, *ibid.*, Chapter Six.

If we take a position between the unlimited community of cognition and the simple positing of an objective nature held in common, we see repeated for each given historical group the problems of the "own" and the "alien" which we have described on the level of each person. To the familiar world of my culture is opposed the alien worlds of other cultures. It is worth noticing that at this level of cultural groups the word "world" is pluralized. While there is "one" physical world, there are "several" cultural worlds. Thus, these higher-level persons present the same kind of problem as that presented by persons properly so-called, for it is always by starting from the own that the alien is understood. In a sense, one can speak of a constitution oriented from the cultural field. Just as one cannot consider the relation of person to person from above, so no view from above permits us to consider the totality of cultures from a position outside of all of them. Thus, all standpointless comparisons are excluded. In our relations to other cultures, the opposition of original and derivative, of the here and the there, is insurmountable. Just as my body is the zero-origin from which I consider all things, so too my community is the zero-member (*Nullglied*) of the human community.

Thus is differentiated the sphere which *Ideas II* calls "spirit" (*Geist*) in order to distinguish it from the psyche, which remains a natural reality. This Diltheyian and, more distantly, Hegelian term (objective spirit) indicates that we have crossed the border which separates nature and culture. Moreover, what we have been calling nature now appears as a simple stratum within a totality of the concrete world obtained by subtraction of all the cultural "predicates" which sociability confers on the world. A few allusions suggest that it is less in a theory of cognition than in a theory of *praxis*—of suffering and doing (*Leiden und Tun*)—that the constitution of these cultural worlds arises. It also appears that the person is completely constituted only at this level, which represents a source of interiorization for these cultural worlds. Thus, the person, in Husserl, is synonymous neither with the ego nor even with "man" (Husserl always speaks of man in relation to the psyche, consequently still on the naturalistic level). Rather, the person is correlative to the community and its "habitual properties." One can say just as well that the person is the ego considered in its communal habits. It is worth observing that only in this context does the notion of *Lebenswelt* appear,[20] the notion which will occupy so considerable a place in the *Crisis*. This "life-world" could not

20. "The systematic progression of the transcendental phenomenological explication of the apodictic ego culminates in uncovering the transcendental sense of the world in all of the concrete fullness in which it is the life-world of all of us" (CM, p. 163:10–14).

appear until the end of the Fifth Meditation, since it represents the concrete fullness toward which the constitution of the Other and of the intersubjective communities points. Hence, we know better than to identify the "life-world" with what we called at the beginning of this analysis the "own sphere of belonging." On the contrary, the *Lebenswelt* forms the counterpole of constitution, not the reduced terminus from which constitution sets out, but rather the attained terminus toward which it is oriented.

Here at the end of our study we can indicate how this long and patient meditation completes the whole of the *Cartesian Meditations.* What has become of the initial project of a philosophical science? By placing these meditations under the patronage of Descartes, Husserl asserted the principle of a universal science beginning from an absolute foundation. What after all has become of this project?

Under the name of philosophical science Husserl means three things: first he means *radicality* in the manner of raising the question of the starting point; next he means the *universality* of a method devoted to the explication of strata and levels of sense; and finally he means the *systematic character* of structures thus brought to light.[21] Do the *Cartesian Meditations,* and in particular does the Fifth Meditation, meet this definition of philosophical science? It can be said that they satisfy this initial requirement, but only at the price of a profound transformation of the project.

(1) Where the radicality of the point of departure is concerned, the most evident result of the *Cartesian Meditations* is to have moved this departure point back further than the Cartesian cogito. Husserl can proudly say in his Epilogue: "There is only one radical coming to awareness of oneself (*radikale Selbstbesinnung*), that of phenomenology" (CM, p. 179:34). We began with a cogito responsive to the Idea of a universal science, one which would be only an epistemological subject. The Fourth and Fifth Meditations forced us to refer the origin of all sense to a singular subjectivity and to a monadic intersubjectivity, for egology and monadology are from now on the locus (*lieu*) of all possible sense. Thus, Husserl breaks with the tradition of the impersonal subject inherited as much from Cartesianism as from Kantianism and Neo-Kantianism. By thus orienting the departure

21. Epilogue, § 64: "Our meditations . . . have essentially reached their goal, in particular to show the concrete possibility of the Cartesian Idea of a universal science beginning from an absolute foundation. The demonstration of this concrete possibility and its practical realization—even though, of course, in the form of endless programs—is nothing other than a necessary and indubitable beginning and an equally necessary method—which, at the same time, allows delineating a system of problems that may be set up without absurdity. This is the point which we have reached" (CM, p. 178:23–33).

point toward the most particularized subject and toward the intersubjective network, Husserl opens the way for the new investigations which form the *Crisis* cycle and which end, seven years later, in one of the major books of Husserlian phenomenology, *The Crisis of the European Sciences and Transcendental Phenomenology*.

(2) As for the method of explication (*Auslegung*), the Fifth Meditation reveals it in all of its richness and perhaps also in its profound contradiction. We have seen it oscillate between an acute sense of the concrete and a no-less-pressing demand for the radical. The taste for the concrete carries phenomenology toward an ever-more-ample recapitulation of human experience, much like the Hegelian phenomenology. Thus, phenomenology becomes a description of an ongoing totalization, whose most distant horizon is the *Lebenswelt*. But in the period of the *Cartesian Meditations*, Husserl is possessed by a more fundamental intention of subordinating this progression toward the concrete and toward the total, to the movement of regression toward the foundation which more than ever consists in the ego.

One can compare this double development with that which in a parallel manner animates the *Logic* of 1929. *Formal and Transcendental Logic* begins with an expansion which opens up formal logic into the mathematical logic of the moderns and issues out in a *mathesis universalis* which leads, as in the *Cartesian Meditations*, toward a primordial experience, toward subjectivity and intersubjectivity. Accordingly, these two contemporary works are to be taken together and read in the same way. Moreover, the phenomenological philosophy, to which the *Cartesian Meditations* opens the way (CM, §§ 59 f.), includes the results of these two contemporary works. What Husserl calls "ontological explication" (*ontologische Explikation*) consists in an unfolding of strata of sense (nature, animality, psyche, culture, personality), the superimposition of which constitutes "the world as constituted sense." This unfolding represents quite well what we have called the movement toward the concrete, that is to say, the movement toward the world of man. But this successive reading of strata of sense remains static for as long as these constituted senses are not attached to the different steps in the constitution of the ego: the primordial ego, the alien ego, and the community of monads. The progressive and synthetic movement toward the concrete thus remains firmly subordinated to the regressive and analytic movement toward the original and the radical.

"Explication," thus, is held midway between a philosophy of construction and a philosophy of description. Against Hegelianism and its successors and against all "metaphysical construction," Husserl maintains that phenomenology does not "create" but instead "discovers"

(CM, p. 168:2–3). This is the hyperempirical side of phenomenology. Explication is an explication of experience.

> Phenomenological explication does nothing else—and this can never be emphasized too much—but explicate the sense that the world has for all of us prior to all philosophy and which manifestly our experience gives to it. This sense can be analyzed (*enthüllt*) by philosophy, but never modified (*geändert*) by it. And in each actual experience it is surrounded—for essential reasons and not because of our weakness—with horizons in need of clarification (*Klärung*) (CM, p. 177:14–22).

But on the other hand, by linking explication in this way with the clarification of horizons, phenomenology seeks to go beyond the static description which would make it a simple geography of sense-strata, a descriptive stratigraphy of experience. For the transferring operations from the ego toward the Other, then toward objective nature, finally toward history—as we have seen—realize a progressive constitution, a gradual composition, finally a "universal genesis," of what we live through naïvely as "life-world."

Thus, the elucidation of the experience of the Other provides the occasion for disassembling the mechanism of the Husserlian explication (*Auslegung*). This explication realizes a harmonious equilibrium between tendencies which, were they separated, would lead back to the constructivism of German idealism and to the empiricism of the British tradition.

(3) It is more difficult to say to what extent the *Cartesian Meditations* satisfy the requirement of system. Phenomenology cannot be systematic in the sense that the cogito for Descartes furnishes the first link in a chain of truths. The Husserlian cogito is not a truth to be followed by other truths in an "order of reasons." The cogito plays, rather, the role of "origin" (*Ursprung*), of "antecedent foundation," instead of that of initial theorem. Even less can phenomenology be a system in the Hegelian sense of the word, inasmuch as it ignores the tragedy of negation and the logical sublation of this tragedy. Nevertheless, in Husserl there is a project of a system which remains in a programmatic state but to which he expressly relates his notion of philosophy as science.

Referring to the "metaphysical results of our explication of the experience of the Other" (CM, § 60), Husserl presents the intermonadic constitution as a "consequential justification of the world of objective experience." He means by this that the intermonadic relation includes a structure resistant to our arbitrary actions; from this structure proceeds the objective order. Between the Cartesian and the Hegelian models of system the Leibnizian model suggests itself here.

Actually, there is a system if one can pass beyond the infinite multiplicity of monads to the unity of the monadological world. Leibniz has seen clearly the condition under which this passage is possible. It rests upon the laws of compossibility: "All possibilities are not compossibilities." In the same way phenomenology would be possible as science if it could be shown that the free intersubjective combinations are limited by a "system of a priori incompossibilities." Husserl affirms this once with much force: my existence has a determinate structure which "prescribes" (vorschreibt), "predetermines" (vorzeichnet) a compossible universe, a closed world of monads (CM, p. 168:8–9).

Can such a program be carried out? Can one determine anything other than a general style of coherence, that is to say, the general conditions of coexistence among subjects? Husserl himself admits the difficulty, after having said in the language of metaphysics that "the first being in itself (en soi) which serves as foundation for all that is objective in the world is transcendental intersubjectivity, the totality of monads which unite into different forms of community and communion" (CM, p. 182:11–14). He declares that this intermonadic structure provides only a framework of ideal possibilities. But once more within this framework all the questions of "contingent facticity" arise: death, destiny, the possibility of authentic life, the problem of the sense of history, and the like. Hence, the "monadological system" is only a prepared structure for ethico-religious problems, "a ground on which every question that might have a possible sense must be raised" (CM, p. 182:22–24). Thus, the only system that phenomenology can conceive remains a system of compossibilities, that is finally to say a system of possibilities. This system leaves out all of the ultimate questions. It is only a system of "sense possible for us."

This is the modesty of ambition which, together with the firmness of rational project, is expressed in the final notion of a universal coming to self-awareness (universale Selbstbesinnung). The word "universal" recalls the project of philosophy as science. But the phrase "coming to self-awareness" brings to mind that every totality of ideal possibilities, no matter how well interconnected, rests finally upon the power of each of us to return to the ego in reflection.

Let us repeat with Husserl the admirable words which conclude not only the Fifth Meditation but also the whole course of the Cartesian Meditations:

> The Delphic motto, "know thyself" (γνῶθι σαυτόν) has gained a new sense. Positive science is a science of being which is lost in the world. But then I must lose this world by epoché in order to regain it by a universal coming to self-awareness. "Noli foras ire," says St. Augustine, "in te redi, in interiori homine habitat veritas" (CM, p. 183:4–9).

6 / Husserl and the Sense of History

THE APPEARANCE of a concern for history in the last phase of Husserl's thought raises a number of questions the most important of which go beyond Husserl's preoccupation and involve the possibility of a philosophy of history in general. Our first question is directed only toward a psychological understanding of the author: What motives stand behind this transformation of Husserl's set of problems? Here we have a thinker naturally unaccustomed to political concerns—apolitical, one could say, by formation, taste, profession, and by his care for scientific strictness—who comes to an awareness of a collective crisis of humanity, a thinker who no longer speaks only of the transcendental ego but also of European man, of his destiny, his possible decline, and his necessary rebirth, a thinker who situates his own philosophy in history with the conviction that it is responsible to this European man and that it alone can show him the way to his renewal. Not content to think about history, to think himself into history, the phenomenologist assumes the surprising task of founding a new age, just as Socrates and Descartes did.

The works we shall call upon date from the period 1935–39. We may suspect that from 1930 on, Husserl began to relate the understanding of his own philosophy to the understanding of history, more specifically to the understanding of the history of the European spirit. On May 7, 1935, Husserl delivered a lecture at the Vienna *Kulturbund* under the title "Philosophy and the Crisis of European Humanity." In November, 1935, this lecture was followed by a series of lectures to the "Prague Philosophic Circle for Research into Human Understanding." All of these manuscripts belong with the large work entitled *The Crisis of the European Sciences and Transcendental Phenomenology.* (The first two parts were published in 1936 by the Belgrade journal *Philosophia;* the third part alone is twice as long as the first two parts.)

[143]

Together these manuscripts compose the group of works referred to as the *Crisis*. They include the first draft of the Vienna lecture, the text probably used at the conference, a reworked version (which I have translated into French),[1] another more complete formulation of this same piece, the whole text of the *Crisis,* and various texts not originally destined for publication which contain meditations following along the same lines.[2]

The political situation in Germany at that time is visibly in the background of this whole course of thought, and in this sense one can surely say that it was the very tragedy of history which inclined Husserl to think historically. Suspected by the Nazis as a non-Aryan, as a scientific thinker, and more fundamentally as a man of Socratic and questioning spirit, the aging Husserl, retired and condemned to silence, could not fail to discover that the spirit has a history which is of importance to all history, that the spirit can become ill, that history is even a place of danger for the spirit and a place of possible failure. This discovery was inevitable, since the sick themselves—the Nazis—were the ones who were to denounce all rationalism as decadent thought and were to impose new biological criteria for political and spiritual health. In any event, it was through awareness of crisis in the time of National Socialism that Husserl actually entered into history. Out of respect for rationalism, someone had to say who was ill and hence to point to the sense and the senselessness of man.

We should add that not far from him his former collaborator, Martin Heidegger, was developing a work which from another angle also signified the condemnation of classic philosophy and called, at least implicitly, for another reading of history, another interpretation of the contemporary drama, and another distribution of responsibilities. Thus, the most non-historic of professors was summoned by history to interpret himself historically.

But it remains to be understood how historical perspectives could

1. "La Crise de l'humanité européenne et la philosophie," *Revue de métaphysique et de morale,* LV (July–October, 1950), 225–58. The German text of *Crisis: Die Krisis der Europäischen Wissenschaften und die Transcendentale Philosophie, Husserliana VI,* ed. Walter Biemel (The Hague, 1954) [cf. n. 1, p. 144]. [For an English translation of the Vienna lecture, cf. Lauer, *Edmund Husserl: Phenomenology and the Crisis of Philosophy* (New York and Evanston, Ill., 1965), pp. 149–92.]

2. [Professor Ricoeur worked from the manuscripts to which he refers and published this article five years before the publication of *Husserliana VI,* the definitive text of *Crisis.* The citations from *Crisis* in this article will be translated from the French article, but the page numbers will refer to *Husserliana VI.* Textual references to *Crisis* will be designated by the letter C, with the page number following; references to *Ideas I* will continue to be indicated by the letter I, followed by the page number, which refers to the *Jahrbuch* edition.—Trans.]

be incorporated into phenomenology. Here the transformation of a set of philosophical problems goes beyond any explication of psychological motivation, for the coherence of transcendental phenomenology is in question. How can a philosophy of the cogito, of the radical return to the ego as founder of all being, become capable of a philosophy of history?

It is possible to answer this question in part through an examination of the Husserlian texts. Up to a certain point, the unity of Husserl's thought is uncovered if one strongly emphasizes the mediating role between consciousness and history which is assigned to Ideas (to Ideas in the Kantian sense). These Ideas are taken as infinite tasks implying an unending progress and hence a history. But if human time is a development ordered by an infinite Idea—as one already sees in Kant (e.g., in *The Idea of a Universal History from the Cosmological Point of View* and in other short writings on the philosophy of history)—this movement from a philosophy of the ego to a philosophy of historical humanity poses a number of radical questions which involve all Socratic, Cartesian, and Kantian philosophies, all philosophies of the cogito in the broad sense. We shall raise these questions at the appropriate time.

[I]   THE OPPOSITION OF TRANSCENDENTAL PHENOMENOLOGY
TO HISTORICAL CONSIDERATIONS

NOTHING in Husserl's foregoing work would appear to prepare for his turning phenomenology in the direction of a philosophy of history. Rather, there seem to be reasons for its never turning in that direction.

(1) The transcendental phenomenology expressed in *Ideas*, in *Formal and Transcendental Logic,* and in the *Cartesian Meditations* does not cancel but rather in a specific manner integrates the logical concern which governs the *Logical Investigations*.[3] Now this logical concern excludes a certain sense of history. The lesson of the *Logical Investigations* is that the sense of a logical structure—either narrowly conceived as formal logic, even if enlarged to a *mathesis universalis* (I, §§ 8 and 10), or broadly conceived as the material ontologies which analyze the supreme genera presiding over the "region" nature, the "region" consciousness, etc.—is independent of the history of the individual consciousness or of the history of humanity which points to the discovery or the elaboration of this sense. The sense is revealed as sense

3. On the relation of "logicism" to transcendental phenomenology, see my "Introduction to *Ideas I.*" [Cf. above, pp. 28 ff.]

to the intuition, which discerns its articulations. The history of the concept, as an expression of the sense, is of no consequence to the truth of the sense. The truth is not acquired like a functional aptitude is acquired among animate species. Truth remains a nonhistorical relation between an "empty" or "unfulfilled" intentive process (*visée*) and an intuitive presence (sensuous perception, introspection, perception of the Other, "categorial" perception,[4] etc., or their modification in imagination or memory) which "fulfills" that process.

Husserlian thought overcame psychologism at the beginning, and this conquest remained the presupposition of all subsequent transcendental philosophy. Thus in the very beginning, philosophy of history was challenged in the respect in which history is grasped as an evolution, as a genesis where the more rational is derived from the less rational, and in general, where the more is derived from the less. In this respect, the atemporality of the objective sense is inaccessible to an empiricistic generation of subjective approximations to this sense.

The philosophy of essence, which at the level of *Ideas I* continues the "logicism" of the *Logical Investigations*, confirms this mistrust of genetic explanations. The "eidetic reduction," which parenthesizes the individual case and retains only the sense (and the conceptual signification which it expresses), is in itself a reduction of history. The real is related to essence as the contingent is to the necessary, for every essence "has" a field of individuals which can be here or there, now or at some other time (cf. I, p. 8).

Note how cautiously Husserl uses the word "origin" (*Ursprung*). Early in *Ideas I* he is careful to observe: "We are not talking here in terms of history. This word for origins neither forces nor authorizes us to think of any genesis understood in the sense of psychological causality or in the sense of a historical development . . ." (I, p. 7 n). The notion of origin cannot reappear except at another stage of thought, at a properly transcendental stage, where it no longer signifies historico-causal genesis but rather grounding.[5]

The "logicism" of the *Logical Investigations* and the "eidetic reduction" of *Ideas I* indicate a clear victory over a certain sort of intrusion of history into philosophy. We can be assured that the history of the spirit (*esprit*), which will be considered below, will never be a genesis of sense that starts from the insignificant, an evolution of the Spencerian kind. The development of the Idea which history will imply will be something other than the genesis of the concept.

(2) Phenomenology's properly transcendental problem-set in-

---

4. Cf. Sixth Logical Investigation, Second part.
5. Cf. the two usages of *Ursprung* in I, § 56 (p. 108) and I, § 122 (p. 253).

cludes no manifest historical concern; rather, it seems to eliminate this concern by the initial operation of "transcendental reduction."

A few words will be useful in order to locate the transcendental reduction within the group of problems belonging to the whole of phenomenology. By means of this reduction consciousness rids itself of a naïveté which it has beforehand and which Husserl calls the natural attitude. This attitude consists in spontaneously believing that the world which is there is simply given. In correcting itself about this naïveté, consciousness discovers that it is itself giving, sense-giving (*Sinngebende*) (I, § 55). The reduction does not exclude the presence of the world; it takes nothing back. It does not even suspend the primacy of intuition in every cognition. After the reduction consciousness continues seeing, but without being absorbed in this seeing, without being lost in it. Rather, the very seeing itself is discovered as a doing (*opération*), as a producing (*œuvre*),[6] once Husserl even says "as a creating." [7] Husserl would be understood—and the one who thus understands him would be a phenomenologist—if the intentionality which culminates in seeing were recognized to be a creative vision.[8]

We cannot dwell here on the difficulties involved in the interpretation of this central theme of phenomenology; just let us say that the natural attitude is only understood when it is reduced, and it is not reduced except when the constitution of all sense and of all being is positively elicited. Thus, one cannot first say what the natural attitude is, then what the reduction of it is, and finally what constitution is, for one must understand these three points of the phenomenological problem-set en bloc.

Now, what interests us here is that at the time of *Ideas I* Husserl counted among the disciplines of the natural attitude not only the sciences of nature but also the human sciences (*Geisteswissenschaften*), for history, the sciences of civilization, and sociological disciplines of all sorts are "mundane" (I, p. 8). In Husserlian language, spirit just like social reality is a "transcendence," that is to say, an object (*Gegenstand*) into which pure consciousness goes beyond itself. Spirit is "outside" just like nature, which is its first basis, just like the body where consciousness objectifies itself, and just like the soul understood as individual psychic reality. The mundaneity of spirit signifies that it is encountered among the objects of a conscious subject and that it must be constituted facing consciousness, "in"

6. On *Vollzug* and *Leistung*, cf. I, § 122.

7. "The spontaneity of what one can call the creative beginning (*le commencement créateur*) . . ." (I, § 122).

8. On "originary giving intuition," cf. I, pp. 36 and 242.

consciousness, as the correlate of certain fundamental acts which posit spirit in the world, in history, and in societies. The "sciences of the spirit" in this sense must initially be reduced (I, p. 108), for instead of losing us in the historical and in the social as in an absolute, we suspend believing in the being-there (*Dasein*) of the spirit just as in that of things. Henceforth, we know that the spirit of historical societies has being only for and even through an absolute consciousness which constitutes it (I, p. 142). Here is the source, we believe, of all subsequent difficulties; for how are we to understand on the one hand that the historical man is constituted in an absolute consciousness and on the other hand that the sense that history develops includes the phenomenological man who effects (*opère*) this consciousness? A difficult dialectic seems to be presented here of the including and the included, between the transcendental ego and the sense which unifies history.

Without going further into this difficulty we can say that the enterprise of constituting man (that is to say, the psycho-physical soul, the psycho-social person, and the spirit as historical reality) was actually undertaken by Husserl in *Ideas II*. In the second part of that major text there is a long analysis of the operations of consciousness by which the body is elaborated as a living organism and then as the expression and mode of action of the Other, and finally there is an analysis of the operations of consciousness by which the social relations among persons are constituted.

Hence, at the stage of *Ideas I* and *II*, there is no privileged place for history. To the contrary, historical man is a moment, a level of mundanity, a "stratum" of the constituted world, since in this sense he is "included," like any "transcendence," into absolute consciousness.

(3) It is true that history, twice excluded—as explanatory genesis and as the relevant reality of the historian and the sociologist—can re-emerge in a more subtle fashion at the very heart of the transcendental consciousness "in" which nature and history are constituted. This consciousness is always temporal. It is a life which goes on. Every sense is constituted in a "multiplicity" (*Mannigfaltigkeit*) of successive adumbrations as a unity binding this succession together. Bit by bit, by convergent movements in time, the blue of the sea, the expression on a face, the technical sense of a piece of equipment, the aesthetic sense of a work of art, the legal sense of an institution, etc., are elaborated. For example, time is the manifest dimension of the most primitive consciousness, the consciousness of things, of that which "gives" the very first stratum of mundane existence. The perceptibility of things yet unknown is the possibility that new aspects will

appear in an infinite time, aspects which will confirm or disconfirm the nascent sense or will motivate a new sense.[9] Hence, absolute consciousness is temporal along a threefold horizon of memory, expectation, and instantaneous compresence.

Cosmic time reduced reveals phenomenological time, which is the unifying time of all subjective processes. It is true that this time is in turn an enigma to the degree that the absolute of the transcendental ego is still an absolute only from a certain point of view (in relation to transcendences) and calls for a proto-constitution rife with difficulties.[10] There is no use involving ourselves here in the radical difficulties which surround the primordial constitution of the phenomenological consciousness of time which Husserl first elaborated in 1905 in *Lectures on Internal Time Consciousness*. These difficulties would take us away from our problem, for, in effect, this primitive mode of connection of one conscious subjective process to another such process, this proto-synthesis, is a time, but it is not yet a history. History is "outside," whereas time is consciousness itself.

If it be said that time is constituted, this is not in the same sense as that which is outside is constituted. Time is proto-constituted in the sense that every movement beyond consciousness into a transcendent object, a movement which unifies adumbrations or aspects of the transcendent thing, presupposes that each present consciousness move beyond itself in an immanent manner, go beyond itself temporally into another consciousness. Thus, the consciousness becomes the immediate past of a new present for which there still is an imminent future. The transcendental time which is constitutive and, furthermore, proto-constituted, is not transcendent history. The latter history is only the correlate of a consciousness which elaborates it by perceiving traces in documents, by understanding Others through these documents, by elaborating the sense of a community which develops in cosmic time (sidereal time, clock time, and calendar time). In this respect phenomenological time is the absolute in which nature, men, cultures, and history are constituted as objects.

All the same, it is not without interest that the ultimate consciousness is temporal itself. If the history of the historians is reduced and constituted, another history much closer to the giving and operating consciousness could perhaps be elaborated. In this way, with the theme of phenomenological time, transcendental phenomenology places a pointer in the direction of a philosophy of history.

(4) Another problem must be indicated where the hiatus appears

9. On all of this, cf. I, pp. 74 ff., 202 ff., and the Second Cartesian Meditation.
10. I, p. 163 and, above all, the Fourth Cartesian Meditation.

between the phenomenological problem-set and that of a possible philosophy of history. With phenomenological time there also appears a transcendental ego, for the ego is not merely mundane, given as a psychological object and thus as something to reduce and constitute. There is an ego which lives in every constituting consciousness, but no word can be said about it, except that it lives a world (thing, man, work of art, etc.) through such an intentive process (I, p. 109). This is the one which perceives, imagines, senses, wills, etc. The ego of the cogito cannot become the object of inquiry; it cannot be "thematized." One can only come upon its "ways of relating itself to . . ." (I, p. 160)—for example, how it pays attention to . . . , suspends or posits, passively maintains a perception, actively advances by joining one act to another. There is then, at the most, a phenomenology of the *how* of the ego, although there is none of the *quid* of the ego. The affirmation that the ego differs numerically with each stream of consciousness emerges from this phenomenology "turned toward the subjective face" of the cogito. Hence, there is an axiom of indiscernibles which institutes a plurality of egos, a plurality which is not the constituted mundane plurality of psychological consciousnesses (I, pp. 165 and 167).

Is this plurality of consciousnesses the chance for a history? In the last analysis, yes, since the unifying sense of a human history will have the plurality of consciousnesses for its field of development. But it is quite necessary to note the extent to which transcendental phenomenology encounters obstacles on the fringes of the notion of history. Just as the time of the ego is not the unique human history but rather the time of each ego, so too the plurality of egos is not history either. Two difficulties remain:

In the first place, the plurality of egos appears to be quite absolute. How, then, can we make one history with many consciousnesses? We shall see that the philosophy of the Idea from the period of the *Crisis* answers to this difficulty. Even if one can strictly understand that the plurality of consciousnesses and the singularity of history can become correlative through the intermediary function of a common task, the second difficulty seems still harder to overcome. "In" which consciousness is the plurality of consciousnesses posited? The plurality which a unifying sense, a historical task, somehow traverses cannot be seen from above in such a way that I, thou, we, others, appear combinable into a totality; such an act would make this totality into an absolute which would dethrone the ego. This obstacle to a philosophy of history stands out with emphasis for the reader of the Fifth Cartesian Meditation. We shall return to this point at the end of this study when we shall have a better understanding of the nature of history.

[II] VIEWS OF THE TELEOLOGY OF HISTORY AND RE

HISTORY, as we were saying, thrust its way into the preoccupations of the most nonhistorical and apolitical of philosophers through the consciousness of crisis. A crisis of culture is like a grave doubt on the ladder of history. Certainly, it does not perform the function of methodological doubting unless grasped as a philosophical questioning by the consciousness of everyone. But, thus transformed into a question which I raise to myself, the consciousness of crisis remains within history. It is a question both about history and in history: Where is man going? that is to say: What is the sense and the goal for us, we who are humanity?

Thus, the initial question for the philosophy of history goes from the crisis to the Idea, from the doubting to the sense. The consciousness of crisis calls for a reaffirmation of a task, but a task which by its structure is a task for everyone, a task which develops a history. In return, history lends itself to a philosophical reflection only through the intermediary of its teleology, for it appears to be implied by an original type of rational structure which specifically requires a history. There is no direct reflection on history as a flux of events, but there is an indirect reflection on it as the advent of a sense. In this way, history is a function of reason, its own mode of realization.

From the first lines of his Vienna lecture Husserl's perspective is fixed; the philosophy of history and teleology are synonymous. He writes:

> I wish to try . . . [to give] its whole breadth to the Idea of European humanity, considered from the point of view of the philosophy of history or even in the teleological sense. On this occasion in explicating the essential function which can be taken over by philosophy and by the sciences which are its ramifications, I am also trying to submit the European crisis to a new elucidation (C, p. 314).

We shall return later to the two convictions which are immediately presupposed here: that it is in Europe that man has a "teleological sense," an "Idea," and that this Idea is philosophy itself as the totality of understanding and as the infinite perspective of the sciences.

Even more neatly, the beginning of the first part of *Crisis* links history to philosophy through the intermediary of the "teleological sense":

> This writing . . . seeks to found the ineluctable necessity of a conversion of philosophy into transcendental phenomenology as a means to teleologi-

cal-historical investigation of sense (*Besinnung*) applied to the origins (*Ursprünge*) of the critical situation where we now find ourselves in the sciences and in philosophy. Hence this writing constitutes an independent introduction to transcendental phenomenology.

Thus, history is so little a secondary addition to philosophy that it becomes a privileged way of access to its set of problems. If history is only to be grasped through the Idea realized in it, then the movement of history can become for the philosopher the original revealer of transcendental themes, if it is true that such themes are those which give history its properly human quality.

But before entering further into the methodological questions raised by the notion of historical teleology and by the use of this teleology as an "independent introduction to transcendental phenomenology," it will be useful to give a brief notion of how the method is applied. In this respect, the reworked text of the Vienna conference is more illuminating than the second part of *Crisis* which, by reason of its fragmentary character, does not let major agreements become evident. *Crisis,* Part Two, is a history of philosophy from Galileo to Kant. Its over-all views of the European spirit and the relations of philosophy of history to reflective philosophy in the transcendental style are quite rare though quite precise (in particular §§ 6, 7, and, above all, 15; we shall return to this).

Only Europe has an "immanent teleology," a "sense," while India and China have merely an empirical-sociological type. Europe has the unity of a spiritual form. It is not a geographic place but a spiritual connection which is the intention of "a life, an action, a spiritual kind of creation." The elevation given to the notion of spirit (*Geist*) is already visible. It is no longer stuck into a corner of nature but is kept beside constituting consciousness, to the extent that the connection among men is not that of a simple sociological type but rather that of a "teleological sense."

The affirmation that only Europe has an Idea appears less astonishing if complemented in two ways. In the first place, it is necessary to say that, absolutely speaking, it is humanity as a whole which has a sense. Europe did not cut itself off geographically and culturally from the remainder of humanity (*Menschenheit*) except by discovering the sense of man (*Menchentum*), for what sets it apart is precisely Europe's universality. In addition, the only Idea that can be an Idea for everyone is philosophy. Philosophy is the "innate entelechy" of Europe, the "proto-phenomenon" of its culture. Indeed, to be European is less a glory which particularizes than a responsibility which relates to all. Again, it is necessary fully to understand this term: philosophy. Understood as the sense of European man, it is not a system, a school, or a work with a date, but an Idea in the Kantian sense of the term; it is a task. The Idea of philosophy, this is the teleology of history. This is why the philosophy of history in the end is the history of philosophy, itself indistinguishable from philosophy's coming to self-awareness.

But, what is philosophy as an Idea, as a task? What is its relation to the whole of civilization? From the start, to designate philosophy as an Idea is to emphasize its two traits of totality and infinity. Husserl even calls it a telos, an end aimed at, for it is the telos of the science of the whole of being. Because it is directed toward the achievement of the science of all that is, the Idea of philosophy can be only a "normative form situated at infinity," a pole at "infinity." Each historical realization of philosophy still has the inaccessible Idea for its horizon.

By means of its infinity the Idea signifies a history, an unending process. Before history and outside of history, man does have a historicity; still, he has only finite tasks, closed ones, tasks without horizons, measured by short-range interests, and governed by tradition. In the Sixth Century there appeared in Greece "the man of infinite tasks." The Idea of philosophy was borne along by a few isolated individuals, by a few groups who immediately destroyed the limited tranquillity belonging to "the man of finite tasks." Then, the leap was made from the will-to-live to astonishment, from opinion to science. A doubt was born in the heart of the tradition. The question of truth arose. The universal was demanded. An "inner community" gathered around the enterprise of knowing. This philosophizing community spread its influence out beyond itself through culture and education and bit by bit transformed the sense of civilization.

Thus, Husserl sees Occidental history led by the philosophical function, understood as free, universal reflection, embracing all ideals both theoretical and practical as well as the ideal of the totality of these ideals, embracing, in short, the infinite whole of all norms. This function is the "archon-function":

> Without a doubt universal philosophy and all the particular sciences represent a partial aspect of European culture, but all of my interpretation implies that this part exercises, so to speak, the role of the brain. The true spiritual sanity of Europe depends upon its normal functioning (C, p. 338).

If such is European humanity, a Europe having signification through the Idea of philosophy, the crisis of Europe can be only a methodological distress which affects understanding not in its partial realizations but in its central intention. For there is no crisis in physics, in mathematics, etc., but there is a crisis in the very project of knowing, in the directive Idea which gives science its scientific character (*Wissenschaftlichkeit*) (C, §§ 2 ff.). This crisis is objectivism, the reduction of the infinite task of knowing to the mathematico-physical knowing which has been its most brilliant realization.

We shall return later to the signification of this crisis, and we shall follow the reverse path of reflection, the return from the history of philosophy to philosophy. Then phenomenology will be envisaged as the catharsis of the sick man. Now that we have summarized the Husserlian interpretation of the history of the Occident, we are in a position to envisage the methodological problems implied in it.

The relations between philosophical reflection and the interpretation of history clearly shape the critical issue: How is one to recognize the historical teleology? By direct inspection of history? But will the professional historian agree to read the entire history of the Occident as the advent of philosophy? If philosophy whispers the password into the historian's ear, what good is this detour through history? Why not take the short way of reflection?

The Vienna conference contains only a few allusions to this difficulty which manifestly dictates the rhythm of the philosophy of the *Crisis*. But on the other hand, some sections of the *Crisis* directly broach this major methodological issue.[11]

For one thing, it is clear that a philosophical presentiment leads to understanding history as the advent of a sense, as a development (*Entwickelung*) in the direction of an eternal pole, thus as a passing from social typology to the Idea of man—all the more reason for avoiding the delusion of a zoology of peoples. "This presentiment serves us as an intentional guide for discerning within the history of Europe an interconnection of the highest signification, for in following it step by step we elevate the presentiment to the dignity of controlled certitude. Presentiment is in all orders of discovery the affective detector" (C, p. 321).

More emphatically, § 15 of *Crisis*, entitled "Reflections on the Method of Our Historical Considerations," emphasizes the contrast of this method with the historical method of the historian. The investigation of a teleology is inseparable from the project of "creating clarity within oneself." History is a moment in the understanding of ourselves insofar as we cooperate in this history.

> We are trying to disengage the *unity* which prevails through all historical setting up of goals, by way of the contrast and continuity of their transformations. As the consequence of a constant critique which holds fast only to the interconnectedness of the whole of history (like the

11. In particular, §§ 7, 9 (the end), 15, and some of the manuscripts on *Geschichtsphilosophie*.

coherence of a person), we are trying finally to grasp reflectively the historic task which we alone are able to recognize as being our own personally. One's glance does not start from the exterior, from the fact, as if the temporal becoming in which we ourselves become were only a simple external causal succession. The glance proceeds from the *interior*. We who do not have merely a spiritual heritage, but who from beginning to end are nothing but beings in becoming according to the historical spirit (*historisch-geistig Gewordene*); only by virtue of this fact do we have a task which is truly ours (C, pp. 71 f.).

Because history is our history, the sense of history is our sense:

> That sort of elucidation of history by which we return to ourselves in order to question the original foundation (*die Urstiftung*) of the goals which connect the chain of the generations to come, . . . this elucidation, I say, is only the authentic coming to awareness by the philosopher of the *true end of his willing*, of what is willing in him, *comes from willing*, and is willing *as such* from his spiritual ancestors (C, p. 72).

Perhaps, it will be said, these texts clearly demonstrate that the history of the spirit has no autonomy; rather, this history relates back to self-understanding. Those who say this do not show that self-understanding must come about through the history of the spirit. This is the new fact in Husserl's thought: the fundamental traits of the ideal of philosophy are not to be read in history. History is neither imaginary nor a vain detour. Since reason as infinite task implies a history, a progressive realization, history is the privileged revealer of a suprahistorical sense. I can know who I am through uncovering an origin (*Ursprung*), a primal institution (*Urstiftung*), which is also a project toward the future horizon, a final institution (*Endstiftung*). This historical character of self-understanding is manifest when one relates it to the struggle against prejudice. Descartes affirmed that evidence is a conquest over prejudice. Now, prejudice always has a historical signification. It is ancestral before being childish. It belongs to the order of the "sedimented" (C, § 15). The sort of thing which is "a matter of course" (*Selbstverständlichkeit*) is "the basis (*Boden*) of all private and nonhistorical work" (C, p. 73).

On the other hand, I can free myself from a settled or sedimented history only by renewing contact with the sense "buried" (*verborgene*) under the "sedimentations" by making it again present, by presentiating it (*vergegenwärtigen*). Thus, by a single gesture I apprehend the teleological unity of history and the depth of interiority. I have access to myself only by again apprehending the aim of my forefathers, and this I understand only by instituting it as the present sense of my life.

This process, at once historical and reflective, Husserl terms *Selbstbesinnung*.[12]

In short, history alone restores the breadth of infinity and totality to the subjective task of philosophy. Every philosopher offers an interpretation of himself, a key to his philosophy:

> But when we have inquired by a historical investigation, however precise, into these "private interpretations" (even when made for a whole series of philosophers), we shall be none the wiser about the ultimate *volitional intention* which dwells in the heart of all philosophers, within the hidden unity of their intentional interiority, and which alone constitutes the unity of history. Only in the positing of a final foundation (*in der Endstiftung*) is this intention revealed: for only in starting out from it can one uncover the single direction of all philosophies and all philosophers; in starting out from it one can come upon the light in which one understands the thinkers of the past as they would never have been able to understand themselves (C, p. 74).

After all, nothing is served by citing isolated texts and making explications of each of them separately, for the sense of a philosopher only emerges to a "critical view of the whole" (C, § 15) which reveals his total personal intention in relation to the total intention of the Idea of philosophy.

Hence, during the last decade of Husserl's life, historical considerations prompted a profound transformation of the sense of philosophy itself. The appearance of new expressions like *Selbstbesinnung* and *Menschentum* (humanity) is already a remarkable indication of this evolution of reflective philosophy.

In order to bring all the new acquisitions of Husserl's thought together into a single expression—acquisitions developing out of the encounter with historical reflection—by taking up again the Kantian contrast between reason and understanding, one can say that phenomenology developed into a philosophy of dynamic reason. (This *rapprochement* with Kant could be traced rather far and within the purview of the philosophy of history.) Kant had emphasized the disproportion between the understanding as achievable regulation of the phenomena and reason as inachievable demand for totalization, for the summation of the conditioned within the unconditioned. This

---

12. [*Selbstbesinnung* is translated by Professor Ricoeur as *prise de conscience*, which he also uses to render *Besinnung*. At this point in the text he remarks parenthetically that "Husserl occasionally annotates this word with the expressions *historische Rückbesinnung* and *historische und kritische Rückbesinnung* (§ 7)." Where *prise de conscience* renders *Besinnung* we usually render it as "investigation of sense" and where it renders *Selbstbesinnung* we usually render it as "coming to self-awareness," though the full sense meant might be translated at length as "reflectively investigating the sense of one's own self."—Trans.]

demand, as everyone knows, present in each of the transcendental Ideas, gives rise to the metaphysical illusion of rational psychology, rational cosmology, and rational theology, but it survives the unmasking of the illusions under the form of regulative principles. Now in reintroducing the Platonic expression "Idea," Kant had the sense of remaining true to the genius of the Greek philosopher for whom the Idea was the indivisible principle of intelligibility (like the mathematical and cosmological Idea) and the principle of obligation and of action (like the ethical Idea: justice, virtue, etc.). Reason is always the demand for total order, and, by virtue of this, it develops an ethic of speculative thought and of the intelligibility of ethics.

Husserl picks up and continues in this Platonic and Kantian vein when he gathers under the heading of *reason* the five traits that we have presented in a scattered manner throughout the course of our analysis thus far.

(1) Reason is more than a critique of cognition; it is the task of unifying all the significational activities, speculative, ethical, aesthetic, etc. It covers the whole field of the culture whose indivisible project it is. In *Ideas I* reason had a much more speculative sense and was related to the problem of actuality. It declared the universal validity of seeing, or originary intuition, for founding evidence (on this point, see the whole fourth part of *Ideas I*, entitled "Reason and Actuality"). In this sense reason already demanded an achievement and a completeness, the completeness of all intentions in one vision.

Consequent upon its total character, reason takes on an existential accent in the *Crisis,* for it deals with "questions of the sense or senselessness of all human existence" (C, § 2); it is concerned with man's possibilities, "insofar as he freely decides in his behavior toward his human and extrahuman surrounding world, insofar as he is free in his possibilities to give a rational form to himself and to his surrounding universe" (C, § 2). Section Three emphasizes the "absolute," "eternal," "supratemporal," "unconditioned" character of these Ideas and Ideals which apply to the problem of reason; but these characters are specific in placing the dignity of man's existence beyond all purely speculative definition. Reason is the very essence of humanity (*Menschentum*), insofar as it ties the sense of man to the sense of the world (C, § 5).

(2) Reason is understood dynamically as a "becoming-rational"; it is the "coming of reason to itself." An important manuscript of this period includes this sentence (which gives it its title): "Insofar as philosophy is the coming to self-awareness of humanity, the movement of reason to actualize itself through stages of development requires as its own function that this coming to self-awareness should

develop itself by stages . . ." (C, p. 273). The same text speaks of "*ratio* in its incessant movement to clarify itself" (C, p. 273). In this way a history is possible, but possible only as the actualization of reason. Reason is not an evolution, which would be equivalent to deriving sense from senselessness, nor is it merely an adventure, which would amount to an absurd succession of senselessnesses; it is a permanence in movement, the temporal self-actualization of an eternal and infinite identity of sense.

(3) Reason has an ethical accent which is expressed in the frequently occurring term "responsibility," for as the manuscript just cited says, "Reason aims at the autonomous man's ultimately responsible self-awareness"; and again, "Reason is the will-to-be-rational" (C, p. 275).

(4) A task of an ethical character involves a time having a dramatic character, for the awareness of crisis assures us that the infinite Idea can be buried, forgotten, and even debased. The whole history of philosophy is an open struggle between an understanding of the task as infinite and its naturalistic reduction, or, as the *Crisis* puts it, between transcendentalism and objectivism. The disproportion between the Idea of philosophy and the actual possibilities of a private or common mundane cognition means that man can be a traitor. The drama is born from the fact that every actualization of the task threatens the loss of the task. Likewise, all success is ambiguous: Galileo is the greatest witness to this victory-defeat because he recovered the Idea in uncovering nature as incarnate mathematics (C, § 9). This ambiguity and this risk, written into the very teleology of history, are not without reference to the power of illusion, which, according to Kant, pertains to the very vocation of reason. Apart from the fact that Husserl regarded the illusion as positivism and not as metaphysics, only he succeeded in orienting the conflict between the unrealizable aim and the realized work—a conflict at the very heart of the human enterprise—in the direction of a historical drama. In this respect, Husserl approaches to some extent the meditations that inaugurated the philosophy of Jaspers concerning the disproportion between our quest for the absolute being and the narrowness of our existence. There too objective knowing leads us into narrowness.

(5) The infinity of the task, the movement of the realization of reason, the responsibility of the will, the risk of history, all of these categories of reason culminate in the new concept of man. No longer is there "I the man" (I, §§ 33, 49, 53), for the phenomenological reduction strikes this down as a mundane reality constituted by way of perception, empathy, historical accounts, sociological induction. There is only man as the correlate of his infinite Ideas; the Vienna lecture

speaks of "the man of infinite tasks." The manuscript cited above contains the following: "Philosophy, as the function of humanizing man . . . as human existence under its final form, this is at the same time the initial form from which humanity set out. . . ." And again: "Reason is the specific element of man. . . ." Later: "This reason makes his humanity . . . ; reason designates that towards which man insofar as he is man strives in his most intimate being, that which alone can satisfy him, make him 'happy.' "

All of § 6 of *Crisis* is devoted to this identification of European man with the struggle for reason. What distinguishes the "telos innate in European man" from the "simple empirical anthropological type" of China or India is this rational task. It is owing to reason that denumerable humanity (humanity in extension, *Menschenheit*) is subordinated to significational humanity (or humanity in comprehension, *Menschentum*), for

> the human quality (*Menschentum*) is essentially human being (*Menschsein*) within human groups (*Menschheiten*) linked by descent and social relations. And if man is a reasonable being—a rational animal—he is so only to the degree either that his humanity is humanity according to reason (*Vernunftmenschheit*), or that it is oriented latently toward reason, or manifestly toward the entelechy which *consciously* leads human becoming—once this entelechy has come to itself and become manifest for itself. Philosophy and science would from then on be *the historical movement through which universal reason is revealed,* "innate" in humanity (*Menschentum*) as such.

Thus, the notion of man qualifies the notion of reason in an existential and historical manner, while reason gives man a signification. Man is the image of his Ideas, and Ideas are like the paradigm for existence. This is why a crisis which affects science in its intention, in its Idea, or as Husserl says, in its "scientific character" (*Wissenschaftlichkeit*) is a crisis in existence. "Sciences of fact engender men of facts" (C, § 2).

> This is why the crisis in philosophy signifies the crisis of the modern sciences which are the roots of the universal philosophical trunk: a crisis at first latent, but becoming more and more manifest, which affects European man in his over-all capacity to give a sense to his cultural life (*in der gesamten Sinnhaftigkeit seines kulturellen Lebens*), in his global "existence" (*Existenz*) (C, p. 10).[13]

13. In the same way, § 7 speaks of the "existential contradiction" of contemporary culture which has lost the Idea, although it can live only from the Idea, and opposes to it the "very existential" character of our fidelity and our treason.

Husserl thus expresses the possibility of connecting a critical philosophy to an existential purpose through a philosophy of reason in history: "Every coming to awareness that develops from 'existential' premises is critical by nature" (C, p. 60).

In order to complete this tour of the horizon of the new categories of reason, let us observe the shift in sense which the notion of apodicticity has undergone. This notion, speculative par excellence, is now enlivened by the new Idea of man. *Ideas I* would call the necessity of a judgment which particularizes a general proposition of the eidetic order "apodictic" (I, § 6), and contrasts it to the simple "assertoric view of an individual" (I, § 137). In the *Crisis* group apodicticity is synonymous with that achievement which reason demands; this would be the truth of man as perfected reason; in this respect reason is the infinite pole of history and the vocation of man. The manuscript entitled "Philosophy as the Coming to Self-Awareness of Humanity" (which was not intended for publication) calls for:

> . . . the man reaching ultimate self-understanding. This man reveals himself as responsible for his own being, he understands himself as a being which consists in being called (*Sein im Berufensein*) to a life under the sign of apodicticity. This understanding would not give rise to an apodictic science of an abstract sort and in the ordinary sense of the word; it would be an understanding which would realize the totality of its concrete being under the sign of apodictic freedom, carrying this being to the level of an apodictic reason, of a reason that it makes its own throughout its whole active life. This reason makes its humanity, as we have said, through rational self-understanding.[14]

Thus, apodicticity still expresses a constraint, but the constraint of a total task. In consequence, it is not incorrect to say that Husserl's historical considerations are only the projection onto the level of collective becoming of a reflective philosophy already completed on the level of interiority. For it is in understanding the movement of history as the history of spirit that consciousness gains access to its own sense. Just as reflection gives the "intentional guide" for reading history, so history offers the "temporal guide," one might say, for recognizing the infinite reason in consciousness which struggles to humanize man.

---

14. In the same sense, see the *Crisis* (*passim* and particularly §§ 5 and 7). The philosophy of history borrows its concept of apodicticity from formal logic, just as it borrows that of entelechy from Aristotelian ontology and that of the Idea from Kantianism.

[III] FROM THE CRISIS OF EUROPEAN HUMANITY TO TRANSCENDENTAL PHENOMENOLOGY

WE CAN NOW GIVE an account of Husserl's views on the crisis of philosophy and contemporary science. These views constitute the core of the second part of *Crisis*. The analysis of the several manuscripts cited above permits us properly to situate this interpretation as limited to the contemporary period. The Renaissance is the new beginning of European man; by contrast, the Greek conversion is left in the shadows and even minimized in relation to the second birth of modern man.[15]

The three principal traits of this interpretation of the whole of the modern spirit are as follows: (1) "Objectivism" is responsible for the crisis of modern man; the whole modern enterprise of cognition is summed up in Galileo. (2) The philosophical movement which represents the Idea of philosophy in opposition to objectivism is transcendentalism, in the broad sense; it goes back to the doubt and cogito of Descartes. (3) But, because Descartes dared not follow his immense discovery to its end, it fell to transcendental phenomenology to radicalize the Cartesian discovery and victoriously to resume the struggle against objectivism, for it is thus that transcendental phenomenology feels itself responsible to modern man and capable of healing him.

This interpretation of modern philosophy as a unique combat between transcendentalism and objectivism leaves no place for strictly particular problems. Philosophers are placed in perspective, situated within this particular history, and confronted by a single dilemma: either the object or the cogito. Only the unity of the philosophical problem-set permits us to safeguard the principle of a teleology of history and finally the possibility of a philosophy of history. Let us consider these three points more closely:

(1) The originality of Husserl's views on "objectivism" resides in the fundamental distinction between the Idea of science and the methods proper to the sciences, for Husserl never dreams of carrying the debate to the area of scientific methodology or of physical theory. The crisis of principles which interests scientists like Einstein or de Broglie, or methodologists like Duhem, Meyerson, or Bachelard, is not

15. It is very curious that, contrary to the reworked text of the Vienna conference, the first part of *Crisis* goes back to Greek thought and in particular to Euclidean geometry, to assign the glory of having conceived of an infinite task of knowing (§ 8).

under consideration here, for their crises take place entirely within objectivity, concern only scientists, and can be resolved only through the progress of the sciences. The crisis in question concerns the "significance of the sciences for life" (C, § 2 is entitled: "The Crisis of Science Regarded as a Loss of Its Significance for Life") and is on the level of the Idea, of the project of man. This is a crisis which is a crisis of existence.

While partially realizing the vow to understand everything, the two genuine conquests of the modern spirit have altered the ideal of philosophy. These two conquests are the generalization of Euclidean geometry to a *mathesis universalis* of the formal type and the mathematization of nature. The first innovation is still in line with ancient science, but it goes beyond this science as infinity goes beyond the finite. It goes beyond the ancient science first by elaborating an axiomatics which circumscribes the closed field of deduction and then by carrying the abstraction of its object to the extreme. For, thanks to algebra, then to geometric analysis, and finally to a purely formal universal analysis, the new science opens out into a "theory of multiplicity" (*Mannigfaltigkeitslehre*) or "logistic," following Leibniz's old project of a universal calculus whose object would be the pure "something in general" (C, §§ 8 and 9).[16] Thus, the realm of absolute exactness is conquered. The first part to be conquered is the "limit-forms" of pure geometry, with respect to which every perceived or imagined figure is only an approximation. This realm is a closed whole, rationally connected, and susceptible to being dominated by a universal science.

The second innovation is connected with the name of Galileo; the longest and closest analyses of the second part of *Crisis* are devoted to him (§ 9 on Galileo contains no less than forty pages). He is the man who projected a science of nature where nature would be treated as a "mathematical multiplicity" similar to ideal figures. Now the motivation of this brilliant plan must be entirely reconstituted because it rests upon a "sedimented stratum" of presumptive evidences which we need to bring up to the level of consciousness. These presumptive evidences are at the base of the objectivism which has engendered our troubles.

In the first place, Galileo is heir to a geometric thought already consecrated by tradition. In drawing upon it, living consciousness no longer apperceives the "origin," to wit, the idealizing operations (*Leis-*

16. On the concept of "multiplicity," cf. the First Logical Investigation, §§ 69–72, I, § 72, and, above all, *Formal and Transcendental Logic*, §§ 28–36. In addition, see J. Cavaillès, *Sur la logique et la théorie de la science* (Paris, 1947), p. 44 ff.

tungen) which wrench the limit-forms from the perceived bedrock, from the "surrounding life-world" (*Lebenswelt* or *Lebensumwelt*) serving as the matrix of all works of consciousness.[17] "Galileo lived in the naïveté of apodictic evidence."

The second piece of petrified evidence coming from Galileo is the evidence that perceived qualities are purely "subjective" illusions and that the "true reality" is of a mathematical order. From this point on, the demand for treating nature mathematically "follows of itself." This invention, formidable in its consequences, is "naïve" and "dogmatic" in its presuppositions. The stroke of genius lay in proposing to overcome the obstacle which quality opposed to measure and calculation by treating all "subjective" qualities as the index, the announcement (*Bekundung*), of an objective quantity. But this working hypothesis, for lack of self-criticism, is not recognized as the audacity of spirit at work. Soon this "indirect mathematization of nature" could verify itself only by the success of its extension, without which the circle of hypothetical anticipation and unending verification could never be broken, for every enigma of induction is inscribed within this circle. Only a more radical reflection which relates all of physics to the foregoing presence, to the "pregivenness" of the life-world, can escape from this circle. We shall see that phenomenology performs its critical function with regard to objectivism only by way of this radical reflection.

To the pseudo-evidences that contemporary reflection discovers in Galileo's motivation must be added the speeding up of the process of "sedimentation" which followed him. Algebra brought all mathematics and mathematical physics to a "technical" stage where the manipulation of symbols as in a game of cards or checkers eliminates understanding from its own steps of thinking. Thus, science is "alienated" (*veräusserlich*) and consciousness loses the key to its own working.

For all these reasons, which could not be elucidated in Galileo's time, the founder of mathematical physics is the ambiguous genius who, in uncovering the world as applied mathematics, covers it over again as a work of consciousness (C, § 9). Here we can grasp the actual style of Husserl's historical explication, for it is clear that this inspection of Galileo's motives can only be a retrospection; the current crisis illuminates the originating motivation (*Ursprungmotivation*) at the same time that this latter renders the present disorder intelligible. The question is less one of understanding Galileo psychologically than of understanding the movement of the Idea which passes through him

17. We shall return to these two cardinal notions of *Bewusstseinsleistung* and *Lebenswelt*.

historically. Also, the only important thing is the sense of the whole which proceeds from his work and which was decided in the history that issues from that work. One could call the analysis of motivation a rational psychoanalysis much as Sartre speaks of an existential psychoanalysis, history being the special revealer of the project.

(2) The twofold illness might already have suggested that the naturalistic dogmatism had to be criticized. Why do two logics subsist, one a *mathesis universalis* and the other an experimental logic—or, if you will, two mathematics and two justifications: on the one hand, an ideal mathematics and an a priori justification, and on the other hand, a mathematics indirectly applied to nature and an a posteriori justification?

Still the most insupportable illness appears on the side of psychology, for if nature is universally mathematizable, it would be necessary to separate the psychic from the physical, since the physical is mastered only in consequence of abstraction from consciousness. Yet it would be necessary to construct the psychic after the model of physics, since the method of the natural sciences is in principle universally applicable. But the difficulties brought on by dualism and psychological naturalism vaguely attest to the fact that something was lost, namely subjectivity.

The first radical reflection on the priority of consciousness over its objects must be attributed to Descartes. By virtue of this, he is the originator of the transcendental motif, which alone is capable of destroying the dogmatic naïveté of naturalism. The first two Meditations have a further reach than one would ever expect, further than Descartes himself ever supposed. His doubt initiates every imaginable criticism of the sufficiency belonging to mathematical, physical, and sensuous evidences. He is the first to undertake to

. . . cross over the hell of the quasi-skeptical *epoché*, which no one knew how to get beyond, in order to reach the entrance to the heaven of an absolutely rational philosophy and even make this into a systematic edifice (C, p. 78).

Going almost to the end of the universal "suspension" of being, he made the "apodictic foundation" emerge: *ego cogito cogitata*. This fully elaborated formula indicates that the world, lost as the disclosure of an in-itself, can only be reaffirmed as "that which I think"; the cogitatum of the cogito is the sole indubitable being of the world. In enlarging the sphere of the cogito, which is impervious to doubt, to the cogitata, which he called ideas, Descartes implicitly posited the important principle of intentionality (C, § 20) and by this means undertook to bring all objective evidence back to the primordial evidence of the cogito.

Descartes, however, was the first to betray himself. He remained a prisoner of the evidences of Galileo; likewise, as he saw it, the truth of the physical is mathematical, and the whole enterprise of doubt and the cogito served only to reinforce objectivism. Thereafter, the I of the I-think is understood as the psychological reality, the *res cogitans* or the real psyche, which remains when one subtracts the mathematical nature. But on the other hand, it is necessary to prove that this soul has an "outside," that God is the cause of the idea of God, that the material "thing" is the cause of the idea of this world. Descartes did not see that the ego "de-mundanized" by the *epoché* is no longer soul, that the soul "appears" just as the body does, for "he did not discover that all distinctions of the type I and thou, internal and external, are 'constituted' only in the absolute ego" (C, § 19).

This misapprehension, joined with the project of confirming objective science, explains the strange destiny of Cartesianism, which engendered the rationalism of Malebranche, as well as that of Spinoza, Leibniz, and Wolff, all turned entirely toward absolute knowledge of being in itself, and also engendered skeptical empiricism, which draws out all the consequences of the psychologistic interpretation of the cogito. The first current eliminated the motif of doubt and the "reduction to the ego"; the other grossly deluded itself about the nature of founding subjectivity and destroyed truth entirely.

(3) It may appear strange that Husserl lingers longer over Galileo and Descartes than over Kant. Is Kant not the transcendental philosopher par excellence, according to his very own terminology? Why so much reticence in praising Kant at Vienna and Prague? The *Crisis* gives reasons for this mitigated admiration. The interpretation of Kant is linked with that of Hume; but the hidden sense of Hume is more profound than that of Kant, because Hume, if viewed correctly, is closer to the Cartesian doubt than Kant is. It is taken for granted that Hume, accepted as he presents himself, signifies the "bankruptcy of philosophy and the sciences" (C, p. 90). But "the true philosophical motive for unseating objectivism, hidden in the absurdity of Hume's skepticism," is finally to allow the radicalization of the Cartesian *epoché*. While Descartes swerved away from the *epoché* and thus helped to justify objectivism, the skepticism of Hume reveals every cognition of the world, both pre-scientific and scientific, to be a gigantic enigma. An absurd theory of knowledge was necessary to uncover the fact that knowledge itself is an enigma. Finally, the riddle of the world (*Welträtsel*) reached the status of a philosophical "theme." One can even go all the way and be assured that:

... the life of consciousness is a performing life (*leistendes Leben*), that it works out a legitimate or vicious being-sense (*Seinsinn*); but as intuitive consciousness on the sensuous level, and even more as scientific consciousness, it is already just such a performing life (C, p. 92).

In short, it is objectivism in general, the objectivism of both mathematical rationalism and sensuous empiricism, whose age-old foundations are shaken.

This final rehabilitation of Hume in the name of his "hidden motive" is the key to all of Husserl's reservations regarding Kant, for the philosophy of Kant responds not to the question "hidden" in the depths of Hume's skepticism but only to its manifest sense. This is why, in a profound sense, Kant is not the true successor to Hume. He remains closed up within the problems of post-Cartesian rationalism up to Wolff, and in this rationalism the momentous discovery of the first two Meditations is not present. This is why Kant returns not to the ego but rather to the forms and concepts which are still an objective moment of subjectivity. To be sure, he certainly merits the title of transcendental philosopher in that he refers the possibility of all objectivity to these forms. Thus, for the first time and in a new way "the Cartesian return to the subjectivity of consciousness is manifested in the form of a transcendental subjectivism" (C, p. 98). Still the consolidation of objectivity by this subjective founding preoccupied him more than the operation of the subjectivity which gives sense and being to the world; the reconstruction of a philosophy of the thing in itself beyond the philosophy of the phenomenon is a weighty indication of this.[18]

Thus, we must return to the Cartesian set of problems, radicalized by the "true Hume," the "true problem which animated Hume himself." This problem deserves the name of transcendental more than the Kantian theory does (C, § 26). We shall not linger over the traits belonging to this transcendental philosophy, which is the explication of this "radical transcendental subjectivism." The particular interpretation of the two closely related notions, "performance of consciousness" and "life-world," which are the chief centers of this last philosophy of Husserl, would themselves constitute a vast critical problem. In any event, the second part of *Crisis* treats them not directly but rather, by way of the philosophy of history, as an elaborated question or as a set of problems which is searched into and radicalized through the pseudo-evidences of Galileo, the Cartesian cogito, the problem of Hume, and the Kantian critique.[19]

18. Part Three of *Crisis* connects with Part Two by picking up the critique of Kant.

19. The theme of the third part of *Crisis* is specifically the life-world.

Since the "telos of European man" coincides with the advent of this transcendentalism, we shall limit ourselves to stating this "transcendental motif" in a few brief formulas.

(1) Transcendentalism is a philosophy in the form of a question. It is an inquiring back which leads to the ego as the ultimate source of every positing of being and value.

> This source bears the title: *myself*, and includes in this all of my actual and possible life of knowing, in short my concrete life in general. The whole set of transcendental problems turns about the relation of this self—of the "ego"—to what is at first posited in its place as a matter of course, viz., my psyche; then it bears once more upon the relation of this ego and my conscious life to the world of which I am conscious and whose true being I recognize in my own products of cognition (C, p. 101).

By its questioning form this philosophy holds close to the very Idea of philosophy.

(2) The "performance" (*Leistung*) is a giving of sense and being. It is necessary to go on to a radical disturbance of objectivity in order to reach the extremity of this conviction. The enigma of the world (*Welträtsel*) reveals to us the *Leistung* of consciousness.

(3) The original ego is called a life (*Leben*); in effect its first work is pre-scientific and perceptual. All mathematization of nature is "dressing" (*Kleidung*) and is secondary in relation to the original giving of a life-world. This regression to the life-world founded in the ego renders all higher level work and all objectivism in general only relative.

The second part of *Crisis* stops at this point. The reworked text of the Vienna conference allows us to place this fragment of the history of philosophy within the perspective of the whole, where the third part will take it up again. The aim of this entire history of philosophy is the catharsis of the sick modern spirit. The return to the ego is modern man's opportunity. Descartes, in omitting religion and morals from the doubt, did not conceive of such a historical design. The crisis of humanity reveals no irreducible absurdity, no impenetrable fatalism, and the teleology of European history shows its actual motivation.

How is this crisis to be resolved? Two ways remain possible: either the "growing alienation" within "barbarism and hate for the spirit" or the rebirth of Europe through a new understanding and a new affirmation of the sense of the history to be carried forward. Here the responsibility of the philosopher appears, the recognition of which is the leading note among all of these developments, for: "We are . . . , through our philosophical activity, the servants of humanity."

[IV] CRITICAL REMARKS

THESE REFLECTIONS by Husserl on the sense of history and on the function of the history of philosophy have at the very least the merit of provoking an interrogation which places in question the very possibility of a philosophy of history. Three groups of questions present themselves:

(1) The first group bears on the role of Ideas in history, and more particularly on the guiding role of philosophy in Occidental history. The reader is immediately struck by the contrast between the thought of Husserl and that of Marx. However, this contrast should not be taken rigidly, if Marxism is not to be reduced to its positivistic caricature. A dialectical conception which remains open to the return shock of ideas upon the infrastructure of societies cannot fail to reflect on the very origins of human capital equipment, for the tool which incarnates the technique proceeds from science, and the very project of natural science is specifically connected to the over-all project whose explication Husserl provides when he deals with the "motivation of the mathematical sciences of nature in Galileo." There is, thus, the advent of the Idea which up to a certain point accounts for an important aspect of history. This reading is the more legitimate to the degree that it shares in the responsibility of the philosopher who, by means of this understanding, practices his vocation as philosopher.

On the other hand, this reading of history as the history of Ideas seems to require self-criticism in two ways: by confronting itself continually with the history of the historian and by reflectively correcting its notion of the Idea.

The dialogue of the philosopher of history with the pure historian begins as soon as one affirms that the Idea is not only the task, the "obligation," but also the historical reality of the Occident. It is then quite necessary that the proposed reading be compared with other possible readings of history, for example, as history of labor, of law, of the state, of religion, etc. Would a philosophy of history worthy of this name not then have the initial task of enumerating the various possible readings, of assaying them critically and perhaps ordering them? One cannot say that philosophy has an "archontic" role, that it is the "brain" of the Occident, without elaborating a system of the whole which would justify the privileged position of the philosophical explication over all others. Instead of following a single melodic theme— history of philosophy, history of law, economic and social history, or the like—one could try to compose a sort of counterpoint which would include all the melodic themes; or, to give another image with the same dialectical tendency, one could try to correct each of the "longitudinal" readings of history by a "vertical" reading. Thus, only the Husserlian interpretation, too simple and too a priori to suit the historian's taste, might bring about a coincidence at infinity of the a priori and the a posteriori explication. But in the current state of the history of civilizations, this coincidence seems hardly to be accessible.

The confrontation with the history of the historians, that is to say, the confrontation with an inductive and changing synthesis, would not reach Husserl's interpretation in any essential way, since the conviction that the Idea of philosophy is the task of European man is not an inductive conclusion or an ascertainment of fact but rather a philosophical requirement. If history is rational—or, if it be preferred, to the degree that history is rational—it should realize the same signification as that which self-reflection can attain. This identity of the sense of history and the sense of interiority founds the philosophy of history in Husserl. And this identity gives it its a priori character in relation to the history of the historians. But does it not then call for a properly philosophical critique whose theme would be something like this: under what conditions can the same Idea give an inner coherence both to history and to interiority? Just at this point the sense of history can manifest itself as more recondite than any philosophical Idea, at least in speculative form. Certainly, Husserl did understand this Idea as an infinite totality; but he constantly tends to interpret it as a science or even as the project of a theory of knowledge, thus sacrificing the ethical and aesthetic aspects and the other cultural traits of the Idea. Is the demand for justice, love, and saintliness a task which contains the Idea of science, even if a greater extension is attributed to this Idea than to the whole of objective knowledge? Moreover, should not the Idea capable of founding history and subjectivity at the same time also be an act—an act powerful enough to produce history and intimate enough to institute the interior man? But then, is a philosophy of the cogito, of a transcendental subjectivism, sufficient for the job?

A critique of the philosophy of history would, therefore, have the task of making the a priori sense of history coincide at some point: first, with the a posteriori sense which a properly historical induction could formulate, and second, with the more radical subjectivity of the ego. Under its second form, this critique would lead to a residual difficulty common to all of the philosophies which Husserl calls "transcendental." Let us examine this last.

(2) We should like to ask if history could have the Idea of philosophy as its sense and as a task to realize. This question leads to

another: Does an Idea or a task in general develop a true history? Does an advent make an event? The paradox of the notion of history is that it becomes incomprehensible if it is not a unique history unified by a sense; yet it loses its very historicity if it is not an unforeseeable adventure. One way, there would be no more philosophy of history; the other way, there would be no more history.

Now, although the unity of history is forcefully conceived by Husserl, the historicity of history, to the contrary, is understood by him with some difficulty. This weakness appears on several occasions: the outline of the history of philosophy in the second part of *Crisis* systematically sacrifices each philosopher's particular set of problems to a single problem-set which is termed the "true" problem, the "hidden" problem (of Descartes, Hume, etc.). Putting them in such a perspective is not without its dangers, for the aspects of a philosopher which do not lend themselves to this unifying reading of history are omitted. The interpretation of the philosopher by himself is considered as negligible. Yet we may wonder if the character peculiar to each philosopher is not an aspect of history quite as important as the rationality of the history in which it is recorded. To understand a philosopher, is this not also to come to grips with the question which he alone encountered and posed? In the sense in which the question is identified with the philosopher himself, it becomes a kind of living process. The question is not only thought out; it is actually thinking. Is not the attempt to identify oneself with this question by a sort of "loving struggle" quite akin to the efforts we make in order to communicate with our friends?

For such reasons, perhaps it will be necessary to say that history is at once continuous and discontinuous—discontinuous like particular existences which organize their systems of thought and life around one task belonging to each and continuous like the common task which renders their pursuit reasonable.

We may come to suspect that history has a paradoxical structure in another way through reading Husserl himself. For the danger of reducing philosophies to *the* philosophy lies in construing the latter entirely according to the interpretation of the last philosophy which considers the matter. The philosophies of history which orient the whole movement of history toward their own problems run a risk which is the risk of putting the accent too readily upon the task which "comes of itself"—which "advenes"—rather than on the particularity of the existents which "emerge" to philosophical reflection. Hegel's philosophy of history and Brunschvicg's progress of consciousness would be open to the same objections.

A considerable difficulty at this point must be acknowledged, for in the end a paradox in history conceals a paradox concerning truth. If an author attaches some value to his efforts, may this mean that he recognizes some truth in them for which he is not an adequate measure? May he not rightfully expect others to recognize it and hope that history will realize it? Whoever reflects calls on the authority of truth and by so doing seeks the consecration of history to the extent that his thought is rational.

On the other hand, how will one not admit that, from the point of view of a modest understanding, the intention or intuition of each philosopher resists adsorption within one single task? Shall I not put aside recounting the sense of history, if it is true that this claim presupposes that I survey all thinking existences and that I set myself up as the final outcome and the suppression of history? Thus, transposed in terms of truth, the difficulty of the philosophy of history is increased, for the rationality of history implies a nascent dogmatism for which history is an Idea and an Idea thinkable by me. The historicity of history suggests a nascent skepticism for which history is incurably multiple and irrational.

Perhaps the second task for a philosophy of history is to set up the terms of this paradox correctly. This is not to say that a philosophy is to be built with paradoxes. However, one must begin by taking them on if one thinks oneself able to overcome them.

Husserl's reflection does not always sacrifice the event to the advent. It also has something which leads us to the brink of this paradox: that history which we understand as the "coming to itself" of reason is also of such sort that there can be defection, for after all there is a crisis of European humanity. The rational character of history does not exclude its dramatic movement. Is there need to emphasize that the very birth of philosophy in Greece, the lapse of invention into tradition, the corruption of the Idea of philosophy by objectivism, the awakening of Descartes, the question of Hume, the birth of Husserlian phenomenology itself, all are so many quite unforeseeable events, particular events without which there would not have been the advent of sense? Husserl's own language carries a trace of this tension: "The apodicticity of foundation," that is to say, the force of the Idea, presupposes the responsibility of the thinking man, who can make the Idea advance, stagnate, or become pointless. Finally, Husserl's views of what is to come are tinged with paradox. On one side, he recovers courage with an optimism founded on the rationality of history, for "Ideas are the stronger." On the other side, he makes a claim upon the responsibility of whoever thinks, for Europe can "always" render itself "yet more estranged from its own signification" or "be reborn from the spirit of philosophy, thanks to the heroism of reason."

Optimism of Idea and *tragedy of ambiguity* refer to a structure of history where the plurality of responsible beings (the event of thinking) are the inverse of the unity of the task (the advent of sense).

(3) All the questions that Husserl's attempt at instituting a philosophy of history bring to mind culminate in one final difficulty. If history does draw its sense from a task that it develops, what is the ground or reason for this task? Two contrary tendencies seem to participate in the philosophy of the *Crisis*. On the one hand, Husserl seems to approach Hegel, even coming to speak of the spirit (*Geist*) in a manner quite like the great idealist: "Only the spirit is immortal." But on the other hand, the whole sense of European history is borne along by "transcendental subjectivity." This latter philosophical motif is called "the return to the ego," "my ego," "my conscious life," the "performance of consciousness," whose first work is "my life-world." Has Husserl married water and fire, Hegel and Descartes, the objective spirit and the cogito, and moreover, the cogito radicalized by Hume's skepticism?

The question is all the more troubling, since the theory of *Bewusstseinsleistung* and *Lebenswelt* reaches its full development in the *Crisis*. Hence, one and the same work initiates a philosophy of the historical spirit and brings a philosophy of the ego cogito to its point of culmination. How is this possible? To give this question a general bearing, let us ask if a Socratic, Cartesian, or transcendental philosophy—whatever be the name for a philosophy of the "return to the ego"—is capable of a philosophy of history? On one side, does not a transcendental philosophy (in the broad sense Husserl proposes) found all being, including that of the Other and of history in the ego cogito? On the other hand, does not a rationalistic philosophy of history found all private tasks in one great common project and the ego itself in the historical Idea?

The great interest of Husserl's last philosophy is to have taken on the apparent antinomy and to have attempted to overcome it. The contrast between the Fifth Cartesian Meditation and the cycle of the *Crisis* is very illuminating in this respect. The Fifth Cartesian Meditation tries to fill in the great lacuna of Cartesianism, which includes no theory of the existence of the Other. It establishes that the Other is a being which is constituted "in" my ego but which is constituted there precisely as another ego, one which gets away from me, which exists like my ego, and with which I can enter into a reciprocal relationship. This text is one of the most difficult in Husserl but also one of extraordinary force and lucidity. One can well say that the entire enigma of a history which includes its own including—that is, I, the one who understands, who wills, who makes the sense of this history— was already taken up in the theory of *Einfühlung* (empathy or experience of the Other).

Proceeding to a final *epoché*, this Meditation "suspends" all certitudes and all experiences which we owe to our relations with the Other: the belief in a common world of perception and in a common world of culture. Thus, the sphere "belonging" to the ego, its "primordial sphere of ownness," is stripped bare. This sphere is nearly what the *Crisis* will call the "life-world." "In" this final sphere of life and experience, "within" this owned being, the experience is elaborated of the Other as precisely an alien or outsider in this sphere. This bursting forth toward the "outsider" in the very bosom of one's "ownness" is just the problem to be attacked. The inherence of the Other as Other in my own life is the whole enigma of *Einfühlung*. On the one hand, it is quite true that all being is a "phenomenon" for and in the ego; and yet what is "in" my ownness sphere is not at all a modality of myself, a content of my private consciousness, for the Other is given in me as other than me.

At this point we omit the concrete analysis of this "apperception by analogy" which Husserl calls "appresentation" (i.e., that the body of the Other is "presented" over there but not his own subjective life).[20] Here we consider only the movement of the whole of this Meditation, insofar as it leads us to the apparent circle formed by the ego and history together.

The whole theory of phenomenological constitution—be it a question of things, animals, persons, etc.—places us face to face with the paradox of an immanence which is a bursting forth toward transcendence. This paradox culminates in the apperception of the Other, for on this occasion the intentional object is a subject like me. Directly linked with his body, the Other and the world of the Other are constituted as another monad by "eppresentation in mine" (CM, § 52). If one comes to understand correctly what this constitution is, this inherence which is an inclusion not as a really inherent part but as an intentional object, it is no longer enigmatic

> that I can constitute another ego in myself, or to speak in an even more radical fashion, that I can constitute another monad in my monad, and, once constituted, grasp it precisely as Other. We also understand this fact, inseparable from the first, that I can identify the nature constituted by me with the nature constituted by the Other, or to speak with all

20. "The existence of the Other is founded in this indirect but true accessibility of what is directly and in itself inaccessible" (CM, § 52, p. 144).

precision necessary, with a nature constituted in me as constituted by the Other (CM, § 55, pp. 155 f.).

Later on: "To admit that it is in me that Others as Others are constituted is the only way of understanding that for me they can have the sense and being-status of determinate existence" (CM, p. 156). But these are just those monads "which exist for themselves in the same way that I exist for myself" (CM, p. 156). At this point I can say that "the Other grasps me just as immediately as Other for him, as I grasp him as Other for me" (CM, § 56, p. 158).

Such is the ultimate attempt to overcome the difficulties which the notion of history encounters in a philosophy of the ego cogito. From the period of the *Cartesian Meditations* Husserl saw the bearing of his theory of *Einfühlung* on a theory of cultural and social life; §§ 56–59 lead up to the principal analyses of the *Crisis*.

Did Husserl succeed in maintaining that history was actual and simultaneously that the ego is the only fundamental thing? He expected to succeed where Descartes and Hume failed because he was the first to have conceived of an intentional idealism, that is to say, an idealism which constitutes all other being—even the other person—"in" the ego, but for which constitution is an intuitive intending, a passing beyond, a bursting forth. This notion of intentionality in the last resort permits the founding of man on history and history on my consciousness. Its final claim is to justify a true transcendence of history on the basis of a transcendental subjectivism.

One must wonder if constitution is an effective production and the true solution to the problem of the various transcendences, or if it is only the name given to a difficulty whose enigma remains unaffected and whose paradox still gapes. At least Husserl did mark out the shape of the true problem: How can one escape from the solipsism of a Descartes seen through Hume, in order to take seriously the historical character of culture and its evident power to form man? How at the same time can one avoid the Hegelian trap of an absolute history elevated to equal an external God, in order to remain faithful to the disturbing discovery in Descartes's first two Meditations?

7 / Kant and Husserl

THE GOAL OF THIS STUDY is to locate the difference between Husserlian phenomenology and Kantian Criticism with some exactness. This task of differentiation follows from a study of the major works devoted to Kant during the past twenty years (to his metaphysics in particular) and from a thorough reading of the published and unpublished works of Husserl. I would like to show that this difference is not situated where the Neo-Kantians who criticized *Ideas I* think it is (cf. Natorp, Rickert, Kreis, Zocher). Their criticism remains too dependent upon an overly epistemological interpretation of Kant. The difference should be located on the level where Kant determines the ontological status of the phenomena themselves and not on the level of an exploration of the world of phenomena.

(1) To begin with, taking Husserl as our guide, we shall distinguish an implicit phenomenology behind the Kantian epistemology which Husserl might then be said to have revealed. In this respect Husserl develops something that was frustrated in Kantianism and which remained there in an embryonic state, even though necessary to its general economy.

(2) Then, in return, taking Kant as our guide and taking his ontological intention seriously, we shall inquire whether or not Husserlian phenomenology simultaneously represents the exfoliation of an implicit Kantian phenomenology and the destruction of an ontological problem-set which had found its expression in the role of limiting and founding the thing-in-itself. We can then ask whether the loss of the ontological dimension of the object *qua* phenomenon was not common to both Husserl and his turn of the century Neo-Kantian critics. If so, this would be the reason why they located their dispute in an area of secondary importance. We shall, then, be led to reinterpret the Husserl-

[175]

ian idealism with the guidance of that sense of limits which is perhaps the soul of the Kantian philosophy.

(3) Since the process of disontologizing the object led Husserl to a crisis in his own philosophy which he himself termed "transcendental solipsism," we shall ask if it is possible to overcome this obstacle and move on to intersubjectivity without the aid of a practical philosophy in the Kantian style. Then, taking our point of departure in Husserl's difficulties with the constitution of the alter ego, we shall return a last time to Kant in order to look for the ethical and practical determination of the person.

[I] The *Critique* as Implicit Phenomenology

SINCE HUSSERL is going to serve us as guide in bringing an implicit phenomenology of Kantianism to light, it is necessary to state briefly those characteristics of the Husserlian phenomenology which we take to be essential for this revelatory enterprise.

(1) I must first insist forcefully on the necessity of a distinction in Husserl between the method as it was actually practiced and the philosophical interpretation which it received, above all in *Ideas I* and in the *Cartesian Meditations*. This distinction will take on its full sense when the Kantian philosophy of limits will have opened our eyes in turn to the metaphysical decision implicit in Husserlian phenomenology.

When distinguishing between the method practiced and the philosophical interpretation of this method, in no way do I mean to exclude the well-known phenomenological reduction. To do so would be to reduce phenomenology to a rhapsody of lived experiences and to baptize as "phenomenology" any concern for the curiosities of human life, as is too often the case. The reduction is the straight gate to phenomenology. But in the very act of reduction a methodological conversion and a metaphysical decision intersect, and just at that point one must distinguish between them.

In its strictly methodological intention the reduction is a conversion which causes the "for-me" to emerge from every ontic positing. Whether the being (*être*) is a thing, a state of affairs, a value, a living creature, or a person, the *epoché* "reduces" it to its appearing. A conversion is necessary here because the "for-me" is initially disguised by the positing of the particular being (*étant*). This dissimulating positing, which Husserl called the natural attitude or the general thesis of the world, is hidden from reflection. Thus, a special spiritual discipline (*ascèse*) is necessary in order to destroy its charm. Probably, one can speak only in negative terms of this "natural thesis," since its sense appears only in the movement of reducing it. Hence, it is said that this thesis is not belief in existence, and even less intuition of it, because reduction leaves this belief intact and reveals the "seeing" in all its liveliness. It is rather an operation which insinuates itself into intuition and belief and so makes the subject a captive of this seeing and believing to the degree that he overlooks himself in the ontic positing of this or that.

This is why the natural attitude is a restriction and a limitation. But in return, the reduction, despite its negative appearance, is the reconquest of the entire relationship of the ego to its world. To put it positively, the "reduction" becomes the "constitution" of the world for and in the subjective life of consciousness. The act of reduction uncovers the relativity of what appears to performing (*opérante*) consciousness. This relativity defines the phenomenon very exactly. Henceforth, for phenomenology, nothing *is* except as a sense in consciousness. Phenomenology seeks to be the science of phenomena conquered by a spiritual discipline from the positing of particular beings. We have said enough about this topic to outline the distinction between method and doctrine. The matter will not become clear until the Kantian ontology reveals a set of problems in addition to that of the reduction.

Is the whole set of problems concerning being (*être*) annulled by the reduction? In order to affirm this, it is necessary to decide whether this problem-set is entirely contained in the natural attitude, that is to say, in the positing of each particular being (*étant*) absolutely, without relation to consciousness. It must be admitted that Husserl never brought this problem directly into the open. Likewise, if the emergence of the for-me-ness of all things and if the thematization of the world as phenomenon exhaust the questions that could be raised with regard to the being of what appears, is it the case that we are then obliged to lay aside the problem of knowledge? My feeling is that the method practiced by Husserl leaves this problem intact. I will say more. The natural attitude is at once the dissimulation of the appearance for me of the world and the dissimulation of the being of the appearance. If the natural attitude loses me into the world, sticks me into the world as seen, sensed, and acted upon, its being-in-itself is the false in-itself of an existence without me. This in-itself is only the absolutization of the ontic, of the "this" and the "that," of "particular beings." "Nature exists"; this is the natural thesis. In putting an end to the omission of the subject, in uncovering the for-me-ness of the world, the "reduction" opens rather than closes the true problem-set of being. For these problems assume the conquest made by a subjectivity, and they imply the reconquest of the subject, that being to whom being opens itself.

(2) The phenomenological reduction, which made the phenomenon of the world emerge as the very sense of consciousness, is the key that opens the way to an original "experience," the experience of the "subjective process" (*vécu*) in its "flux of consciousness." This is called "immanent perception" in *Ideas I;* and in the *Cartesian Meditations* there is a "transcendental experience," which like all experience draws its validity from its intuitive character, from the degree of presence and plenitude of its object. The Jamesian sound of these words "subjective process" (*vécu*) and "flux of consciousness" should not mislead us. The accent is fundamentally Cartesian. Even though perception of the transcendent thing is always dubitable because it is produced in a flux of adumbrations or perspectival shadings which can always cease to come together into a unity of sense, the subjective process of consciousness *schattet sich nich ab*—it does not "adumbrate." It is not perceived by successive aspects or adumbrations. Hence, phenomenology is based upon an absolute perception, that is to say, upon one which is not only indubitable but also apodictic (in the sense that it is inconceivable that its object, the subjective process, should not be).

Is this to say that phenomenology is a new empiricism? A new phenomenalism? What matters here is to remember that Husserl never separated the transcendental reduction from that other reduction which he terms eidetic and which consists in grasping the fact (*Tatsache*) in its essence (*eidos*). Hence, the ego that the *epoché* reveals as the one to which all things appear should not be described in its accidental singularity but rather as eidos ego (*Cartesian Meditations*). This change of levels, obtained principally by the method of imaginative variation, converts "transcendental experience" into science.

There are two reasons why Husserl's phenomenology can serve as a guide within Kant's work. These concern (1) the reduction of the particular being to the phenomenon and (2) the descriptive experience of the subjective process in the eidetic mode. Kant himself is the authority in this matter. In the letter to Markus Herz of February 21, 1772, he announces that the great work he is projecting on the limits of sensibility and reason would include in its theoretical portion two parts: first, phenomenology in general, and second, metaphysics considered uniquely in its nature and method. Yet the *Critique of Pure Reason* is not called a phenomenology and properly speaking is not a phenomenology. Why? This question will permit us to situate the *Critique* in relation to the "reduction."

(1) Two reasons can be offered which show why the *Critique* is not a phenomenology. The first, to which we shall return in our second part, concerns the philosophy of limits which has as large a role in the *Critique* as the investigations of the domain of phenomena. In the preface of the second edition, Kant refers to the "revolution" in metaphysical method brought about by the *Critique* and declares, "It is a treatise on the method, not a system of the science itself. But at the same time it marks out the whole plan of the science, both as regards its limits and as regards its entire internal structure" (B 22–23).[1] Thus, the two intentions of the *Critique* are set forth neatly: to limit the phenomenon and to elucidate its internal structure. It is this second task that could be a phenomenological one.

This reason why the *Critique* is not a phenomenology is not the only one; in addition, the elucidation of the internal structure of phenomenality is not conducted in a phenomenological fashion. Here it is necessary to question the particularly epistemological preoccupation of the *Critique*. The fundamental question, "How are synthetic a priori judgments possible?" forbids a genuine description of subjective life. The problem of justification that appears in the foreground of the "Transcendental Deduction" virtually eliminates the intention of composing a genuine physiology of the mind (*Gemüt*). It seems less important to describe how the mind (*esprit*) knows than to justify the universality of knowledge by the synthetic function of the categories and ultimately by the unifying function of transcendental apperception. The three correlative notions of nature, experience, and objectivity bear the mark of this epistemological preoccupation. Nature defined (to some degree phenomenologically) as the "totality of all phenomena" in epistemological terms is "nature in general, considered in its conformity to laws (*Gesetzmässigkeit*)." And since nature is the correlate of experience, the *Gesetzmässigkeit* of nature is identical with the conditions of the possibility of experience. Regarding its epistemological task, the *Critique* searches for such a priori concepts as will render possible "the formal unity of experience" or "the form of an experience in general." It is within this framework that the problem of objectivity is presented. Objectivity is the cognitive status conferred on the empirical understanding by its *Gesetzmässigkeit*.

To be specific, the *Critique* is not limited to a purely epistemologi-

1. [Quotations in English are based on Immanuel Kant's *Critique of Pure Reason*, trans. Norman Kemp Smith, 1st ed. (London, 1929); 2d ed. (London, 1933). Ricoeur uses both the German edition of the *Gesammelte Schriften*, sponsored by the Royal Academy of Prussia, Vol. V, and the French translation by Tremesaygues and Pacaud (Kehrbach edition, 1909). Our citations denote the first German edition by *A* and the second by *B*.—Trans.]

cal determination of objectivity, that is, to a justification of constituted knowledge (mathematics, physics, metaphysics). The "Analytic" more than meets the needs of Newtonian physics and the "Aesthetic" those of Euclidean and even non-Euclidean geometry. It is in this marginal area where the *Critique* goes beyond a simple epistemology that there is a chance of finding the beginnings of a genuine phenomenology.

The Copernican Revolution, disengaged from the epistemological hypothesis, is nothing other than the phenomenological *epoché*. It constitutes a vast reduction which moves not merely from the constituted sciences, from successful knowledge, to their conditions of legitimacy; it also moves from the totality of appearing to its conditions of constitution. This descriptive design, usually overshadowed by the justificatory intention of the *Critique*, appears every time Kant renounces dependence on a constituted science and directly defines what he calls receptivity, spontaneity, synthesis, subsumption, production, reproduction, etc. These embryonic descriptions, quite often masked in definitions, are necessary to the epistemological enterprise itself, for the a priori which constitutes the formal determinations of all knowledge is itself rooted in the acts, operations, or functions whose description by and large gets beyond the strict domain of the sciences. Can one, then, say that the *Critique* includes a "transcendental experience"?

(2) The transcendental experience which opens up to the phenomenologist beyond the threshold of the phenomenological reduction at first glance seems totally foreign to the Kantian spirit. Is not the very notion of an "experience" of the cogito some sort of a monster for a Kantian? To examine and describe the cogito, is this not to treat it as a phenomenon, hence as an object in nature and no longer as the condition for the possibility of phenomena? Does not the combination of the transcendental and the eidetic reductions remove us still further and more decisively from Kant by the use of a suspect mixture of psychologism (the subjective process) and Platonism (the eidos ego)? Is this not the place to recall that the "I-think" of originary apperception is in no way the ego grasped in its eidos and reduced to the unifying function that supports the synthetic work of cognition? So then, how will "transcendental experience" escape from this dilemma: either I am "conscious" of the "I-think" but it is not knowledge, or I "know" the ego but it is a phenomenon in nature? It is on just these grounds that the Neo-Kantian criticisms of Husserl are founded.

It must be recognized that the *Critique* beats a difficult trail around this dilemma which lies purely on the epistemological plane, for the "I-think" and the "self phenomenon" are defined in terms of objective knowledge. In fact, however, Kant escapes from this dilemma every time he proceeds to a direct inspection of the *Gemüt* (mind). The very term *Gemüt,* so enigmatic, designates the "field of transcendental experience" which Husserl thematizes. *Gemüt* is not at all the "I-think," the epistemological guarantee for the unity of experience, but rather what Husserl calls *ego cogito cogitata.* In short, it is the theme of the Kantian phenomenology itself, the theme that the "Copernican Revolution" brings to light. When this revolution is not reduced to the *questio juris,* to the axiomatization of Newtonian physics, it is none other than the reduction of particular beings to their appearance in the *Gemüt.* With the guidance of a transcendental experience of the *Gemüt* it is possible to grasp the features of the Kantian phenomenology.

Certainly, the "Transcendental Aesthetic" is the least phenomenological part of the *Critique.* The description of the spatiality of the phenomenon—the only description that Kant undertakes, and then because it concerns mathematics—is squeezed between the epistemological preoccupation with justifying the synthetic a priori judgments of geometry [2] and the characteristic constructibility of mathematical reasoning,[3] by means of the concept of pure intuition on the one hand and on the other the ontological concern for situating exactly the being of space.[4]

Nevertheless, a phenomenology of spatiality is implied as long as space is related to the "subjective constitution of our minds" (*subjektiven Beshaffenheit unseres Gemüts*) (A 25). Only this phenomenology can establish that the purely epistemological notion of a priori intuition coincides with that of a "form situated in the subject." Kant is led to describe space as the manner in which the subject is disposed to receive something before the appearance of that something. "To render possible an external intuition" is a phenomenological determination far broader than "to render possible the synthetic a priori judgments of geometry." This possibility is no longer on the order of legitimation but is on the order of the constitution of the *Beshaffenheit unseres Gemüts.*

Nevertheless, the "Transcendental Aesthetic" is still quite deceptive, not only because of its embryonic but also because of its static character. Space and time are considered not in the movement of the entire experience but rather as forming a prior stratum, finished and inert. This too is to be understood by reference to the emphasis on

---

2. Cf. "The Transcendental Exposition of the Concept of Space" (A 25, B 40).
3. "Transcendental Doctrine of Method" (A 712 ff., B 740 ff.).
4. The initial question is of an ontological order: "What, then, are space and time? Are they actual beings?" (Was sind nun Raum und Zeit? Sind es wirkliche Wesen?) (A 23, B 37).

epistemology. Spatiality is not a stage in the constitution of the "thing" for the geometrician. Its determination as pure intuition must be terminated within itself in order to assure the complete autonomy of mathematics.

Once Kant has placed his foot across the phenomenological threshold and relates space to the possibility of being affected by something, he is led into the actual movement of a dynamic constitution of experience and thinghood. The provisional juxtaposition of space and time is suddenly once more in question. Space must be "traversed" in temporal moments, "retained" in a total image, and "recognized" as an identical sense (A 95 ff.). The schematism accentuates even more the dynamic character of spatial constitution (A 137). This grasping of space through time ("Time is a necessary representation which founds all intuitions") marks the triumph of phenomenology over epistemology.

What is more, to the degree that we move away from the concern for axiomatizing geometry, all that appeared clear epistemologically becomes phenomenologically obscure. If space is on the level of sensibility, we still do not think anything in it; we only dispose ourselves to receive something. But then we are below all syntheses, and it is necessary to say that this (epistemological) form is a (phenomenological) manifold (A 76 f.). Kant even goes so far as to observe that space concerns the status of a being which is dependent "in its existence as well as in its intuition (and which through that intuition determines its existence in relation to the given objects)" (B 72).

At the same time, he identifies space—or the formal property of being affected by objects or receiving an immediate representation of things—with the intentionality of consciousness. This is the movement in consciousness toward something, considered as the possibility of spreading out, discriminating, or pluralizing any impression whatsoever. Thus, the more explicit phenomenology of the "Analytic" dispels the false clarity of the "Aesthetic," so feebly phenomenological.

The phenomenology of the "Analytic" stands out emphatically if one reads it in reverse order, ascending from the transcendental theory of judgment (or "Analytic of Principles") to the transcendental theory of the concept, pausing at the "Analogies of Experience" before plunging into the difficult chapter on the "Schematism" (this difficulty will be discussed below). It is to be expected that the phenomenology of Kant should be primarily a phenomenology of judging. Such a phenomenology is most apt to offer a propaedeutic to epistemology. On the other hand, it is to be expected that Husserl's phenomenology should be, preferably, a phenomenology of perception, for this is most apt to illustrate a concern for evidence, for originariness, and for presence—although, the *Logical Investigations* begins with judging, and in phenomenology the place of judging comes to be marked out in the strata of subjective life on the level of founded syntheses. (We shall see in the second part that there are other reasons which explain this difference in accent and preference in the descriptions of Kant and Husserl.) In any case no difference between them in descriptive theme hides their kinship in method of analysis.

If we begin the "Analytic" at the end, therefore, with the "Analogies of Experience," we shall see a full analysis of judging developed as the act of subsuming perceptions under the rules of intelligibility. Kant the epistemologist holds this operation to be a simple "application" of the laws of previously constituted understanding. But the tendency of the description leads the analysis in another direction as subsumption reveals itself to be an actual constitution of experience inasmuch as it is experience which is understood, judged, and expressed on the predicative level.

The "Principles," which from the epistemological point of view are the axioms of pure physics, the first synthetic judgments a priori of a science of nature, yield an admirable description of the constitution of thinghood (*Dinglichkeit*). In this regard, the intellectual character of the percept is thematized in addition to the principles of permanence, causality, and reciprocity. It is admirable that Kant linked the structures of thinghood with the structures of temporality long before Husserl. The different ways in which experience is "connected" are also the diverse ways in which time is intellectually structured. The second analogy in particular contains a veritable phenomenology of the event which answers the question: What does "to happen" signify? The phenomenologist elaborates the notion of an ordered succession upon (*sur*) the object in the world. In Husserlian language one would say that the "Analogies of Experience" develop the noematic side of the subjective process in the judgment of experience. They consider the judgment from the side of the "judged" where it connects to the object. (On the other hand, the preceding chapter on the "Schematism" yields a noetic analysis of the "event" and reflects on the operation of connecting as "the synthetic power of the imagination" [B 233]. We shall return to this matter later.)

If one considers that this second chapter of the doctrine of judgment, whose heart is the theory of the "Analogies of Experience," shows the noematic side of the judgment of experience, then one sees that this noematic analysis is completed in the "Postulates of Empirical Thought in General" (A 218 ff.). In effect, the "postulates" add no new determination to the object, but they do thematize its existence according to the modalities of the actual, the possible, and the necessary. Now, what do these postulates signify? They simply posit the fundamental correlation of the existence of things with their perceptibility: "Our knowledge of the existence of things reaches, then, only so far as perception and its advance according to empirical laws can extend" (A 226). Spatiality has furnished us with the style of intentionality as the opening to the appearing. The postulate of empirical thought determines the effectiveness of intentionality as the perceived presence of the thing which appears.

It is not by accident that Kant inserts the "refutation of Idealism" (B 274 ff.) into a corner of the second edition; it is a definition of intentionality before its time: "The mere yet empirically determined consciousness of my own existence proves the existence of objects in space outside me" (B 275). In fact, the correlation of "I am" and "something is" is intentionality itself.

If Chapter Two of the "Transcendental Doctrine of Judgment" develops the noematic side of the judgment of existence, then Chapter One, devoted to the schematism, deals with the noetic side. Hence the obscurity of Chapter One. It incessantly anticipates in a reflexive way the "Analogies of Experience" which reveal the work of judging on the object. One should always read this chapter after the one that follows and then return to Chapter One by a reflexive movement which finds "in" the *Gemüt* (mind) what was revealed "on" the object. The anticipatory character of this chapter explains Kant's brevity in elaborating the schemata. Nevertheless, these few hundred lines (A 144–47) are the subjective side of the immense noematic analysis of the following chapter.

If one considers it in this way, the theory of the schematism comes very close to being what Husserl calls auto-constitution or the constitution of the ego in temporality. We know that Kant himself was astonished at this "art concealed in the depths of the human soul whose true modes of activity nature is hardly likely ever to allow us to discover and to have open to our gaze" (A 141). Never is Kant more free with regard to his epistemological preoccupations. Likewise, he is never closer to discovering the originary time of consciousness beyond constituted time (or time as representation, according to the "Transcendental Aesthetic"). The time of the schematism is at the union of receptivity and spontaneity, of the manifold and the unitary. Time is my power of ordering, and it also offers the constant threat of escaping and defeating me. It is the indivisible, possible, rationality of order and the ever renascent irrationality of the subjective life. It looks toward affectivity, whose pure flux it is, and toward intellectuality, since the schemata mark its possible structuration in respect to "series," "content," and "order" (A 145).

Should we follow this phenomenology of the *Gemüt* to its conclusion, we would have to relate what Kant was repeatedly led to say concerning the existence of consciousness to this noetic analysis of the operation of judging. While the noematic analysis culminates in the "Postulates of Empirical Thought" that coordinate the existence of things with their perceptibility, the noetic analysis culminates in the self-determination of the I-exist. But with regard to this theme one only finds occasional notes in the *Critique*. And in effect it is here that the implicit phenomenology encounters the most formidable resistances deep within Kantianism. The whole epistemological conception of objectivity tends to make the "I-think" a function of objectivity and imposes the alternatives to which we referred at the outset. Either I am "conscious" of the I-think but do not "know" it, or I "know" the ego, but it is a phenomenon within nature. This is why Kant's phenomenological description tends toward the discovery of a concrete subject who has no tenable place in the system. However, Kant moves in the direction of this subject whenever he moves toward originary time at work in judgment by means of the schematism. Likewise, he approaches this subject when he determines the existence of the things as correlative to my existence. At this point he remarks: "I am conscious of my own existence as determined in time . . . consequently the determination of my existence in time is possible only through the existence of actual things which I perceive outside me" (B 275–76; see also the note to the preface of the second edition on B xi).

The great difficulty was in thematizing an existence which was not the category of existence, which was not, in other words, a structure of subjectivity. This difficulty is confronted for the first time in § 25 of the second edition (an existence which is not a phenomenon). The note that Kant adds here (B 158) proposes the task of grasping existence in the act of the I-think that determines this existence, hence before the temporal intuition of myself that raises my existence to the level of a psychological phenomenon (B 157). The difficulty here is great, especially if one considers that the I-think only passes into act upon the reception of a manifold which it determines logically. Above all the famous text comes to mind in the critique of "Rational Psychology," where the "I-think" is considered as an empirical proposition that includes the proposition "I-exist." Kant attempts to resolve the problem within the framework of his epistemology by linking existence to an "undetermined empirical intuition" anterior to all organized experience. This allows him to say, "Existence is not yet a category" (B 423).

Is not this extracategorial existence that very subjectivity without which the "I-think" would not merit the title of first person? Is it not in connection with this originary time that the "Analytic" stands forth from the time representation of the "Aesthetic"? In short, perhaps this is the existence of *Gemüt,* the mind, which is neither the I-think as principle of the possibility of the categories nor the self phenomenon of psychological science, but rather the mind which is offered to transcendental experience by the phenomenological reduction.

[II] THE *Critique* AS ENVISAGEMENT OF LIMITS

OUR FIRST GROUP of analyses depended on a provisional limitation. We granted that in Husserl the actually practiced method could be distinguished from the philosophical interpretation which he constantly mixed with it, especially in his published works. We made use of this actual phenomenology to reveal an implicit phenomenology in the *Critique.* Hence, the kinship of Kant and Husserl was established at the price of a legitimate but precarious abstraction applied to the total intention of the work of each man.

Now the *Critique* is something quite different from a phenomenology, not only by its epistemological preoccupation but also by its ontological intent. Only in this respect is the *Critique* more than a simple investigation of the "internal structure" of knowledge; it is also an investigation of the limits of knowledge. The rooting of the knowledge of phenomena in the thinking of being (*être*) which is not convertible into knowledge gives the Kantian *Critique* its properly ontological dimension. To destroy this tension between knowing and thinking, between the phenomenon and being, is to destroy Kantianism itself.

So then one can wonder whether the phenomenology of Husserl, which served us as guide and revealer for Kantianism's descriptive phenomenology, should not be considered in turn from the standpoint of the Kantian ontology. Perhaps the philosophical interpretation involved in the transcendental *epoché* participates in the destruction of the Kantian ontology, sanctions the loss of *Denken* in *Erkennen,* and thus thins out the philosophy into a phenomenology without ontology.

First, let us take account of the function of the positing of the thing-in-itself in relation to the inspection of phenomena as Kant sees it. There is no knowledge of being. This impossibility is somehow active and even positive. In spite of the impossibility of knowledge of being, *Denken* still posits being as that which limits the claims of the phenomena to make up ultimate reality. Thus, *Denken* confers on phenomenology its ontological dimension or status. One can trace this connection between a deception (regarding knowledge) and a positive act of limitation throughout the *Critique*.

As early as the "Transcendental Aesthetic," where the ontological intention is constantly present, Kant posits that a priori intuition is determined in contrast with a creative intuition which we do not have. Kant's very important note on *intuitus originarius,* at the end of the "Aesthetic," is clear. The *Gegen-stand* (object) holds itself up before me to the degree that it is not the *Ent-stand* (original), which would spring up from its own intuition.[5] Now, from the beginning this metaphysical deception is incorporated into the very sense of space and time and gives a negative tone to every page of the "Aesthetic." "Our whole intuition is *only* the representation of the phenomenon. The things that we intuit are not in themselves as we intuit them." In some way the phenomenon's lack of being is incorporated into it. But this shortcoming is itself the inverse of a positive act of *Denken* which in the "Aesthetic" takes the fanciful form of a supposition, the supposition of the destruction of our intuition: "If we depart from the subjective condition . . . the representation of space stands for nothing whatsoever."[6] And the same is said a bit further along with respect to time (A 37). This possible nothingness forms part of the notion of transcendental ideality since space is nothing outside of the subjective condition (A 28). This bit of fancy expresses what is positive in the negative of our lack of originary intuition. The *Denken* is the positive. It is not reducible to our being-affected and in consequence not reducible to that "dependence" of man "in his existence as well as in his intuition" (B 72) which was pointed out near the end of the "Aesthetic." The *Denken* is what imposes the limit.[7] It is not the phenomenal understanding that limits the usage of categories of experience; it is the positing of being by *Denken* that limits the claim of knowing the absolute. Knowledge, finitude, and death are thus linked by an indissol-

5. In the letter to Markus Herz of February 21, 1772, the problem of the *Vorstellung* was presented by reference to the strange possibility of an intuition generating its own object.

6. A 26. And later on: "If without this condition of sensibility I could intuit myself, or be intuited by another being, the very same determinations which we now represent to ourselves as alterations would yield knowledge into which the representation of time, and therefore also of alteration, would in no way enter" (A 37, B 54). "If we take away from our inner intuition the peculiar condition of our sensibility, the concept of time vanishes" (A 37, B 54).

7. "But these a priori sources of knowledge, being merely conditions of our sensibility, just by this very fact determine their own limits, namely, that they apply to objects only insofar as objects are viewed as appearances and do not present things as they are in themselves" (A 39, B 56).

uble pact which is only recognized by the very act of *Denken* that escapes from this condition and somehow views it from without.

There should be no difficulty in showing that this supposition of the nothingness of our sensible knowledge clarifies Kant's constant affirmation that transcendental philosophy stands on the dividing line that separates the "two sides" of the phenomenon (A 38), the in-itself and the for-us. "For what necessarily forces us across the limits of experience and all appearances is the unconditioned that authorizes us to speak of the things "only so far as we do not know them" (A 38).

This limiting function of the in-itself finds a striking confirmation in the "Transcendental Analytic." It touches on the sense of "nature." By indicating the empty place of an impossible science of creation, the in-itself protects knowledge of the phenomena of nature from falling into a dogmatic naturalism. This limiting function of the in-itself is given its most complete expression in the chapter on the "Distinction of all Objects into Phenomena and Noumena." The concept of the in-itself even though "problematical" (from the standpoint of knowledge; problematical, however, does not mean doubtful, but rather non-contradictory) is necessary "to prevent sensuous intuition from being extended to the things-in-themselves" (A 254). To be even clearer: "The concept of a noumenon is thus a merely limiting concept, the function of which is to limit the presumptions of sensuousness" (A 255). Hence, there would be a sort of *hubris* of sensuousness—not, correctly speaking, of sensuousness as such, but of the empirical usage of the understanding, of the positive and positivistic praxis of the understanding.

This notion of the usage of categories is of first importance. Kant expressly distinguishes it from the sense of the categories (A 147, A 248). This distinction clarifies what Kant understands by the presumption of sensuousness. He says nothing else when he shows the vanity of this pretension by means of the play of transcendental illusion and the check of failure (paralogism and antinomies). It is not reason that is unsuccessful in the "Transcendental Dialectic"; it is rather sensuousness in its claim to apply to the things-in-themselves.[8]

If we believe ourselves able to use this Kantian doctrine as a guide for interpreting the implicit philosophy of Husserl, we need to be assured that Kant truly succeeded in reconciling this function of limitation with the idealism of his theory of objectivity, such as it is

8. "The understanding accordingly limits sensuousness, but does not thereby extend its own sphere. In the process of warning the latter that it must not presume to claim applicability to things-in-themselves but only to appearances, it does indeed think for itself an object in itself, but only as transcendental object . . ." (A 288, B 344).

developed in the "Transcendental Deduction." Is not objectivity reduced to the synthesis imposed on the manifold of sensibility by
apperception through the categories? If this conception of objectivity
as the operation of transcendental subjectivity is truly the center of
the "Transcendental Deduction," how can it be linked with another
signification of the object as the in-itself? At times it seems that the
word "object" can only designate "the totality of my representations"
and that the intellectual structure of experience is sufficient for detaching my representations from me and opposing them to me as
something over against me (there is the familiar example of the house
passed through, apprehended, and recognized) (A 190–91). In this
sense the object is just "appearance, in contradistinction to the representations of apprehension" (A 191). Causality consolidates the object
of my representations into a counterpole to consciousness in the process of distinguishing succession *in* the object from the succession *of*
representations "insofar as one is conscious of it" (A 189). And one can
speak of truth, that is to say, of the agreement of the representation
with its object, since by this process of objectivation of representations, there is truly "an object distinct from them," (A 191). Was it not
Husserl who pointed to the constitution of the object *in* consciousness
as something *over against* consciousness?

Moreover, Kant does not doubt that what radically situates the
object outside is the thing-in-itself. The intending of the phenomenon
beyond itself is toward the non-empirical object, the transcendental X.
This is why Kant balances the texts where objectivity emerges from
the separation between my representations and the phenomenon with
others, where the phenomena remain "representations, which in turn
have their object" (A 109). The transcendental object is "what can
alone confer upon all of our empirical concepts in general relation to
an object, that is, objective reality" (A 109).

Now, the realistic function of intentionality (the object X as "correlative of the unity of apperception") penetrates through and through
the idealistic function of objectifying my representations. How is this
possible? The key to the problem is the distinction, fundamental in
Kant but totally unknown in Husserl, between *intention* and *intuition*.
Kant radically separates from one another the relation to something
and the intuition of something. An object = X is an intention without
intuition. This distinction subtends that of thinking and knowing and
maintains the agreement as well as the tension between them.

Rather than juxtapose the two interpretations of objectivity, Kant
posits their reciprocity. It is because the relation to the object = X is an
intention without an intuition that it refers to objectivity as unification
of a manifold. From that point on, the relation to the object is nothing

other than "the necessary unity of consciousness, and therefore also of the synthesis of the manifold." [9] Thus, the objectivity that issues from objectivation and the objectivity prior to this objectivation refer to each other (A 250–51). The transcendental ideality of the object turns back to the realism of the thing-in-itself, and this latter leads to the former. The preface to the second edition says nothing else when it posits the mutual implication of the conditioned and the unconditioned (B xx).

This structure in Kantianism has no parallel in Husserlian phenomenology. Like the Neo-Kantians, Husserl lost the ontological dimension of the phenomenon and simultaneously lost the possibility of a meditation on the limits and foundations of phenomenality. This is why phenomenology is not a "critique," that is to say, an envisagement of the limits of its own field of experience.

Here we have the true guide for discerning the simple methodological conversion within the phenomenological reduction, the one whose complications we saw in the first part, and also the methodological decision mixed in with it. The Second Cartesian Meditation clearly shows this clandestine shift from an act of abstention to an act of negation. In refraining (*mich enthalten*) from positing the world as absolute, I conquer it as world-perceived-in-the-reflective-life; in short, I gain it as phenomenon. Husserl can legitimately say that "the world is for me absolutely nothing else but the world existing for and being accepted by me in such a conscious cogito." Yet, notice that Husserl dogmatically posits that the world "finds in me and draws from me its sense and its being-status." [10] Ingarden has already expressed reservations regarding such expressions which, he says, anticipate the result of constitution, "for these expressions involve a metaphysical decision, a decision that one can assimilate to a categorial thesis having to do with something that is not itself an element of transcendental subjectivity." [11]

The most basic reason behind Husserl's view is that he confused the problems of being (*être*) with the naïve positing of particular beings (*étants*) in the natural attitude. Now, this naïve positing is precisely the omission of the connection of particular beings to our-

---

9. A 109. "But it is clear that, since we have to deal only with the manifold of our representations, and since X (the object) which corresponds to them is nothing to us—being, as it is, something that has to be distinct from all of our representations—the unity which the object makes necessary can be nothing else than the formal unity of consciousness in the synthesis of the manifold of representations" (A 105).

10. *Cartesian Meditations*, p. 60; cf. also p. 65, lines 11–16.

11. *Bemerkungen von Prof. Roman Ingarden*, Appendix to *Husserliana I*, pp. 208–10.

selves, and it arises from that *Anmassung* (presumption) of sensuousness discussed by Kant. Furthermore, the interlacing of the significations of objectivity which we found in Kant, an objectivity constituted "in" us and a founding objectivity "of" the phenomenon, is not to be detected in Husserl. This is why this world that is "for" me in respect to its sense (and "in" me in the intentional sense of "in") is also "from" (*de*) me in respect to its *Seinsgeltung*, its "being-status." Thereupon the *epoché* is also the measure of being and cannot be measured by anything else. It can only be radicalized; it cannot be penetrated by an absolute position which, like the Good in Plato, would give the power of seeing to the subject and would give something absolute to be seen.

I would now like to show how this implicit metaphysics of the non-metaphysical explains certain traits in Husserl's own description. Certainly it does not explain the fidelity and submission of his regard for "the things themselves"; phenomenology would be ruined entirely by this reproach. But it does explain the preferences that orient the attention toward certain constitutive strata of subjective life rather than toward others.

(1) In the first place the function of reason differs profoundly in Kant and Husserl. In Kant, reason is the *Denken* itself reflecting on the "sense" of the categories beyond their empirical "usage." We know that this reflection is at once a critique of transcendental illusion and a justification of the "Ideas" of reason. Husserl employs the word reason, generally associated with the words actuality and truth, in an entirely different way. Every discernment of the claims of the subjective process to indicate something actual is a problem of reason (I, Part IV). Now this discernment of actual validity consists in measuring each type of signification (the percept as such, the imaginary, the judged, the willed, the sensed as such) by the corresponding type of originary evidence.

The problem of reason is not at all oriented toward an investigation of some sort of intention without intuition, of some intending without intuiting, that would give the phenomenon something beyond itself.[12] Quite to the contrary, reason has the task of authenticating the phenomenon itself on the basis of its own plenitude.

12. At first § 128 of *Ideas I* seems to proceed in this direction. Husserl, remarking that it is the same object that incessantly gives itself differently, calls the object the "X of its determinations." In addition, he proposes to elucidate the way in which the noema "as meant" can have a relation to an objectivity (I, p. 315): "Every noema has a content, namely its sense, and it relates through it to its object" (I, p. 316). But after this start in the Kantian style, the analysis turns to a specifically Husserlian theme: the new intending of the noema towards its object, which seems to go out to something beyond the "sense," designates the degree of plenitude, the mode of "fulfillment" of the sense by intuition (I, §§ 135 ff.).

Henceforth, the phenomenology of reason will be entirely concerned with the notion of originary evidence, whether this evidence is perceptual, categorial, or otherwise. Thus, it is clear that phenomenology should develop a critique to replace that of Kant. In fact it does more than describe in the intuitive mode; it measures every claim by a seeing. Its virtue is no longer only descriptive, but now it is also corrective. Every empty signification (for example, a symbolic signification whose formative rule is lost), is referred back to the presence of actuality, such as it would appear if it would show itself, in its *Leiblichkeit*, in flesh and blood. Reason is this movement of referring from the "modified" to the "originary."

Thus, phenomenology has become critical, but in a way opposite to that of Kant. With Kant, intuition refers to the *Denken* that would limit it. With Husserl, "simply thinking" refers back to the evidence that fulfills it. The problem of fullness (*Fülle*) has replaced that of limitation (*Grenze*). In defining truth by evidence and actuality by the originary, Husserl no longer encounters the problem of the in-itself. While Kant was careful not to let himself be closed up in the phenomenon, Husserl is careful not to let himself be abused by inactualized thoughts. His problem is no longer one of ontological ground but is rather a problem of the authenticity of subjective life.

(2) But this critique of authenticity is to lead Husserl to reduction after reduction and first to a reduction of evidence itself. Every philosophy of seeing, of immediacy, threatens to return to naïve realism—that of Husserl more than any other, insofar as he insists on the presence of the thing itself in "flesh and blood." This is a danger which Husserl never ceased to invite. The more he insists on a return from the thought to the originarily evident, the more he has to compensate for the latent risks of this intuitionism in ever further radicalizing the idealistic interpretation of constitution.

The Third Cartesian Meditation and, likewise, the unpublished material of the last period are directed to this point. These writings try to reduce the repeatedly revived discord between the idealistic requirements of constitution—those that make the object a purely ideal unity of sense—and the intuitionistic requirements of reason. Hence, the reduction from the learned and the acquired must be practiced on evidence itself. Completely freed from old, sedimented, and suppressed evidence, evidence is reduced to the living present (*die lebendige Gegenwart*) of consciousness. Here once more is seen a new effect of the "metaphysical decision" that we have just discerned in the Husserlian reduction. Every presence remains an enigma for description because of the "addition" (*Zusatz*) that it contributes in comparison to my expectation and most exact anticipation. Husserl, crushing this last prestige of the in-itself, which might still insinuate itself into presence, decides that the presence *of* the thing itself is *my* present. The radical otherness attaching to presence is reduced to the nowness of the present; the presence of the Other is the present of myself.

Hereafter, Husserl will look on the side of temporality for the secret of the constitution of all supposed being-in-itself. Former evidences, destroying the movement of constitution where they were primally instituted (*Urstiftung*), present themselves as a mysterious transcendence. The in-itself is the past of evidence and the possibility of reactivation of it in a new present. An entire group of manuscripts, Group C, struggles at the breach opened by the Third Meditation. We find the great problem of temporality in the place of honor here. Because Husserl discerned the originary temporality, which is the advance of consciousness, beyond the time-representation of the "Transcendental Aesthetic," he can defy the most hallowed enchantment: absolute reality. The question is whether he ever saw the problem of being.

(3) The disontologizing of reality leads to a new climax: the passage from "static" to "genetic" constitution, a problem which is indicated by the intersecting role of temporality in the problems of origin and authenticity. Now, "genetic" constitution is largely "passive" genesis. *Experience and Judgment* indicates this orientation in Husserl's investigations. Every positing of sense and presence includes an abridged history which is sedimented and then suppressed. We have already seen this with regard to evidence. This history constitutes itself in the "anonymous" strata of subjective life. At the time of *Ideas I*, Husserl was not unaware of this aspect of the "passivity" of consciousness. However, he considered it rather as the obverse of consciousness (as hyle in relation to intentional form). What remained on the first level was the active anticipation of a "sense," of a unity of signification (thing, animal, person, value, or state of affairs). Above all, Husserl did not fail to emphasize that consciousness is a diversity which the phenomenologist cannot approach without the "transcendental guide of the object." In other words, it is noematic analysis which takes precedence over reflection on subjective life in the noetic perspective. Such concern to identify consciousness with synthesis, with the claiming of a unity, is basically very Kantian. But Husserl's interest moves progressively from the problem of the unity of sense to the problem of primal institution (*Urstiftung*), that is, to the problem of the rooting or founding of all sense in the evident actual subjective process. This shift of interest leads from logical reason to perceptual reason (the articulations of judgment actively seizing upon passively elaborated structures in the antepredicative sphere of perception).

Likewise, it leads from perceptual reason to the sensuous impression with its mnemonic retentions and its kinesthetic protentions.

Thus, the most important unpublished writings of Groups C and D in the Louvain classification elaborate a new "Transcendental Aesthetic" which is not absorbed by a "Transcendental Deduction." According to this new "Transcendental Aesthetic," the object perceived by everyone "refers back" below intersubjectivity to the primordial world such as it would appear to the *solus ipse*. Within this primordial sphere the "external" object refers to the "immanent object"—to the *Urimpression*—by means of the retentions and protentions of temporal constitution. In this way Husserl was called from the genius of Kant to that of Hume. Kant would found the impression on the a priori of sensibility and the entire perceived order on intellectual objectivity. In the late Husserl founding no longer signifies elevating to intellectuality, but on the contrary it signifies building up on the basis of the primordial, of the pre-given. Hume's genius is precisely that of regressing in this way from signs, symbols, and images to impressions.

(4) Owing to this identification of reason with a critique of evidence, to the reduction of evidence to the living present, and to the reference to the impression, one might say that Husserl entirely identifies phenomenology with an egology without ontology.

The most manifest purpose of the *Cartesian Meditations* leads to this identification. The Second Meditation initially contends that if every actuality is a correlate of the cogitatio, every cogitatio is a mode of the cogito. The cogito in turn is the expression of the ego. And thus phenomenology is an egological analysis (CM, § 13). Husserl immediately saw the formidable consequences of this view:

> Without a doubt it begins in the style of a pure egology, of a science which condemns us, it seems, to solipsism, at least transcendental solipsism. At this stage one absolutely cannot foresee how, in the attitude of reduction, it could be possible that we would have to posit the existence of other egos, not as simple mundane phenomena, but as other transcendental egos, and that thus we make them also the legitimate theme of a transcendental egology (CM, p. 69).

Husserl heroically accepts the difficulty and lets it be suspected that transcendental solipsism must remain a "preliminary philosophical stage" which must be assumed provisionally "in order that the problems of transcendental intersubjectivity may be stated and attacked correctly as founded problems and hence as problems belonging to a higher level" (CM, p. 69).

We shall see in the third part of this study whether Husserl succeeded in crossing the threshold to intersubjectivity. For the present let us note how radical a stage egology has been led to by Husserl and to what a paradox he has brought transcendental solipsism. In the Fourth Cartesian Meditation the ego itself, insofar as it is the ego of the ego cogito, is thematized: "It is continuously constituting itself as existing" (CM, p. 100). Thereafter, Husserl must go beyond the old thesis of *Ideas I* according to which the ego is the "identical pole of subjective processes." Henceforth, "the ego, taken in full concreteness, we propose to call by the Leibnizian name: monad" (CM, p. 102).

This shift from Cartesian to Leibnizian language signifies the total triumph of interiority over exteriority, of the transcendental over the transcendent: everything which exists for me is constituted in me, and this constitution is the concrete life of the ego. From here one can correctly say that all the problems of constitution are included in those of "explicating this monadic ego phenomenologically (the problem of his constitution for himself). . . . Consequently the phenomenology of this self-constitution coincides with phenomenology as a whole" (CM, pp. 102–3). Thus, phenomenology aspires—as a philosophical discipline—to cross the desert of solipsism. Phenomenology is the science of the only ego of which I have evidence originarily—my own.

Kantianism would never encounter such a problem. Not only because in its epistemological perspective it could encounter only a consciousness in general, the subject of true knowledge, but also because the *Gemüt* that the *Critique* presupposes as concrete subject is always tending toward "the transcendental-object = X" that escapes from the phenomenon and which could be the absolute existence of another person. In Husserl the disontologizing of the object virtually implies the disontologizing of the bodies of Others as well as the disontologizing of other persons. Thus, the description of the concrete subject leads, under the aegis of idealism, to a metaphysical solitude whose consequences Husserl accepted with exemplary probity.

This is why the constitution of the Other, which assures the passage to intersubjectivity, is the touchstone for the success or failure not only of phenomenology but also of the implicit philosophy of phenomenology.

[III] The "Constitution of the Other" and "Respect"

ALL ASPECTS of phenomenology, therefore, converge upon the problem of the constitution of the Other. Have we, consequently, left Kant's problem behind? Are we pushing into a new area which the Kantian genius has not cleared? Not at all. The final turning point of Husserlian phenomenology, the product of what is least Kantian in

Husserl's "transcendental experience," leads us in an unexpected manner to the heart of Kantianism, not, to be sure, to the *Critique of Pure Reason* but rather to the practical philosophy.

Kant has no phenomenology of the knowledge of Others. The phenomenology of *Gemüt* is too implicit and too blurred by epistemological considerations to contain even some hints of a theory of intersubjectivity. In the *Anthropology* at most the premises of such a theory might be found within the framework of the theory of the passions which in effect Kant conducts like a theory of intersubjectivity. But all this is slight in comparison with Husserl's admirable phenomenological essays on *Einfühlung* (empathy). The theory of empathy belongs to descriptive phenomenology before taking on the task of resolving the paradox of transcendental solipsism. It merges with the phenomenology of perception, the perception of Others being incorporated into the significations of the world that I perceive. It is inscribed in the constitution of the thing and determines the last stratum of objectivity. It is implied in the constitution of cultural objects, languages, and institutions. Hence, it is not on the properly descriptive level that phenomenology has something to learn from Kant. Here Husserl guides, not Kant.

On the other hand, we shall come back to Kant again in order to resolve the difficulties entailed by the philosophical interpretation of the reduction, difficulties which culminate in the paradox of transcendental solipsism. Husserl not only proposed to describe how Others appear, or in which perspective, or in which affective or practical modes the sense of "the Other" or "alter ego" are constituted; he also tried to constitute the Other "in" me and yet to constitute it as "Other."

This is the task of the Fifth Cartesian Meditation. One might say that this difficult attempt is a losing bet. The author tries to constitute the Other as a sense that forms in me, in what is most intimate to the ego, in what Husserl calls the sphere of my ownness. But at the same time that he constitutes the Other in me according to the requirements of idealism, he intends to respect the very sense that is attached to the presence of Others. This presence is that of someone different from me yet that of another me who has his world, who perceives me, addresses himself to me, and who forms relations of intersubjectivity with me out of which arise a unique world of science and the multiple worlds of culture.

Husserl wants to sacrifice neither the requirements of idealism nor compliance with the characteristic traits of *Einfühlung*. Idealism demands that the Other, like a thing, be a unity of modes of appearing which is a claimed ideal sense. The compliance with the actual requires that the Other "invade" my own sphere of experience and force an excess of presence through the boundaries of my subjective life in a fashion incompatible with the inclusion of sense into my subjective life.

The problem of the Other thus brings out the latent separation between the two tendencies of phenomenology, the dogmatic tendency and the descriptive tendency. The genius of Husserl is to have maintained his bet until the end. The descriptive care in respecting the otherness of Others and the dogmatic care for founding the Other in the ego's primordial ownness sphere find their balance in the notion of an analogical grasping of the Other. The Other is there himself, and yet I do not live in his subjective life. The Other is at best *appräsentiert* (appresented) on the basis of his body, which alone is *präsentiert* (presented) with an originary evidence in the sphere of my subjective life. "In" me a body is presented that appresents a subjective life other than my own. This life is a subjective life like mine in virtue of the *Paarung* (pairing) between my body here and the other body there. This coupled configuration founds the analogy between the subjective life *erlebt* (lived) and the subjective life *eingefühlt* (empathetically grasped).

Does Husserl succeed in constituting the outsider as outsider in one's own experiential sphere? Has he won his bet on the defeat of solipsism without the sacrifice of egology? The enigma is that the Other appresented in his body and grasped analogically by "passive synthesis" has a being-status (*Seinsgeltung*) that tears him out of my primordial sphere. Let us suppose that I do know the Other analogically. How can such an analogy have this transcendent intending when all other analogies go from one thing to another within my experience? If the Other's body is constituted "in" me, how is the subjective life belonging to him appresented "outside" me? How can a simple concordance of behavioral modes of appearing indicate (*indizieren*) an alien life and not just a more subtle thing of "my" world? Does Husserl succeed in escaping from the extraordinary temptation of the constitution of the thing as thing, of *Dinglichkeit*, in the flux of adumbrations? Is the Other more than a simple unity of concordant adumbrations?

In the third part of *Ideas II* Husserl does contrast the constitution of persons with the constitution of nature (things and animate bodies). In one of the appendices he even goes so far as to contrast "the unity of appearances" (*Erscheinungseinheit*) of the thing to "the unity of absolute manifestation" (*Einheit absoluter Bekundung*) of the person. Thus, the person would be much more than a display of adumbrations; he would be an absolute emergence of presence. But this opposition between the person who "announces himself" and the thing that "appears" is an opposition that description imposes and the philosophy of the reduction minimizes. It implies the complete destruction of the idealistic sense of constitution. What the person announces is precisely his own absolute existence. To constitute the person is, then, to localize the subjective modes in which this recognition of otherness, of foreignness, of other-existence is effected. Husserlian idealism is obliged to oppose this reversal of the sense of constitution.

Here we propose a return to Kant, not in the least for the purpose of perfecting a description of the appearing of the Other but rather in order to understand the sense of the existence which is announced in this appearing. It is remarkable that the philosopher most unprepared on the terrain of phenomenological description is the one who should go straight to this sense of existence. In the *Foundations of the Metaphysics of Morals*, Kant introduces the second formulation of the categorial imperative: "Act so that you treat humanity, whether in your own person or in that of another, always as an end and never as a means only." [13] One could find this brusque introduction of the Other into the Kantian formalism a shock, and one could complain that no description of the knowledge of the Other precedes this practical determination of the Other by respect. Is it not first necessary to know the Other as Other and then to respect him? But Kantianism suggests an entirely different response. The existence of the Other resides only in respect as a practical determining.

Let us examine the Kantian procedure a bit more closely. The existence in-himself of the Other is at first posited hypothetically as identical with his value:

> Suppose, however, there were something whose existence has in itself an absolute value, something which as an end in itself could be a principle of determinate laws; then in it, and in it alone, would there be the principle of a possible categorical imperative—that is, of a practical law (K, pp. 427–28).

In this hypothetical positing of a foundation, there appears no difference between the existential and the practical determination of the person. The contrast of person and thing is directly practico-existential. As object of my desires, the person belongs to the order of

---

13. [This translation, like others from this source, is that of Lewis W. Beck found in *The Critique of Practical Reason and Other Writings in Moral Philosophy* (Chicago, 1948), p. 429. This pagination, preferred by Ricoeur, is found both in Beck and in the Cassirer edition of *Kants Werke* (Berlin, 1922). Vol. 4 contains the *Grundlegung der Metaphysik der Sitten* and Vol. 5 contains the *Kritik der praktischen vernuft*. Textual references to this work appear with the letter K followed by the page numbers.]

ends in themselves: "Rational beings, on the other hand, are called *persons* because their nature already marks them out as ends in themselves . . ." (K, pp. 428–29).

It will be objected that respect, like sympathy, is a subjective feeling and no more has the power of attaining to an in-itself than sensuous perception or desire has. But to align respect with perception, desire, or even sympathy is an error, for respect is the practical moment that founds the transcendent intending of sympathy. Sympathy, as an affection, has no more privilege than hate or love. This is why the enlargement of the Husserlian phenomenology in the way indicated by Max Scheler, MacDougall, or by the French existentialists, although legitimate, changes nothing with respect to the problem of existence, even though it does enrich the inventory of the modes of the appearing of the Other. Respect, as a practical feeling posits a limit to my ability to act. Thus, speaking of humanity, Kant establishes that it is not a "subjective end" which my sympathy would aim at—this would mean including humanity among my inclinations "as an object which we of ourselves really make our end" (K, p. 431). Humanity is an "objective end," like a law of a series, which constitutes "the supreme limiting condition of subjective ends" (K, p. 431). Later on Kant calls it even more emphatically "the supreme limiting condition in the usage of all means" (K, p. 438). The same is true for the person. He is "an end that exists in himself," which I can consider only negatively "as an end against which one should never act" (K, p. 437).

Through respect the person is seen to be directly situated in a field of persons whose mutual otherness is founded on their irreducibility to means. Should the Other lose the ethical dimension which Kant calls his dignity (*Würde*), or his absolute price, should sympathy lose its quality of esteem, then the person becomes nothing more than a "merely natural being" (*blosses Naturwesen*) and sympathy merely an animal affect.

But, it will be said, the proposition "Rational nature exists as an end in itself" (K, p. 429) is only a postulate. Kant would willingly agree (see his note on p. 429). This postulate is the concept of a reign of ends, that is to say, of the systematic interconnection of reasonable beings by communal laws. The historian has no difficulty here in recognizing the Augustinian notion of the City of God and the Leibnizian notion of the reign of grace. What is properly Kantian is compliance with this notion by a regressive movement toward the foundation of good will, that is, by radicalizing the advance toward freedom. The plurality and the communication among consciousnesses cannot be made the object of description unless they are initially posited by an act of foundation laying (*Grundlegung*). Communication among consciousnesses is, then, what renders possible the coordination of freedom and what makes each subjective will a freedom.

Doubtless, one can regret the narrow juridical turn that this mutuality of freedoms takes under the notion of an a priori legislation. But this is not the most remarkable thing in Kant. The notable thing is his not having sought a "situation" for the person other than in his "belonging" (as member or as leader) to a practical and ethical totality of persons. Outside of this, one is no longer a person. One's existence can only be a value-existence (*existence-valeur*). The affective manifestations which the other person exhibits do not of necessity get beyond the level of equipment or merchandise. Thus, the absolute existence of the Other originarily belongs to the intention of good will. Only a reflexive movement of foundation laying (*Grundlegung*) reveals that this intention includes the act of situating oneself as legislating member in an ethical community.

At the same time the determination of the person as an existent end-in-himself leads us to the problem of the thing-in-itself. In the second part we emphasized the limiting function of the thing-in-itself with respect to the claims of the phenomenon. This philosophy of limits, totally absent from phenomenology, finds its own exfoliation on the practical plane, since the Other is the one against whom I must not act. But at the same time the notion of a reign of ends brings out the positive character of the founding of the in-itself. Only the determination of the in-itself never becomes theoretical or speculative but remains practical and ethical. The only intelligible world in which I can "place" myself is the one with which I have complied through respect. By the autonomy of my will and the respect for the autonomy of the Other, "we transport ourselves into the intelligible world as members." But upon entering into this world, I can "neither see nor feel myself in it" (K, p. 458). "By thinking itself into the intelligible world, practical reason does not overstep its limits in the least: it would do so only if it sought to intuit or feel itself into that world" (K, p. 458).

Has not Kant shown in this way the limits not only of the claims of the phenomenon but also the limits of phenomenology itself? I can "see" or "sense" the appearing of things, persons, values. But the absolute existence of the Other, the model of all existences cannot be sensed. It is announced as alien to my subjective life by the very appearance of the Other in his behavior, his expression, his language, and his work. But this appearance of the Other does not suffice to announce it as a being-in-itself. His being must be posited practically as that which limits the intention of my sympathy to reduce the person to his desirable quality, and as that which founds his appearance itself.

The merit of phenomenology is to have elevated the investigation of the appearing to the dignity of a science by the "reduction." But the merit of Kantianism is to have been able to coordinate the investigation of the appearing with the limiting function of the in-itself and with the practical determination of the in-itself as freedom and as the totality of persons.

Husserl *did* phenomenology, but Kant *limited* and *founded* it.

8 / Existential Phenomenology

TAKEN ALONE the term "phenomenology" is not very illuminating. The word means science of appearances or of appearings. Thus, any inquiry or any work devoted to the way anything whatsoever appears is already phenomenology. The way in which things, animate beings, or human beings show themselves could be described. Thus, the phenomenology of a "region" of reality, the region thing, the region animal, the region man could be produced. Likewise, the phenomenology of a feeling (e.g., fear, if one describes the way in which fear, the thing feared, and the world under the sign of fear show themselves) and in general the phenomenology of any subjective process of consciousness could be elaborated. In this diluted sense the word "phenomenology" covers every sort of popular presentation of appearances. The term is a long way from a disciplined limitation of its usage.

Phenomenology becomes strict when the status of the appearing of things (in the broadest sense of the term) becomes problematical. In short, it becomes strict when this question is raised: What does "appearing" signify for a thing, for an animate being, for a person, for a conscious experience, for a feeling, for an image, and the like? How do the "regions" of reality (thing, animal, man, etc.) relate to the subjective processes of consciousness (perceiving, imagining, positing an abstraction, judging, etc.)? In this strict sense the question of being, the ontological question, is excluded in advance from phenomenology, either provisionally or definitely. The question of knowing that which *is* in an absolute sense is placed "between parentheses," and the manner of appearing is treated as an autonomous problem. Phenomenology in the strict sense begins as soon as this distinction is reflected upon for its own sake, whatever the final result may be. On the other hand, whenever the act of birth, which brings appearing to emergence at the expense of being or against the background of being, is no longer perceived and systematized, then phenomenology ceases to be a philosophical discipline and falls back to the level of ordinary and popular description.

If what is implied in this first strict determination of the notion of phenomenology is developed and if one calls "transcendental" any attempt at relating the conditions of the appearance of things to the structure of human subjectivity, in short to the very life of the subject to whom and for whom things appear, then it will be said that all phenomenology is transcendental. Long before Husserl, Kant and Hegel understood the word "phenomenology" in this way. If this is how things stand, how can we speak of "existential" phenomenology? Is it another branch alongside transcendental phenomenology? But how could there be another branch if all phenomenology is transcendental? We shall show that the phenomenology termed "existential" is not another division juxtaposed to "transcendental phenomenology"; rather, this phenomenology becomes a method and is placed in the service of a dominating problem-set, viz., the problems concerning existence.

Phenomenology of the existential sort brings together investigations and writings from several sources: (1) Under this rubric the last investigations of the founder of contemporary phenomenology, Edmund Husserl, can be placed. In these researches we can observe "transcendental" phenomenology turning toward an investigation of the various aspects of man's insertion in the world. (2) In addition, we must draw out the whole function of the rigorous description incorporated in the great philosophies which proceeded from Kierkegaard and Nietzsche in France and Germany (and also from the Hegel of the *Phenomenology of the Spirit,* not to mention that species of phenomenology of economic existence which can be discerned in the work of Marx). These existential descriptions constitute an original source of contemporary phenomenology. In comparison with these philosophies born of the opposition to Hegel's *Logic,* in which classical philosophy is brought to its completion, Husserl's work seems to stand closer to certain currents of Neo-Kantianism than their author believed. (3) A third cycle of existential phenomenology is constituted by the works, particularly the French ones, which are situated at the confluence of the phenomenological method deriving from Husserl and the existential problem-set received from post-Hegelian philosophy. These works best merit the title "existential phenomenology."

[I] The "Existential" Turn of "Transcendental" Phenomenology

HUSSERLIAN PHENOMENOLOGY became more and more existential to the degree that the problem of perception took precedence over all other problems. This development deserves an explanation. In Husserl's first works, from the *Logical Investigations* to the *Cartesian Meditations,* consciousness is defined not by perception, that is to say, by its very presence to things, but rather by its distance and its absence. This distance and this absence are the power of signifying, of meaning. The intending of signifying can be empty (and even incapable of fulfillment, as is the case with absurd propositions). Then perception is only a privileged mode of fulfillment by intuition. Thus, consciousness is doubly intentional, in the first instance by virtue of being a signification and in the second instance by virtue of being an intuitive fulfilling. In short, in the first works, consciousness is at once speech (*la parole*) and perception.

It is in the works and manuscripts of the last ten years that perception is described as the initial basis and genetic origin of all operations of consciousness. This is the consciousness which gives, which sees, which effects presences, and it supports and founds the consciousness which signifies, which judges, and which speaks. This shift in accent marks the passage to existential phenomenology. In fact, the sense of the existence of things and that of the existence of the subject are revealed simultaneously in perception thus reinterpreted.

From its encounter with the Platonic and then with the Galilean tradition, which suppose that the true reality is not what one perceives but what one conceives and measures, the "thing" acquires transcendence in relation to consciousness. This transcendence certainly is not the absolute transcendence of an "in-itself" which could do without any conscious witness but is the relative transcendence of an object (*un vis-à-vis*) into which consciousness comes to transcend itself (*se dépasser*). Consciousness defined by its intentionality is outside, beyond. It ties its own wandering to the "things" to which it can apply its consideration, its desire, its action. Correlatively, the world is "world-for-my-life," environment of the "living ego." And it has this sense only with reference to the "living present," where the pact between daily living and every revealed presence is continuously renewed. Retained and anticipated, time is once more, as Kant said of the imagination, "the art hidden in nature" thanks to which the living present never ceases to move beyond itself into the project of a total world.

Yet, in becoming more and more existential the phenomenology of the late Husserl became more and more empirical, for the whole order of the understanding—predicative judgment, affirmation and negation, activity of synthesis and consecution—henceforth proceeds from "passive synthesis" initiated on the very level of perception. Thereafter it is clear that this progression toward an ever more originary original destroys every claim of constituting the world "in" consciousness or "beginning from" consciousness. The idealistic tendency of transcendental phenomenology is thus compensated for by the progressive discovery that one does not constitute the originary but only all that one can derive from it. The originary is just what could neither be constituted nor reduced.

The "world" consequently, is not what Kant said it was, viz., the Idea of reason, which commands us to unify scientific experience. For this cosmological Idea there is substituted the altogether existential notion of the horizon of subjective life. The "world" is prior to every "object." It is not only presupposed in the intellectualistic sense of a condition for possibilities, it is pre-given in the sense that every present activity surges into a world already there. Moreover, this world is the totality which, not being composed from parts and by means of addition, is inaccessible to doubt. It is the "passive pre-given universal of all judgmental activity," the "one basis of belief upon which every experience of particular objects is erected."

[II]   THE IMPLICIT PHENOMENOLOGY OF THE PHILOSOPHY OF EXISTENCE

(1) NOT ALL of existential phenomenology is in Husserl—far from it. This is the place to recall that Hegel's first great work is called *The Phenomenology of Spirit*. Now this great book nourished the most determined opponents of Hegelianism more than they believed, particularly the opponents of Hegel's *Logic*. It is one of the sources of the philosophy of existence.

In this book philosophy, passing from consciousness to self-consciousness, incorporated for the first time the most dramatic experiences of humanity which previously had yielded only to poetic, dramatic, or religious expression and not to essays having an economic, political, or historical turn. The pages on the desire of a desire which would be another self, on the struggle for recognition through the dialectic of master and slave, on stoicism and skepticism, on unhappy consciousness, and the like—today all of these pages are well-known. Hegel's concern to let human experience appear and speak for itself in its integrity is quite comparable to Husserl's precept: "Back to the things themselves." But at the same time Hegel introduced into the field of phenomenological analysis the "negative" experiences of disappearance, contradiction, struggle, and frustration which impart the tragic tone to his phenomenology. This tone is utterly foreign to Husserl's works which never drew on the "work of the negative"—as Hegel terms it—in the explication of self-consciousness.

This difference is fundamental. At the very moment that it promises an immense enrichment of the description, properly so-called, of human experience, this promotion of the "negative" paradoxically announces the end of phenomenology. In fact, these experiences of the negative are intended to assure the "transitions" from one form to another, and by that very fact to give a systematic cohesion which the old logic of identity and noncontradiction was quite incapable of introducing into the profusion of human experience. The "negative" is the possibility of a system no longer of the analytical type, after the fashion of the Leibnizian combinatorial logic, but of the dialectical type in which the "negative" mediates the becoming of spirit through its forms. Thus, phenomenology discovers the "negative." This negative brought in the new logic, and this logic eliminated phenomenology. This is why the philosophy of existence, though it may elaborate one or another of the Hegelian analyses taken in isolation, is set up over against the Hegelian system and against Logic, where tragedy is swallowed up.

(2) The term "existence," in the sense given it by contemporary philosophy, comes from Kierkegaard. The existent par excellence is the individual who emerges in sadness and solitude, in doubt and exaltation—and in passion—this is the individual whom the System does not include. This strange and irrational birth to itself of the existential thinker initially escapes every methodological concern; hence, it is beyond phenomenology—if its strict character as the science of phenomena be emphasized.

Nevertheless, in two respects Kierkegaard's thought contains the outlines of a quite strict phenomenology. In the first place, his almost sickly concern for self-justification initiates one of the most extraordinary apparatuses for the description of subjectivity ever constructed. For example, the description of "stages on life's way" is set out in an unusual key, one in which the intimacy of the most individual confession coincides with the generality of the barest abstraction. In the same way a vertiginous dread, even fear of the vertigo, which grasps freedom when confronted with the infinity of its possibilities and the finitude of its engagements and under the goad of the forbidden—a dread in which innocence turns aside to sin—elicits a description whose subtlety mobilizes the resources of a casuistical psychology, of dramatic art, and of theological anthropology. In short, the *Concept of Dread* is, properly speaking, already a phenomenology of freedom.

Beyond this concern for justification which generates a pitiless lucidity, Kierkegaard's work conceals within its irrationality a second motive for rigor. In fact, as against Hegel, it was a matter of framing the charter of the anti-system and thus little by little of rendering the opposition to the System coherent. The *Philosophical Fragments* and the *Postscript* develop this methodology of the anti-system by elaborating actual "categories" of the individual over against those of logic: the instant in place of the eternity of logic, the individual in place of the whole, paradox in place of mediation, and existence in place of the System. With the same stroke—and not without contradiction—the existential thinking tends toward a strict elaboration of the "concepts" of the anti-system and thus toward a phenomenology, which, unlike Hegel's, will never be swallowed up in logic. In these two ways, Kierkegaard is at the origin of existential phenomenology.

(3) But Nietzsche is also one of its fathers. He also used strict description, though for other than Kierkegaard's reasons. To be sure an aphoristic form and a symbolic, even mythological, construction belong to the essence of his thinking; an attempt to find a system in it would prove vain. But strict description is required by Nietzsche's plan just as it was by Kierkegaard's. It is set in motion not by concern for self-justification and for setting up a sort of indirect communication with the Other, but rather by the pitiless taste for unmasking the moral and spiritual falsehoods on which our culture is built. Nietzsche's work—at least the negative, nihilistic, side of it—is an enormous enterprise of methodical disillusionment. The *Genealogy of Morals*—did Husserl not call one of his last works a "genealogy of logic"?—is a genuine phenomenology, at once reductive and genetic, applied to the totality of moral phenomena.

A powerful and wily instinct for dissimulation is discovered at the center of human existence, which philosophy vows to track down, to denounce, and to destroy. Thus, long before the Husserlian phenomenology issued from the technique of reduction, the philosopher of "suspicion" followed the path from the derived to the originary. It matters little to us that he mixed in with this technique of truth a dogmatism of instinct and an evolutionistic scientism which are antiquated today. It even matters little that Nietzsche should have lost himself in his destructive passion. The fact remains that he is the first to have practiced what Jean-Paul Sartre later called "existential psychoanalysis." The genesis of the spirit of humility from the will to power and of the demonic form from the project of saintliness are the most remarkable, and in certain respects the most frightening, examples of this critical phenomenology, a phenomenology noticeably more inclusive than the phenomenology of cognition to which the greatest part of Husserl's work had to be limited. This phenomenology includes both a critique of the self by the self, a coming to awareness of the sense of the times, and a recapitulation of Western history in its totality.

[III] EXISTENTIAL PHENOMENOLOGY

IT IS NOW POSSIBLE to distinguish the main themes of contemporary existential phenomenology deriving from the conjunction of Husserlian phenomenology and the philosophy of existence. But these descriptive themes cannot be torn out of their philosophical context without injury. Even when they are elaborated by the same method and at times in the same terms by different philosophers, they are each traversed by a different intention which profoundly alters the sense. Existential phenomenology never describes merely for the pleasure of describing. The examples of Hegel, Kierkegaard, and Nietzsche are sufficient indication that description is effective only in the service of a great plan: to denounce an alienation, to rediscover the place of man in the world, or, on the other hand, to recover his metaphysical dimension, and so on. For each of these senses given to man's existence, there are so many descriptive styles in existential phenomenology. Let us take as examples three themes which are like the three melodic lines of existential phenomenology:

(1) First, the example of the "owned body." In Gabriel Marcel this theme has a function of break and recovery: on the one hand, break with the idolatry of the anonymous epistemological subject which is without situation, unmenaced, inaccessible to drama and to personal death, and, on the other hand, recovery of the concrete, restoration of an experience at once personal and integral which extends between the two poles of the carnal and the mysterious. This dual path, both critical and restorative, orients the patient, subtle, and sometimes evasive descriptions of the "owned body." It oscillates between being and having (I am it, and I have it), between the organ and the instrument, between the same and the different. Thought, misled by the object, works to restore the complete sense of "I exist." But at the very moment when this existential phenomenology seems to be identified with a philosophy of incarnation, it escapes this philosophy and repays it with an investigation of experiences which can be called ontological because they reveal the insertion of my being into being: fidelity, hope, etc. Existential phenomenology then signifies the "positing and concrete approach to the ontological mystery." In other words, the phenomenology of the "owned body" plays the equivocal role of a rerooting in the concrete and of a counterpole to the ontological mystery.

In Merleau-Ponty, on the other hand, the description of the owned body is entirely in the service of a philosophy of finitude or of an exorcism of standpointless thinking; ultimately it is in the service of a philosophy without an absolute. The *Phenomenology of Perception* should be followed from one end to the other without reference to the true object, seen from nowhere, which would justify the possibility of perception, even without ever denying the inherence of consciousness in a point of view. To be sure, this program assumes that the other operations of consciousness—principally science and also all that is amenable to speech and to the λόγος—bear the same fundamental structures, "the same syntheses of transition, the same sort of horizon" as perceptual experience; in short, it assumes that "every consciousness is perceptual, even the consciousness of ourselves." Thus, the first pact concluded between cognition and finitude orients the whole phenomenology of perception. The description of the "owned body" is its touchstone. This description, just as in both Husserl and Gabriel Marcel, goes hand in hand with a critique of sensation as reconstructed by psycho-physiology, i.e., as the simple effect of a physical stimulus. Phenomenology calls description from the sensation, from that late developed object of scientific consciousness, to perception, just as it is given. This perception is given as at once significational, in contrast to the pretended sensation of sensualism, but not intelligible, in contrast to the judgment of experience according to the intellectualist tradition which runs from Lachelier and Lagneau to Alain and Brunschvicg.

The theory of the "owned body" is then the critical point where the breakdown of objective thinking is consummated and where the perspectivist doctrine of perception is established. Neither the psychic, according to reflective philosophy, nor the "physiological," according to scientific thinking, accounts for the owned body. For it is the movement of being-in-the-world (*être au monde*), indivisibly voluntary and involuntary, as projected and as given. Beginning at this point, every analysis of behavior is conducted in such a way as to avoid the alternatives of automatism and abstract intelligence. The "owned body" is the locus of all ambiguities between the nascent sense and facticity, between the enacted and the reflected. Merleau-Ponty's existential phenomenology thus represents the strictest disagreement with the Platonic conversion of the here-below to the beyond. Placed in the service of a reconversion from reflection to the pre-reflective, existential phenomenology becomes identified with the justification of being-in-the-world. One can only wonder, though, how the moment of reflection on the unreflected, how the devotion to universality and to truth, and finally how the philosophical act itself are possible if man is so completely identified with his insertion into his field of perception, action, and life.

(2) The theme of freedom gives rise to contrasts even greater than those of the "owned body" and confirms the subordination of the descriptive method to the existential intention in this sector of phenomenology. The reason is clear: in the case of freedom the ontological status of man is in question. Heidegger had already placed phenomenology in the service of a fundamental ontology where the explication of the being of man was to open the horizon to a theory of being qua being. Thereafter, it is not surprising that a phenomenology of freedom, such as is at the center of Jean-Paul Sartre's work, should carry an ontological title—*Being and Nothingness*—and a subtitle which combines phenomenology and ontology. Even so, we have scarcely left the field of existential phenomenology, for with freedom, the existential and the ontological become synonymous. The being of man consists in existing, in the emphatic sense which Kierkegaard has conferred on this word.

The overthrow which Sartre introduced into the problem-set of freedom consists precisely in having inverted the ontological index of freedom. Did we just say that the being of man consists in existing? Let us rather say that existing consists in being its own nothingness. Here is where phenomenology comes into play, for it has the function of collecting the experiences where I discover my freedom in the negative style of absence, of rapture, of distance, of failure to cohere, and of constancy, of anguish, of rejection, in short, where freedom is revealed as the nihilation of the past, of the completed, in a word, of being. Evidently it is presupposed that being was previously reduced to the being of a thing, to thinghood. It is then clear that the abandonment of the great metaphysical tradition, whereby being is act par excellence, is what directs this phenomenology of nihilating acts. Moreover, this phenomenology manifests an abundance, a perspicacity, and a force rarely equaled. The "sense of the negative" of which Hegel took possession on behalf of philosophy (and to which, as we have seen, Husserl lost the key), re-emerges in contemporary philosophy with Sartre. This dialectical sense is enriched along the way with the Kierkegaardian and Marxian themes of anxiety and conflict. In addition, Sartre uses an agile imagination of concrete situations which as philosopher he takes over from the playwright. Finally, Husserl's concept of intentionality takes on a new look after this bath in negativity. It becomes the original distance, the stepping away of the self from itself, the nothing which separates existence from its having-been. But the step which carries this phenomenology of nihilating acts to the level of an ontology of nothingness is made by the philosopher, not by the phenomenologist.

Yet the same patience, the same descriptive strictness can serve an entirely different purpose, for one can describe, with Gabriel Marcel, another level of freedom, which consists less in tearing oneself away from oneself, in annulling every datum in-itself and beyond oneself, than in letting oneself be opened up by a liberating presence. A phenomenology of liberation, which describes the passage of unavailability to availability (*disponibilité*), from avarice to generosity, here becomes the harbinger of a quite different ontology, one where the main accent is on participation in being rather than on the nihilation of being. But this descriptive spirit is not what makes for the difference between the two phenomenologies. The difference lies rather in the sense of the word "being," which for one signifies act, the giving of existence, and for the other signifies the brute datum or dead thing.

In Merleau-Ponty the phenomenology of freedom can also take form within the phenomenology of the "owned body" which, as we have seen, joins the ego to the world instead of completing the break between the "for-itself" and the "in-itself." If in fact the body is the movement of my being-in-the-world, if it is a spontaneity which offers itself to a situation in order to form it, then the decisive experience of freedom is to be sought not in the dramatic moment of breaking away but rather in the moment of engagement which includes the whole involvement in situation. To project our past, our future, our human milieu around ourselves is precisely to situate ourselves. Henceforth, concrete freedom is not to be sought elsewhere than in this general power to place oneself in situation. And the all or nothing of Sartrean freedom appears to have no measure in common with actual experience, which does not know the sovereign "in-itself" and never encounters anything but a relative freedom which incessantly "busies itself in taking up some proposition about the world." The phenomenology of freedom follows up the metaphysics of finitude which the theory of the owned body began.

(3) The theme of the Other supports our analysis of the relations between the phenomenological method and the ontological intention in existential phenomenology. Jean-Paul Sartre initiates his analysis of

the existence of the Other with the experience of being seen, of being caught by a gaze which freezes me in my tracks, reduces me to the condition of an object, steals my world from me, and takes away my freedom along with my subject position. The existence of the Other thus constitutes my "original fall," that is to say, the movement by which I fall into the world and am condemned to parry and thrust, i.e., to the struggle which is pursued in incipient or indirect ways even in sexual activity. But the choice of this glance that encroaches, fixes, determines, this glance which menaces because it is menaced, this freezing gaze—this choice comes to phenomenology from far away. If the Other appears to me by primordial right as power of encroachment (*d'empiètement*) and of theft, is this not because freedom itself has been described without the experience of generosity or of giving? Is it not only in a foregone project of unavailability, as Emmanuel Mounier says somewhere, that the Other's gaze is a gaze that petrifies and not instead a gaze that overthrows?

However such things stand, when it is a question of the Other, just as when it is a question of freedom or of the owned body, the field of existential phenomenology is an oriented field. One does not describe just anything simply for the pleasure of making brilliant analyses. The privilege accorded to misunderstanding, to conflict, to encounter, to reciprocity, to the collaboration of a teammate or of a galley slave betrays a different ontological style, according to whether being renders the constitution of a *we* possible or not, wherein the difference and the distance between me and the Other would somehow be overcome.

Thus, existential phenomenology makes the transition between transcendental phenomenology, born of the reduction of every thing to its appearing to me, and ontology, which restores the question of the sense of being for all that is said to "exist."

9 / Methods and Tasks of a Phenomenology of the Will

AT SEVERAL POINTS in *Ideas I* Husserl indicates that the problems of the will could and should be entirely repeated and recast by the method of intentional analysis which had already borne its first fruits on the level of the perceptual consciousness and more generally on the level of objectivating acts. He outlined this transposition of the method to the "affective and volitive subjective processes" in two directions. Phenomenology applied to these new subjective processes will first have to exemplify the universality of intentional analysis, and in particular the universality of the distinction between noema and noesis (cf. I, p. 95). Thus, the question is to determine whether the analysis of noetic and noematic structures is still valid for the enormous affective and practical sector of consciousness—the whole project of this analysis having been elaborated with regard to perception, imagination, memory, the sign, enunciative belief, the reality judgment, and in general with regard to the whole level of "representation" (*Vorstellung*). According to Husserl (cf. I, § 116) this new extension of intentional analysis ought further to confirm that the composite or, as he says, "synthetic" subjective processes, among which he classifies affections and volitions, do not call into question the primacy of "objectivating" acts within the totality of consciousness. These acts are varieties of "simple" representations; they have a single "ray." Affection and volition should be instituted "on" representations, as complex "founded" processes on the "simple" (*schlicht*) "founding" subjective processes.

(1) The goal of the present study is, first, to show the fruitfulness of this patient method of description when applied to the practical functions of consciousness. On this first level, to "constitute" simply means to spell out intermingled intentionalities, in some fashion to spread them out before a distinct consciousness, and to identify the

aspects of the world, of the Other, and of my body which stand as correlates of affective and volitive intendings.

(2) But on a second level, the results reached by extension to the will of the intentional method must be turned against the transcendental doctrine erected on the narrow base of the analysis of "representations," i.e., all the operations of consciousness whose primary type is perception. At that level the "constituting" power of consciousness can be interpreted with the resources developed from a description of the voluntary and the involuntary. Husserl's transcendental idealism can then be criticized in light of this new description.

(3) Finally on a third level, we shall outline the transition from a descriptive and constitutive phenomenology to an ontology of consciousness. We shall attempt to circumscribe a privileged experience which, on the level of the voluntary and the involuntary, is constituted as revelatory of my ontological situation. As we shall see, this experience can be an experience of deficiency, of non-being. This experience at least will allow us to denounce as naïve the pretensions of the subject to set himself up as the primitive or primordial being under the pretext that he has, in a limited but authentic sense, the transcendental function of "constituting" the involuntary aspect of his life and world.

[I] THE LEVEL OF DESCRIPTIVE ANALYSIS

PROVISIONALLY SETTING ASIDE the interpretation which Husserl gives of the "founded" character of affective and volitive subjective processes as related to "representation"—an interpretation which is perhaps no more than a prejudice which phenomenology ought to abandon—we need to take the practical life of consciousness as it is given and apply the method of intentional analysis directly to it without going through a prior phenomenology of perception and objectivating acts in general.

This study primarily tends toward a defense and illustration of intentional analysis. We can hardly stress this point enough, for, at the primary level at least, phenomenology is a description which proceeds by analyses. Thus it asks, what does it mean to speak of willing, of acting, of motive, or of situation, and so on . . . ? The fruitfulness of the noetico-noematic analyses of the period of the *Ideas* has probably been underestimated by the generation of phenomenologists which went immediately to the writings of the period of the *Crisis*. That school of phenomenologists has sought inspiration in the theory of the *Lebenswelt* for a description which is too quickly synthetic for my liking. In dealing with a problem, if we go straight to the "existential project," to the "movement of existence" to which all authentically human conduct leads, then we risk missing the special character of the problem and blurring the outline of different functions within a sort of indistinct existential monism which ultimately leads to a repetition of the same interpretation of "existence" with respect to imagination, emotion, laughter, gesture, sexuality, speech, etc.

In the early stages at least, phenomenology must be structural. More precisely, this technique of distinguishing and spelling out interwoven intentionalities must be guided by what Husserl called "noematic reflection." He meant by this, to be sure, a reflection on subjective life but also a reflection on the "side" of the subjective process which is not the intending itself but rather its correlate, a reflection on the object of the various conscious intentive processes. By reflecting on the willed as such, on the emotionally moving, on the imagined as such, we gain access to the distinction among acts themselves, among the intentive processes of consciousness. Willing and moving, for example, are different because their correlates have a different signification.

We must emphasize in addition the concept of signification. To say that phenomenology must distinguish the "significations" from functions or structures means, in the first place, to recognize the task of testing the ordinary and scientific terminology of psychology, in order, for example, to remove the confusing and damaging extension of the senses of expressions such as "project," "motive," "action," or "situation," which have suffered inflation in contemporary phenomenological literature. Furthermore, it means to discern, through this corrected terminology, the "essences" of subjective life. Nor should we forget that the transcendental reduction, which restores the general sense of consciousness, cannot be practiced without the eidetic reduction that determines significations such as perceiving, seeing, imagining, deciding, acting, etc.—to mention but a few examples. The fear of Platonizing essences should not make us avoid the task of constituting phenomenological objects, meaning by this the ideal contents capable of fulfilling the many and varied significational intendings which language employs every time we say "I wish," "I desire," "I regret," or every time that we understand a situation or occasion of conduct as signifying willing, desiring, or regretting. These significations can be identified and recognized in spite of the flowing character of consciousness and in spite of the uniqueness (*singularité*) of each consciousness. If what is "other" could not signify what is the "same," in short, if some relatively incomparable situation could not be understood and spoken about, then the twofold difference (*altérité*)—the temporal difference within a single consciousness and the mutual difference among several consciousnesses—would render each consciousness ineffable to itself and one consciousness ineffable to another.

Even in the obscure forest of emotions, even in the course of the blood stream, phenomenology gambles on the possibility of thinking and naming. It gambles on that primordial discursivity of each subjective process, a discursivity which keeps such a process open for a reflection which may be implicitly a "speaking" (*dire* λέγειν). If the possibility of speaking were not inscribed upon the "will to speak" (*vouloir dire*) of subjective life, phenomenology would not be the λόγος of the φαινόμενα. This intentional analysis directed into the practical function of consciousness cannot be carried out in this study with the care that it requires. The articulations of the many intentional moments of willing can only be indicated very schematically and proposed as a program for work. It is more appropriate, rather, to linger over the sense of this task.[1]

If we practice what Husserl calls "noematic reflection," that is, reflection on the intentional correlate of such a consciousness of . . . , the willed at first designates what I decide, the project I form. We thus take the term project in the strict sense of correlate of deciding; by it, I signify or emptily designate a future action which is within my power and depends on me. The project is the action in the gerundive, the future *pragma* in which I am implicated (in the accusative) as the one who will do and (in the nominative) as he who can do. This definition abridges a multitude of precise analyses which ought to be explicated: the imperative and nonindicative manner in which the project designates what is "to be done," the categorial modality of that "to be done" in relation to the wish, the future dimension of the project, different from foresight, its index "to be done by me" as opposed to the "to be done by another" of a command, and so on.

Also, it is necessary to show how the intentionality of deciding, turned toward the project, is articulated upon an involvement of myself: "I decide to . . ." includes an "I make up *my* mind."[2] This vague consciousness of responsibility presents for reflection the same impulse of consciousness which moves beyond itself toward a job to be done in the world. Finally, the project includes a certain reference to a

1. For a systematic treatment of that intentional analysis, cf. *Philosophie de la volonté;* Vol. I: *Le Volontaire et l'involontaire* (Paris, 1950), pp. 37–75, 187–216, 319–31. [English translation by Erazim V. Kohák, *Freedom and Nature: The Voluntary and the Involuntary* (Evanston, Ill., 1966).]

2. [The contrast here is between the transitive and irreflexive expression *je décide de* . . . (I decide to . . .) and the reflexive expression *je me décide* (I decide for myself, or I make up my mind).—Trans.]

course of motivation: "I decide (for myself) *because* . . ." This relation of the project to its motives must be carefully distinguished from the naturalistic relation of causality. In fact, this is the relation which contains in principle all the mediations between the body and the will.

The "to be done" is on the way toward the doing. Here the proposed intentional structure is that of action. Willing no longer "emptily" designates; rather, it works in the present. I make use of presences achieved by me; the entire world, with its paths and its obstacles, with the unsolved and the accomplished, is the material and the context of my action. The "done by me," the *"pragma,"* as I shall say, as distinct from the project, is in the world and no longer against the background of the world. It is in the world and not in my body; what I "do" is not a movement, not even a complex gesture caught in the whole posture of the body. In action the body is "traversed." The body is not the object of the action, even in the broad sense of a correlate, but is rather its organ. Moving through its function as an organ, where it fades away, the "done by me" is open to the activity as such (which I express by all of the infinitives of action: to run, to work, etc.). The work is, thus, my practical response to a difficulty opened *in medias res* and is inscribed upon the tissue of the world.

Finally, the will completes itself in a more covert intentive process, which I call "consenting." The internal and external necessity for consent is not merely looked at, instead it is actively adopted; it is my situation, the condition of my existing as a volitive being in the world. The active adoption of this necessity sets it up as a practical category, while at the same time taking it on in the first person. From this point on, a phenomenology of finitude is possible, a phenomenology of the hidden (or of the unconscious) and of the initial condition of being born—*natus*—in short, a phenomenology of the state of existing in the very midst of the act of existing.

Before setting out on the way towards a more synthetic view of the voluntary and involuntary life, we need to emphasize the double advantage of this descriptive method on the level of a phenomenologically reoriented psychology. Paradoxically, I would not say that the first advantage is to give an understanding of the involuntary. Classical psychology constructed man like a house: below were the elementary functions; above was an extra level, the will. Need, desire, and habit were transposed from animal psychology as required. Thus, it was possible to omit the fact that the will is already incorporated in a complete understanding of the involuntary. Yet in the human order of things, need, emotion, and habit only take on complete senses in relation to a will which they solicit, motivate, and in general affect; while reciprocally the will takes on these senses even if only by its resignation. The will determines them by its choices, moves them by its effort, and adopts them by its consent. There is no intelligibility belonging to the involuntary as a mechanism, as emotional shock, as unconscious, as character, etc. Only the living interrelationship between the voluntary and the involuntary is intelligible. Only in terms of this interrelationship is description also understanding.

This reversal of perspective is only one aspect of the Copernican Revolution which in various forms is the first achievement of philosophical understanding. For explanation, the simple is the reason for the complex; for understanding, the one is the reason for the many. Far from demolishing the psychology of the involuntary, this reversal establishes it by giving it a sense. Once we have said that the involuntary is for the voluntary, the elucidation of that "for" is exactly the program for a psychology of the involuntary. The many ways of being for the voluntary yield the concrete categories of the involuntary, such as motive of . . . , organ of . . . , and condition of willing. We can see in what limited sense willing is constitution, i.e., in the sense that it qualifies all of the involuntary as human by taking it as motive of . . . , organ of . . . , situation of . . .

The second advantage of this phenomenology is to lead to the constituting will from the constituted will, with which characterology deals and which fell into the hands of empirical psychology. This phenomenology refers from the will which I more or less have to the will which I am. This will is no longer the object of statistical inquiries, of inductive generalization; rather, once more it is grasped as the primitive act of consciousness.

In what sense is this practical constituting called primitive? In the sense that I cannot bring about an empirical development of it. If I hesitate, my indecision is given as a choice that is absent, impossible, wished for, delayed, or dreaded. But even in the absence of choice, I still remain within the categories of choice, as my silence remains within the categories of speech. A slow, hindered willing, a willing which yields, is still a willing; the world for me remains a sea upon which I am embarked in order to choose. A total absence of willing would be an absence of human being. The same is true of an infantile will. It is still a willing included within the concrete categories of project, motive, involvement, movement, power, etc. By unfolding the great events of affective, active, and intellectual life, developmental psychology shows the advent of a sense which by growing becomes historical and thus becomes what it is.

This brief descriptive outline has at least allowed us a glimpse of the sense in which phenomenology always remains a λόγος, at least at its descriptive and analytical level. We have just presented a dual approach toward the ineffable: from the side of the owned body and the obscure affectivity which it nourishes and from the side of the primitive willing which by its uniqueness transcends characterological generalities. Is it possible to maintain until the very end our commitment to intelligibility and communication in both of these directions?

The notion of a phenomenology of the involuntary is not absurd. I have certainly lost the naïveté of pure feeling; but being human consists precisely in already having begun to assume a position in relation to desiring or suffering. There is no phenomenology of the purely involuntary, but instead there is only a phenomenology of the involuntary as the counterpole of a willing consciousness. That initial understanding of my own involuntary life as diversely affecting my willing is the only intelligible aspect of involuntary life as lived through (*vécue*).

However, phenomenology is not condemned to begin all description and analysis from nothing. The naturalistic cognition of man, which empirical psychology in all of its forms puts into operation, is not purely and simply rejected. Psycho-physiology of willing, experimental psychology of elementary movement and posture, psychology of behavior, psycho-pathology of deficiencies, changes, failures of willing, psychology of social life, etc., tend, as all sciences of nature do, to elaborate empirical concepts, functional notions. These are what the scientists call "facts"; they are always contemporaneous with the elaboration of a "law" if they are to be worthy of the rank of "scientific facts."

These "facts" which, on the plane of objective, mundane, and naturalistic cognition, give an account of the voluntary and involuntary life of man and which are integrated into a science of man, do not belong to the subjective life of consciousness. But, if they retained nothing of conscious subjective life, in no way would they concern man and his consciousness; they would not signify man at all. A good implicit phenomenology is often concealed in the most objectivistic sciences and sometimes comes to the fore through the "naturalistic" concepts of psychology. Good examples of such a progress of phenomenology can be found in the clinic and by way of behavioral psychology in the area of the psychology of language and symbolic function. The phenomenology of the voluntary and the involuntary abounds in examples of the same order: there is a good though nonthematized phenomenology lost within naïve problem-sets such as that of behaviorism (I am thinking in particular of Tolman) and especially in those of Gestalt psychology (Kohler, Koffka, and Lewin and his school). It is possible to recapture this somewhat alienated phenomenology by using the "facts" of scientific psychology as diagnostics of phenomenological subjective processes. By means of this diagnostic relation a naturalistic concept may indicate and after a fashion show up a possible signification of consciousness. Sometimes even a very elaborate empirical concept, such as the psychoanalytic concept of the unconscious, diagnostically indicates a moment of consciousness so hidden that its phenomenology is no longer possible. A phenomenology of the "hidden" is by definition a gamble. Yet only a phenomenology which in a manner fades away can liberate us from the naturalistic mythology, such as that of Freudianism, where the unconscious feels and thinks and where consciousness appears naïvely as a part, an effect, or a function of the unconscious.

By this diagnostic relation, phenomenology, in a given time, participates in the work of psychology and elaborates its "essences" of subjective life in their tension with the concepts of the sciences of man.

The notion of a phenomenology of an individual (*singulière*) consciousness is no longer absurd, for the individual consciousness is you or I. Henceforth, for phenomenology, subjectivity designates the subject function of an intentional consciousness in which I understand myself and others. The understanding of self and the understanding of the Other are elaborated together and thus give access to genuine concepts of subjectivity, valid for my fellow man. Even the notion of the solitary choice is elaborated intersubjectively; solitude is still a possibility common to the human condition. I understand it as that of which "everyone" is capable, which is again to refer to my fellow man.

[II] THE LEVEL OF TRANSCENDENTAL CONSTITUTION

THE ANALYTICAL DESCRIPTION of overlapping intentionalities within the willing consciousness is only a first stage for phenomenology. There remains the task of recapturing the whole movement of consciousness opening from the future, making its landscape with its deeds, and working through what it has not done. The question of the interpretation of the whole of the life of consciousness arises in this passage from intentional analysis to existential synthesis.

We have been led to say that willing is "constituting" in the sense that it qualifies the whole of the involuntary as human by taking it as the motive of . . . , the organ of . . . , the situation of . . . willing. We have added that the same willing is "primitive" in the sense that I can imagine neither its absence nor its genesis without suspending the human being. Does this usage of the two Husserlian expressions, "constitutive" and "primitive," confirm the transcendental idealism erected by the Freiburg philosopher in connection with his analyses of perception? The phenomenology of the will, which initially only extends a method tested elsewhere to a new segment of reality, turns its results against the doctrine, which has gradually become indistinguishable from the method. Has the doctrine of transcendental idealism value only within the limits of a theory of representation, of the spectator consciousness?

For Husserl this problem was not acute. As we said at the outset, affective and volitive subjective processes were in his eyes processes "founded" on representation. That primacy of objectivating acts refers back, it seems, to a logistic prejudice which direct reflection on practical life does not verify. Willing has a way of giving sense to the world by opening up practical possibilities and penetrating the indeterminate zones of the will, by peopling the real with human works, by coloring the very resistances of reality with its patience as with its revolts. Thus, we must restore the whole scope to that "giving of sense" which is consciousness in all of its aspects. As the beginning of *Ideas II* suggests, it is even possible to show that the purely theoretical attitude, the attitude which triumphs in science, proceeds by correction and by subsequent purification of a primary presence to things which is indivisibly spectator observation, affective participation, and active influence on things. This theoretical view is outlined already in what the psychologists influenced by Neo-Criticism call "representation." Husserl was not unaware of this, but he hoped to find in that complex subjective process a "kernel of sense" of an "objectivating" character which was already there and which sustained the affective and practical "strata" of consciousness. But, we believe, noematic reflection on the project (or the correlate of deciding), on the *pragma* (or correlate of acting), and on the situation (or correlate of consenting) reveals nothing of this sort.

Here is how we can explain Husserl's logistic prejudice. If we compare an assertion, a wish, a command, and a project, all are expressed as modalities which can be more or less accurately rendered by the grammatical "modes" of indicative, conditional, imperative, etc. Now it is possible to disengage a sort of neutral mode from all of these modes, the infinitive (to eat, to travel, to paint) which is like a common *quid* of all the noemata. One might be tempted to identify this common *quid*, this "kernel of sense," with representation and to reconstruct the wish, the command, or the project on the basis of that neutral representation: I wish (to travel), I order you (to eat), I desire or want (to paint). But this sense held in common is not a representation at all; it is not even a complete noema or a concrete thing into which a consciousness can transcend. It is an abstraction set apart from the complete noemata of asserting, wishing, commanding. Thanks to a secondary modification identical in each instance, that "kernel of sense," that λεκτόν (to use a term from Stoic logic), is then intended by a new act which is no longer either consent, wish, or command but an operation of a grammarian or a logician. The λεκτόν is then only the logico-grammatical correlate of such an operation.

We must, therefore, consider all the "modes"—indicative, conditional, imperative—as equal and primitive. The very fact that we can develop the world-as-observed by starting from the world of desiring or the world of praxis indicates that all the permutations are possible and that the "I will" is first of its kind within the Cartesian account elaborating the "I think." [3] Thus, it seems incontestable that voluntary life gives us a privileged and irreducible access to the problems of constitution. It has a manner appropriate to expressing the sense-giving (*Sinngebung*) of consciousness, for like the Spinozistic God, consciousness is complete in one of its aspects; it is human existence in its totality which in perceiving, willing, feeling, imagining, etc., "gives sense."

The practical life of consciousness presents original problems which in principle are not resolved by an interpretation of "representation"; an attempt could then be made to save Husserl's idealism by identifying the transcendental and "existence" as praxis.[4] Besides, was this not just what we had in mind from the moment that we took the "I will" as constituting the involuntary in man?

That is only partially true. The phenomenology of the will dispels certain equivocations of sense-giving (*Sinngebung*) which cannot be raised to the level of the theory of "representation." If we still wish to call transcendental the voluntary existence which institutes and discovers the practical aspects of the world, such a transcendental cannot be considered to be creative. In fact, the signification of passivity remains hidden in a theory of "representation." We know the uneasiness occasioned by Husserl's theory of hyle in *Ideas I*.[5] Passivity takes on its functional sense within the dialectic of the voluntary and the involuntary.

Let us pause a moment over the traits of this dialectic. On the one hand, it dispels the elementary dualisms and tends toward the limit of the simple and indivisible person, but in the opposite direction it

3. "What is a thinking thing? That is, a thing which doubts, conceives, affirms, denies, wills, does not will, also imagines and feels?" *Meditation II.*
4. Merleau-Ponty, *Phénoménologie de la perception* (Paris, 1944), pp. 73 ff.
5. I, pp. 172, 203. Cf. Fink, "Die phänomenologische Philosophie Edmund Husserls, *Kantstudien*, XXXVIII (1933), 319–83.

brings out what could be called an existential monism, that is, a reflection which seeks to stabilize itself at the level of that indivisible movement of human existence. Let us clarify successively the two sides of this dialectical relationship which we are trying to suggest.[6]

The phenomenology of the will, in search of the lived-through unity of the voluntary and the involuntary, attacks dualism at its root, in the methodological attitudes which institute it. On the one hand, the thinking, which tends to identify itself with self-consciousness, retains only the most reflexive moments of voluntary life, only the moments by which I come back upon things, upon the resistance of my body, upon my motives, and bury myself in the consciousness of the "it is I who . . ."; "it is I who" makes up my mind, who desires to will, who can be able. I am that effort which opposes itself to a body which resists. I am that liberty which comes upon itself in an alien world of necessity. On the other hand, objective thinking, which posits objects true for everyone in a world devoid of individual perspective, repels involuntary life and the whole corporeal life back among objects and omits itself as consciousness for which there are objects. Thus, a scientific biology and psychology are legitimately born.

The division between soul and body, to use classical terminology, proceeds in one direction from the attitude of consciousness facing its own life. It is, then, not yet an ontological dualism but, so to speak, a preontological one.

Phenomenology, by reinstating these attitudes in relation to a more fundamental attitude, restores the unitary movement of the voluntary and the involuntary. Moving along on this side of the consciousness of self, phenomenology shows consciousness adhering to its body, to the whole of its involuntary life, and through that life, to a world of action which is its work and the horizon of its work. Then in addition, moving along on this side of the objective forms of that involuntary life, phenomenology rediscovers within consciousness itself the adherence of the involuntary to the "I will." In this reflection reaching beyond reflexive aspects of willing and in this recovery of the involuntary in the first person from the forms objectified by scientific psychology, we truly move beyond the purely analytic stage of phenomenology and stop spelling out intentionalities and their correlates in order to recapture the whole of the life of the will.

We shall consider this convergent course by taking it up at its two extremes. Reflection brings the will to a culmination in the determination of the self by itself, for I make up *my* mind (*je me décide*), it is I

6. This movement of thought sums up a more detailed analysis presented before the *Société française de philosophie* (Session of November 25, 1950) under the title, "*L'Unité du volontaire et de l'involontaire comme idée-limite.*"

who determine *myself* and whom I determine. The reflexive form of the verb emphasizes this relation, at once active and reflective, of the self with the self. We need to point out that this judgment of reflection is by no means artificial. It is sufficient that I lay claim to responsibility for my acts or that I charge myself with them in order for this reflexive involvement of myself to show up in my consciousness. Even if I go to the very end of this reflexive movement, I discover myself as the possibility of myself which continuously precedes and reiterates itself in the anguish of what might be. But probing the root of that reflective involvement of myself, I discover an unreflective involvement implicit in my projects themselves. Initially, the decision moves somewhere among places and beings and invokes a novel performance by signs in the imperative mood; and while I project myself into an action to be done, which indicates me to myself, so to speak, in the accusative as an aspect of the project, I thus bring myself into question within the purpose of the action to be done. That self, involved in me there, is not yet a true ego, but only a vague presence of my unrealized powers, themselves projected and grasped in the form of the action which will take place. Prior even to judgments of reflection of the type "it is I who," we discover that prejudicative consciousness which is sufficient for holding the intent of my project ready for reflection. In this sense, the first possibility inaugurated by willing is not my own ability-to-be but the event-like possibility which I open up in the world by the projection of action; it is the possibility-of-being-done seen against the world itself, against that world which remains always at the horizon of my choice as the field of operation of my freedom.

In its turn, a project focuses my life at a given moment only because it is rooted in a definite manner in my involuntary life through motivation. There is no decision without a motive (on the condition that we distinguish motive from cause). An original relation holds between initiative and a search for legitimacy. The progress of my choice and the maturation of my motives are one and the same thing.

How is this possible? Starting from the involuntary rather than from the voluntary and taking the description in reverse order, we should see, for instance in the example of desire, how the body in one way or another nourishes motivation so that it can be balanced by a non-corporeal value. Thus, only man can go on a hunger strike; the sacrifice of need attests to the fact that need is ready to submit to a general evaluation. It was necessary that opaque emotionality should first discover in the representation of the absent object and of the way to attain it a form which is at this point an imagining form; likewise, it was necessary that an imagining anticipation should bear upon the pleasure itself, that I should apprehend the goodness of bread in an affection grasped in some degree as the affective image or the analogon of future pleasure. An affection transfigured by an evaluating intention brings the body to the level of a field of motivation and makes it a human body.

It goes without saying that will and power are united in a voluntary motion and that there the distance to things, that sort of irreality of the project, is annulled. Now we could at this point retrace the same return movement which is prior to the reflexive reiteration of effort right up to where that motion which spreads through the docile body and which is unreflective volition passes through the body to the things themselves. Here again we could show how the stimulated and the habitual spontaneity of the body precedes voluntary movement. Our cognitions are also a kind of body; through rules of grammar and calculation, moral and social knowledge, we move on to new acts and so enact our knowledge as we enact our powers.

The sole purpose of these examples was to show how phenomenology is able to extricate the problem of dualism from an impasse and to propose itself the task of surprising the "practical mediation" of the *cogito* and of the *sum* in the articulations of the voluntary and the involuntary. It again goes without saying that the demonstration would be complete if we could succeed in exhibiting the mutual rootedness of freedom and nature up to the most unmistakable forms of necessity, at the level of the indistinct awareness of being alive.

While the critique of methodological dualism restores to us the lived-through union of pre-reflective willing and the owned body, description brings out and multiplies the ever increasingly subtle forms of duality which I shall call existential duality; these forms of duality destroy the intentional monism of our whole previous endeavor. Certain aspects of this dualism can be explained by the temporal structure of our being-in-the-world (*être-au-monde*), as Merleau-Ponty expresses it,[7] in the sense that a tendency to persistence, to fixation, is inscribed in every living present. Sliding into generality and anonymity hardens persistence into resistance, and thus every new project breaks into a world already there, a world of sedimented projects. A part of my vital energy is dispensed into the organic vigilance by which I keep available previous presences of myself as a sort of an abbreviated acquisition.

If we follow this course through to the end, we no longer have to speak of a reciprocity of the voluntary and the involuntary along with whatever the language still conserves of dualism, but rather we could

7. Merleau-Ponty, *op. cit.*, pp. 98–105.

speak of the ambiguity of a movement of existence which in a single thrust, by way of temporalization, becomes freedom and servitude, choice and situation. But we cannot follow through this reabsorption of resistances into survivals to the end, because the only aspects of the involuntary which appear to be so constituted by sedimentation are those which are near or distant tributaries of habit. The description of the involuntary reveals all sorts of forms of the involuntary which are not accumulations from the past. Above all, such fusion into one another of project and situation is held in check by certain fundamental aspects of voluntary life which authorize us to speak of a dramatic or polemic duality, whose unusual status, oscillating between monism and dualism, we must recognize.

We must start from the more manifest in order to reach the more hidden. The most manifest is the split which suffering introduces between me and myself, between the ego which takes suffering on and the ego which undergoes it. Suffering introduces an existential fault or rent (*faille*) [8] into my own incarnation. Necessity is lived through not simply as affecting me, but as wounding me; this is why, on the other hand, freedom contains the possibility of not accepting myself, of saying "no" to that which curtails and negates me. The active denial of my freedom inflames the diffuse negativity of my condition. The incompleteness of my character, whose impotence I must come to terms with in clear consciousness, the situation in which I fall back upon the nourishing and healing grace of my body, these all unceasingly give rise to an erupting and recoiling movement which leads me to wish to come back, to circle around myself, in order to expel the limitations of character—limitations in the unconscious and in being-alive—into a constituted empirical subject. Thus, the moment of rejection, which may be implicit in reflection, becomes manifest; this is the refusal of the human condition expressed in man's threefold wish: to be complete, without finite perspective of character; to be transparent, without the opacity of the unconscious; and finally, to be of oneself (*être par soi*), not born. Thus, the offending scandal is built into the texture of one's condition.

Turning back from the level of consent to that of action, I notice that the continuity of willing, being able to move, and moving manifests its ever reappearing duality: voluntary motion is always to some degree an effort—to the extent to which the body is spontaneous, that

8. [The French word *faille*, like the English word "fault," is used as a geological term referring to a rent or shift in certain earth strata. Its metaphorical use here refers to a split, rent, flaw, or fault in experience. The term, however, is intended to be neutral, referring to neither moral evil, legal guilt, or religious sin, but rather to something anterior to these. *Faute* is sometimes used with the same force.—Trans.]

is, to the extent to which it gets away from me, goes on ahead, and resists. This concrete dialectic is expressed in the contrasting roles of emotion and habit: the one surprises me in the moment, the other alienates me by interposing duration. And since the one heals the other, it must be that spontaneity is by turns organ and obstacle. The perfect voluntary movement, one may say, would be one in which the body would be completely effaced in its organ function. But I am not such an entire docility to myself, and my grasp on my body remains a constant regrasping. Thus, the unity of effort and spontaneity remains at the horizon of my condition as a limit-Idea, and voluntary life continues to be a conflict.

Finally, our regressive movement brings us back to the source of the voluntary act. If in fact we place decision back into the time in which it came to maturity, what we have called the existential fault once again becomes apparent. It becomes apparent in the quite paradoxical fact that the way choice happens can be interpreted in two different ways: in one sense, it is the cessation of an evaluation (I determine myself *because* of this or that reason), but in another sense, it is the emergence of a new act which definitively fixes the sense of my reasons. This twofold reading is inscribed in the structure of decision. This structure is, on the one hand, the invention of a project and, on the other, a reception of values elaborated in another stratum of consciousness. That is just why there have always been two philosophies of freedom: according to one of them choice is only a cessation in deliberation, a repose of attention, as Malebranche said, while according to the other choice is an emergence, an irruption. To be sure, we can always reconcile them theoretically by saying that putting a stop to the motivation toward a course of action and choosing that course amounts to the same thing, but in the concrete life of consciousness these two readings do not correspond to the same situations. There are some choices which do not attain clarity even after endless evaluation and re-evaluation, others which depend on a wager, a toss of the dice. The extremes would be the scrupulous or gratuitous act, the indecisive valuation, or the choice without value; these two possibilities always stalk me and reveal the inner tension of my choice. The synthesis of legitimacy and inventiveness, of value and audacity, remains as a limit-Idea.

Thus, the unity of the person can be expressed in hesitating language: decision *and* motive, action *and* possibility, consent *and* situation.

This conclusion is central to our interpretation of the constituting power of consciousness, according to the transcendental idealism of Husserl. Indeed, it is still possible to speak of a performance (of a

Leistung) of consciousness because the activity of decision, of motion, and of consent complete the human sense of affectivity, of the spontaneity of the animal body. In this sense the phenomenology of the will revises Husserlian transcendentalism in a more existential direction, but it does not overthrow it. It only reinforces the tendency to move away from Kantianism and from the critical philosophical movement in general. Yet on the other hand, the phenomenology of the will bars all pretension to an interpretation of the giving consciousness as "creative"—the bipolarity of its condition appears irreducible. The reciprocity of the voluntary and the involuntary illustrates the specifically human modality of freedom. Human freedom is a dependent independence, a receptive initiative. The notion of creation is directly opposed to the mode of existence which characterizes human willing.

[III] ON THE THRESHOLD OF ONTOLOGY

THE "CONSTITUTIVE" CHARACTER of consciousness is a conquest of criticism over naturalistic (or mundane) naïveté. But the transcendental level thus won conceals a second-level naïveté—the naïveté of criticism which consists in considering the "transcendental," the "constitutive," as the absolutely irreducible. The reflection capable of unmasking, a "second reflection," to borrow Gabriel Marcel's expression, assures the passage from a transcendental phenomenology to a properly ontological phenomenology.

Here our problem is to show the resources of a phenomenology of the will in the movement toward the threshold of ontology. Phenomenology has, in fact, its own way of eliciting the transition to the problem of the being of the human existent by unveiling a specific non-being of the will, an ontological deficiency belonging to the will. The privileged experience of this non-being, in spite of its negative turn, is already an ontological dimension; it is, so to speak, the negative proof of being, the empty ontology of lost being. The explication of this negative moment consists largely in a phenomenology of passion, without, however, being used up in this. Let us call it, in the broadest possible sense, a philosophical reflection on guilt.

It may seem strange at first to connect the passions (ambition, avarice, hatred, etc.) to a "metaphysical" principle as debatable as that of guilt—itself interpreted as non-being! And yet we can hardly stress enough the extent to which a psychology which wishes to economize in principles vulgarizes the human world of passions. Whether it attempts to derive the passions from emotions and feelings, whether it resorts to the empty metaphors of crystallization, or whether it assimilates passion to fixation (*l'idée fixe*), the psychology of the passions falls short of that density and concrete opacity which "pity" and "terror" are able to conjure up on the stage and to which the fascinated reader of a novel yields in imagination. Passion is not a level of emotion nor, generally speaking, of the involuntary.

There are other ways in which our contention that the phenomenon of passion exceeds the limits of ordinary psychology can be confirmed. Passion, that manner of being situated or of situating oneself, that inconsistent captivity, is something entirely different from a complication of the involuntary, since it characterizes a way that the voluntary and the involuntary have of being a whole, a global image of existence. Passion is not a function, a partial structure, but an over-all style, a modality of bondage which has, indeed, its own intentionality (of jealousy, ambition, etc.), and all the intentionalities of partial functions are drawn along after it. We can easily discover in every function of the involuntary (desire, habit, emotion) the zone of least resistance through which the passions enter and multiply, but the passions are the will itself in an alienated mode.

In fact that is why the phenomenon of passion concerns the human "ethos" in its entirety; under the rule of passion, the values which could be inherent in willing as its basic vectors and to which willing is opened by motivation are opposed to it in the hostile transcendence of obligation. Here we discover the passionate birth of "morality"—of the "*dura lex*"—which condemns without aiding and "arouses sinful passions."

Yet we must admit that the problem of guilt (*la culpabilité*) presents itself as a knot of impasses. In one sense the passions seem only to call for a description which would utilize ordinary observation, literature, and history. For are not the passions the everyday manifestation of willing, in regard to which the functions of the voluntary and the involuntary are still but abstractions, a framework or skeleton which lacks flesh? This is quite true, but it soon becomes apparent that this description is diffused into aberrant, infinitely multiplying forms. The passions lack a principle of order needed to constitute a world, a cosmos; they lack an intelligibility similar to that of the partial functions, such as emotion, habit, desire, etc., which are caught up in the dialectic of the voluntary and the involuntary. We have to decipher the signs of each passion by the usages of life and culture. How then is a phenomeno-*logy* of the passions possible? For want of an order-principle, could phenomenology thematize a principle of disorder? It is here that phenomenology comes up against the irreducibly mythical character of the notion of guilt. Now philosophy would very much like to "reduce" the myth and to extract a purely rational understanding from it which would equate fault or error (*faute*) with suffering and death and even reabsorb it into finitude by assimilating it as a "limit-situation." But the myth resists, because it alone has power to bind *Sinn* and *Bild*, sense and image, into an accident, a catastrophe, which would be a sort of transhistoric event of freedom: the event of the fall. Such is the impasse: only some such myth can, so to speak, regroup the disorder, the anticosmos of the passions, but philosophy tends to reduce the event of guilt to a structure homogenous with other structures of the voluntary and the involuntary. In this respect the philosophies of existence, which have done so much to reintroduce error (*faute*) into philosophical reflection, proceed no differently than Plotinus and Spinoza: for them also finitude is the ultimate philosophical alibi for guilt, a temptation which seems inherent in a philosophical treatment of the notion of guilt.

To the impasse, which can be called methodological, is added another which is, in a sense, constitutional, for the non-being brought about by guilt is indivisibly "vanity" [9] and "power." Passion is the "power of vanity." On the one hand, all passion is organized around an intentive "nothing" which myth represents in the images of darkness, of the nether abyss, of corruption, of bondage. This specific nothingness, this "vanity," lives in suspicion, reproach, injury, and grief and makes every passion a wild-goose chase. And yet, on the other hand, passion indissolubly unites grandeur and guilt, animates the movement of history, and driving man toward well-being and power, founds economy and politics. Passion is powerful and empowering; the falsehood of passion lies precisely in passing responsibility on to an alien fatality which would possess and carry it off. This is why myth calls it a demon as well as nothingness and darkness.

In the presence of these impasses, the phenomenology of the will is embarrassed but not caught without resources. Its task is first to elaborate both an empirical and a mythological description of the will. It needs first to regroup the descriptive traits of the passions, starting from the double notion of nothingness and power, and to elaborate the quasi-intelligibility of the quasi-world of the passions by starting from a mythical accident. In particular, phenomenology needs to join the psychology of the passions in the Stoic and Spinozistic tradition to their dramatization in the novel and the theater. In addition, history will furnish it with illustrations of all the passions, principally those of power, for the universe of concentration camps in our day has carried the alienation of the passion whose theme is power to the dimensions of a caricature. A critical analysis of history as struggle for power is

9. [*Vanité* is used here in the etymological sense of the Latin *vanitas*, meaning "empty," and thus suggesting non-being.—Trans.]

probably more important for the understanding of guilt than an interpretation of the petty passions of private life.

The myth can thus serve as a heuristic guide for a description which otherwise would be in danger of indefinite dispersion into details. On the other hand, it is important to elaborate a philosophical critique of myth which would not be a reductive critique but would restore the significational intention of myth. The principal task of that critique is precisely to recapture the negative ontology of the notion of guilt, to disengage the specific sense of the "powerful vanity," by showing the element which checks the attempt to reduce it to other modes of negativity (the experienced lack of need, the "always future emptiness" opened up before the self by the project, by the negation inherent in denial, and above all by the lack of aseity, that is by the non-necessity of the existing which is constitutive of finitude).

More than to any other notion, finitude is that to which guilt tends to be reduced and so should serve at the same time as guide and contrast for a philosophical critique of guilt. To recognize the divergence of the two notions is to "save the myth," for thus the polarity of finitude as "nothingness" constitutive, so to speak, of guilt, as an event-like "nothing" (*"néant" événementiel*), can serve as the guiding theme of a similar interpretation of the non-being of the will.

If we now return from the threshold of ontology to the preceding transcendental reflection, it will appear that the whole dialectic of the voluntary and the involuntary could have been constructed only by omitting that new reversal (*péripétie*) which introduced being through non-being. Afterward, the transcendental dimension of the cogito is revealed as connected with the *epoché* of guilt and the ontology which it implies. The sense of that omission must now be explicated.

The parenthesizing of the passional modalities of the will is both a gain and a loss. It is first a gain because it makes willing and human existence in general appear as that which "gives sense." Going through to the end of that *epoché*, to the level of the will and its capacity for qualifying all of the involuntary as human, is necessary in order to reach the constituting function of consciousness. A reflection which would begin too soon with the passions, with "man's misery," would risk missing the signification of willing and of consciousness; in particular, the notion of bondage considered prematurely would risk being confounded with a determination or an automatism and would imprison anthropology in objective thought. Thus, in order to dissociate the subjective world of motivation from the objective universe of causality, in order to regain the sense of the spontaneity of the powers which the moving body offers for action, in order to regain, more subtly still, that necessity in the first person which I undergo simply by virtue of being alive, born of the flesh, phenomenology must organize that triple notion of motivation, spontaneity, and lived-through necessity around a constitutive (or, in a limited sense, transcendental) "I will." Thus, we have to suspend the bondage which oppresses willing in order to break through to that fundamental possibility of the ego which is its responsibility. We had to omit fault (*la faute*) in order to understand the reciprocity of the voluntary and the involuntary which renders them intelligible for each other under the limit-Idea of their unity.

The omission of fault alone, moreover, makes possible the subsequent reintroduction of this new dimension, for because freedom is constitutive of everything involuntary, including necessity, freedom is not suppressed by guilt; even servitude is an accident of freedom. The dialectic of the voluntary and the involuntary is the undifferentiated structure of innocence and guilt; it is the condition of the possibility of a paradox such as freedom in bondage. Man is not at all part man and part guilt; he remains an ability to decide, to move, to consent, but his is an ability occupied by the enemy.

The ambiguity, however, of a transcendental reflection is at once a gain and a loss; as conquest of the constitutive power of man, it is also an ontological loss. It is as if a second naïveté were involved in it, a transcendental naïveté which takes the place of the naturalistic one. The transcendental reflection creates the illusion that philosophy could be a reflection without a spiritual discipline (*ascèse*), without a purification of its own seeing; it omits the decisive fact that the freedom which constitutes the involuntary is still a freedom to set free. It must, therefore, cross the levels of consciousness in order to get from its non-being to its being.

This naïveté may be more difficult to overcome than that of the "natural" attitude. If the ego loses itself easily in its world and understands itself willingly in terms of the things that surround it, an even more tenacious illusion imprisons it in the very matrix of its own subjectivity. The omission of being seems connected with the dissimulation which gives birth to freedom-in-bondage. The "vanity" of the ego is stretched like a veil over the very being of its existence.

The conquest of constituting subjectivity by philosophy is, strangely enough, a guilty cultural grandeur, like economics and politics. Transcendental phenomenology is already the work of that ego which wills itself by itself and without ontological roots.

And yet the sense of subjectivity, once acquired, should not be lost again, for to transcend the ego would be both to retain it and to suspend it as the supreme instance. While reaching transcendental phenomenology is the work of a Copernican Revolution, the passage from transcendental phenomenology to ontological phenomenology is in its turn a sort of conversion which removes the ego from the center of ontological concern. The explication of "vanity" should be the point of entry for that second reflection. In revealing a specific non-being, a ψευδὴς οὐσία, "vanity" raises in a negative manner the problem of the being of willing and the problem of the being of man. Perhaps this opening to ontology through the "vanity" of willing is more fruitful than the examination of ontological implications on the level of theoretical consciousness.

If, then, such a second reflection were possible, phenomenology, centered on sense-giving (*Sinngebung*) in general and on the constituting power of the "I will" in particular, presupposes a preliminary step, the suspending of the question of the being and non-being of giving consciousness. This is a useful step, since it alone can bring to light the proper sense of subjectivity. But then passing over into ontology would consist in dropping the parentheses, and, while keeping the advantages of the subjectivity acquired through use of the parentheses, in attempting the adventure of a ποίησις, of a "poetics," of the will.

Index